Subsidizing success

The Export-Import Bank in the U.S. economy

Subsidizing success

The Export–Import Bank in the U.S. economy

RICHARD E. FEINBERG

CAMBRIDGE UNIVERSITY PRESS

Cambridge
London   New York   New Rochelle
Melbourne   Sydney

Published by the Press Syndicate of the University of Cambridge
The Pitt Building, Trumpington Street, Cambridge CB2 1RP
32 East 57th Street, New York, NY 10022, USA
296 Beaconsfield Parade, Middle Park, Melbourne 3206, Australia

First published 1982

Printed in the United States of America

Library of Congress Cataloging in Publication Data
Feinberg, Richard E.
Subsidizing success.
Revision of thesis (Ph.D.)—Stanford University,
1978.
Bibliography: p.
Includes index.
1. Export-Import Bank of the United States.
I. Title.
HG3754.U5F44 1981   332.1'54   81–4702
ISBN 0 521 23427 1   AACR2

To Diane and Sonya

Contents

Contents

Tables and figures

x

Figures

Preface

Politics and economics intersect most evidently in public-sector activity. This book describes and analyzes how the power of one state institution, the U.S. Export-Import Bank, is used to affect the allocation of economic resources. Answers are sought to such questions as: Why did the government enter into international lending? Once created, what outside forces and what internal criteria have governed the behavior of this official credit agency? Which private—and public—interests have benefited?

The Eximbank is meant to serve U.S. domestic interests, but it does so by trying to influence the behavior of foreign actors. Exim is found to function as a useful institutional resolution to the analytical dichotomy between the domestic and international spheres. The extension of Exim loans and guarantees overseas inevitably leads to diplomatic considerations; and although this book focuses primarily on Exim's attempts to solve problems of the U.S. economy, Exim's role in foreign policy cannot be ignored. The health of the U.S. economy depends on foreign economic and political events, and Exim tries to influence these in ways thought beneficial to U.S. interests.

A study of Exim, therefore, must intertwine politics and economics—domestic and international, private and public. Because Exim activity is tangible and ever quantifiable, it offers an excellent opportunity to examine these interconnected factors in a relatively empirical, realistic manner.

Several themes are developed throughout the study: the influence of large customers on Exim, its close integration with the international banking community, the degree to which it replicates at the government level the behavior of ordinary banks at the firm level, its willingness to sacrifice its own profit to secure the profit of private interests, its responsiveness to national priorities as expressed in other government activities, and the importance of foreign competition rather than national allocation in sustaining Exim.

Because so little information is readily available on Exim, several chapters explain Exim operations in sufficient detail to serve as a primer for a prospective borrower. No other comprehensive work has appeared on Exim. To permit easy reference, to allow the reader to skip to the chapter of interest without encountering confusion, I repeat basic points where appropriate. With some of the initial spadework now completed, I hope that other researchers will undertake more thorough studies of those particular aspects of Exim behavior that I was unable to elaborate.

This work is a revised and updated version of a Ph.D. dissertation submitted to the Economics Department of Stanford University; it was written while I was a research fellow at the Brookings Institution (1974–5) and while on leave from the U.S. Treasury Department (Summer 1976). While I was at Brookings, I conducted extensive interviews with officials at Exim, at other government agencies, and in the private sector. Jim Cruse of Exim's Policy Analysis Staff, now a Bank vice-president, was especially generous with his time. The views presented here, however, are mine and should not be ascribed to these officials and institutions or any others.

Like any intellectual effort, this work is the product of many influences. My dissertation advisers—Duncan Foley, Don Harris, and Clark Reynolds— offered me the necessary encouragement and sense of worth. Philip Brenner and Barbara Stallings made insightful comments on earlier drafts. My father and mother, however, deserve the greatest credit for providing me with the means and the interest to pursue the educational journey that this work culminates.

Washington, D.C.   Richard E. Feinberg

Introduction

The major government programs designed to foster U.S. exports and overseas investment, including tax subsidies, loans, grants, and guarantees, were running at annual activity levels of some $22–$25 billion* in the mid- and late 1970s. The Agriculture Department, through the Commodity Credit Corporation (CCC) and Public Law (PL) 480, was providing loans and grants each year for approximately $2 billion in food exports.[1] The development loans and grants of the Agency for International Development (AID), although temporarily declining, still reached $1 billion. Various military and security assistance programs (including the AID-administered security-supporting assistance, renamed the Economic Support Fund), which primarily finance exports, were fluctuating from $3.5 billion to $6 billion. Eximbank was authorizing about $4 billion in credits and another $4 billion in insurance and guarantees for private export credits. From the U.S.-funded multilateral lending agencies, primarily the World Bank and the Inter-American Development Bank (IDB), about $1 billion was being used by the borrowers to procure machinery made in the United States.[2] A tax subsidy, called the Domestic International Sales Corporation (DISC), allowed a 50 percent reduction on the tax rate a corporation must pay on profits made from exports, at a loss to the Internal Revenue Service of some $1.5 billion annually.[3] The Overseas Private Investment Corporation (OPIC) was insuring about $500 million each year in overseas direct investments by U.S. corporations.[4] The foreign tax credit—which allows a corporation to deduct from taxes owed to the U.S. Government any taxes its foreign subsidiaries paid to host governments—and the tax deferral—which permits a corporation to avoid taxes on profits earned abroad until they are remitted to the United States—were costing the Internal Revenue Service, according to some estimates, around $5 billion a year.

This impressive array of focused energies belies the frequent claim that the U.S. Government stands aloof from, or merely devotes itself to erecting barriers against, overseas commerce. To the extent, moreover, that these programs are successful, they move resources well in excess of their own activity levels or tax costs. This list of government programs does not even consider the routine business-promoting activities of the State and Defense departments. In

---

*American billion here and in all subsequent uses.

1

addition, the Domestic and International Business Administration of the Commerce Department is concerned explicitly with the overseas expansion of U.S. firms, and conducts worldwide marketing surveys, attends trade fairs, and encourages other promotional activities.

These programs are quite diverse but are justified generally on the following grounds: The state must undertake a necessary activity the private sector has neglected; since foreign governments have such a program for their firms, the United States must provide its firms with equal competitive backing; overseas sales are vital to the health of the U.S. economy or portions thereof; and U.S. foreign policy goals are advanced. Each of the four rationales has been applied in the case of the Eximbank, or Exim.

Throughout its history, the fundamental activity of Exim has remained the provision of long-term trade finance chiefly for capital equipment exports, although the Bank has chosen to emphasize one official justification or another during different periods. In the mid-1930s, the founders of Exim framed their arguments for an export credit agency primarily in reaction to the inadequacy of the private international capital markets (made especially acute by the collapse after 1929) and the contribution the selling abroad of surplus production could have made toward reviving the depressed U.S. economy. In the late 1930s, Exim's loans were concentrated in Latin America in response to a felt commercial and military threat from an expansionist Germany. In the immediate postwar period, Exim preceded the Marshall Plan by lending massively to Western Europe; the Bank attempted to fill the gap resulting from the termination of the lend-lease program, without which, it was feared, Western Europe would not have the dollars to purchase surplus U.S. production and to begin rapid reconstruction of its economies (and thereby reducing the appeal of communism). During World War II, and in the early 1950s, Exim made numerous loans to develop "strategic" raw materials. In the mid-1960s, the Bank continued to lend to mining projects in accordance with "development assistance" objectives. In the 1960s and especially in the 1970s, Exim returned to its earlier refrain of "meeting the competition," which was coming not only from Germany, but from an array of industrial countries.

Exim loans still serve all of these purposes and more. The intention in this study is to analyze only some of them. The emphasis will be on the relationship of the Bank to the U.S. economy, rather than on Exim's impact abroad, except as it affects U.S. interests. Exim was created, and has persisted, to solve certain problems facing the U.S. economy; it should be treated from that perspective. This book will stress the special role Exim can play as an agency of the State as it carries out, or at least attempts to carry out, activities the private sector has been less willing or able to perform.

Part I begins with a discussion of the origins of Exim. Although the general approach of the book is more functional than chronological, Chapter 1 seeks to explain the emergence and role of Exim in terms of concrete historical problems. Like other New Deal initiatives, Exim was not solely a product of the

Great Depression, but rather a response to systemic needs that preceded—and continued after—the Crash of 1929. Early attempts by private interests to establish a private export credit agency are examined, and archival evidence is presented about the attitude of bankers and businessmen toward the creation of a government bank. Chapter 1 also offers a brief history of Eximbank operations, showing both continuity and change in Eximbank policies against a background of secularly rising volumes of business. This preliminary sketch is meant to give a historical framework for situating the more thorough analyses of particular Exim policies discussed in the remainder of the book.

The interested reader is provided with a detailed presentation of Exim's main programs; the absence of such a collection of information has hindered previous research on the Bank, which has been very limited in both quantity and scope. Chapter 2 is an extensive description of Exim's most important program—its direct loans. The discussion touches on such operational matters as application procedures, repayment terms, disbursement methods, and interest rate determination; it proceeds to give data on the distribution of loans by geographic region, economic sector, and U.S. corporate suppliers. Exim loan volume is compared to total U.S. exports and to capital goods exports.

Chapter 3 examines closely a major aspect of the direct loan program—the long-term nature of the maturities—and considers their volume relative to that of the multilateral lending agencies and to the private U.S. capital market. The comparative importance of Exim may surprise many readers. Exim is shown to be a major supplier of the long-term finance required for internationally traded capital goods.

The commercial banks concentrate their loans in the short-term end of the maturity spectrum. In the 1970s, the private market gradually became more willing to venture some of its capital in longer-term trade finance, and Exim's "financial guarantee" program became more active. In a given transaction, the commercial banks (and perhaps suppliers) provide a substantial portion of the finance but are repaid first, while Exim waits for the later maturities. Exim's financial guarantee covers a portion or all of the private finance. This "cofinancing" arrangement, which Exim pioneered, is shown to be consistent with Exim's principle of encouraging and complementing but not competing with private capital.

Chapter 4 outlines the basic workings of the Foreign Credit Insurance Association (FCIA), a composite of some fifty private insurance companies operating under the Exim umbrella. This Exim affiliate was created in 1961 to offer short- and medium-term credit insurance for U.S. exporters and their banks. The private makeup of the association, and its own desire for financial success, is contrasted with its responsibility, as a publicly reinsured agency, to assist exporters to penetrate newer and riskier markets—a contradiction that also haunts its parent, Exim.

Part II examines the relationship of Exim lending patterns to private trade and capital flows and scrutinizes the Bank's criteria for creditworthiness. In Chapter 5, the distribution of Exim loans among the developing countries is compared to the paths etched out by U.S. exporters and private creditors, with explanations offered for Exim's preference for the higher-income lesser developed countries (LDCs). The relationship between the geographic distribution of Exim loans and of U.S. aid is examined, and the impact of U.S. foreign policy attitudes toward potential borrowers and actual Exim lending is discussed. Exim tries frequently to influence political events at important historical moments: This traditional Exim motif is illustrated with two examples dating from the 1930s—Cuba and the Soviet Union—and two more contemporary instances—Peru and Chile. Algeria offers a case study of Exim's attempts to woo a postrevolutionary regime closer to the United States.

In Chapter 6, to unveil Exim's creditworthiness criteria, a series of rejected loan applications is examined and the reasons for denial noted. No quantified formula is developed to predict Exim's loan patterns, but factors dominating the Bank's decisions are identified. The contradictory nature of certain of the creditworthiness criteria shows the potential for subjectivity in the Bank's decision-making process. The sometimes artificial distinction between commercial and political risk is also discussed.

Part III develops from several perspectives the relationship between Exim and the U.S. economy. Chapter 7 examines how Exim (one among many state agencies) uses subsidies to alter the behavior of private firms. In Exim's case, subsidies are offered to induce private firms to direct their energies toward the external sector. The cost of the subsidy had become quite substantial at times during the 1970s, whenever the margin between Exim's interest rate and market rates widened; the subsidy value becomes even greater if the rate by which the later maturities are discounted reflects properly what the borrower would have paid eventually for such scarce long-term finance. A simple formula based on the subsidy concept is developed to measure the net benefit from Exim loans, although it suffers from several features common to cost–benefit analyses. Exim's ability to subsidize U.S. trade without receiving annual appropriations from congress is found to depend on its possession of a capital base and reserve that total $3 billion, which the Bank holds as interest-bearing assets (loans). The use of these funds costs the Bank $50 million only, its annual dividend paid to the U.S. Treasury. On those funds that Exim does borrow, it receives the preferential rates accorded to government-backed borrowings.

Chapter 7 also examines Exim's claim to be an agent of job creation and economic stimulation. The problems inherent in Exim's attempt to act as a macroeconomic stabilizer are analyzed. Neither graphic nor an econometric analysis discovers patterns in annual Exim lending that move counter to fluctuations in gross national product (GNP). The main trend in Exim loan volume, which has varied widely from year to year, has been secularly upwards, without relation to the business cycle.

Chapter 8 reveals that Exim has been of special interest to U.S. firms with overseas subsidiaries and affiliates. Exim's financing of exports to affiliates of U.S.-based transnational corporations (TNCs) is not surprising considering the weight such transactions have in U.S. trade. Startling, however, is the apparently sizable contribution Exim makes to the flow of long-term investment capital from the United States to overseas affiliates of U.S. firms. Exim also serves TNCs in ways related only incidentally to export promotion, ways that include deterring expropriation and forestalling nationalization by injecting fresh (foreign) capital at moments when the U.S. firm is too frightened to risk its own funds. Examples illustrate the various functions Exim as a state agency performs for U.S. firms. The hypothesis is forwarded that Exim also has fostered the spread of foreign branches of U.S. banks that have accompanied their manufacturing clients. In Chapter 8, to determine the degree of support for TNC affiliates, a loan-by-loan analysis is made of Exim activity in four countries.

Exim's extensive involvement in infrastructure development—more than 60 percent of all Exim loans go to public-sector agencies—has provided the base for profitable private, including foreign, investment. These lending patterns, which relegate private local capital to a subordinate role, implicitly foster development models emphasizing state and transnational capital.

The special needs of the aircraft and nuclear power industries and the ways in which Exim meets those needs are discussed in Chapter 9. The logic for Exim's support of these industries lies in the heavy backing they have received from the U.S. Government. Because of insufficient absorptive capacity in the United States, both industries look to export markets to attain the high volume of sales needed to spread out massive research and development (R&D) costs and to realize scale effects. The Bank's long-term, large loans are well suited to solving an important export problem facing these expensive products, that is, adequate trade finance. Exim's willingness to disburse during the long construction periods also helps to meet the firms' heavy demand for working capital.

Chapter 10 focuses on some of the conflicting pressures and contradictory objectives that complicate Exim decision making. Some general conclusions are formulated, which analyze Exim's position within the panoply of international financial institutions and offer some policy prescriptions.

Part I

Origins and programs of Eximbank

Chapter 1

The birth and historical evolution of the Bank

The birth of the Bank

The "General Policy Statement" released by the Export-Import Bank (Exim) in the year of its founding, 1934, explained that: "The object and purpose of said Bank is to aid in financing and to facilitate exports and imports and the exchange of commodities between the United States and other nations or the agencies or nationals thereof." The "general powers" delegated to the Bank were broad, allowing it to borrow and to lend money, guarantee evidences of indebtedness, issue letters of credit, and "to do a general banking business."[1]

After a period of some debate and sifting of options, the Eximbank came to concentrate its energies on making loans tied to U.S. exports, discounting commercial export paper, and guaranteeing private export credits against commercial and political risks. Although some of the loans and guarantees supported agricultural exports, the Bank increasingly emphasized producers' goods requiring long-term finance.

The Eximbank was created in the first term of the New Deal. The following discussion will situate the Bank within the framework of New Deal policies and philosophies, while not losing sight of the private interests that played an important role in molding Exim's programs. Special attention will be given to Exim's functions as they related to the trade policies of the 1930s, notably the Reciprocal Trade Act. To begin, however, it is necessary to look back and examine structural shifts in U.S. trade patterns that occurred in earlier decades. Long-term trends in the U.S. and the international economy had produced a felt need for an export credit and insurance agency even before the depression. The prompt failure of a major private effort to establish such an institution suggested that the government would have to seize the initiative.

When the United States entered the twentieth century, two important trends were noticeable in its external financial accounts. First, the nation had progressed from a chronic net importer to a maintainer of a large and growing trade surplus. Second, the composition of U.S. exports was gradually shifting away from agricultural and raw material goods toward manufactured items and even capital goods. By 1928, capital goods including transportation equipment accounted for 21 percent of the $5.1 billion in total U.S. merchandise exports.[2]

The development of a trade surplus and an export trade in heavy investment goods had important implications for trade finance. The trade surplus threatened to deprive foreigners of the dollars necessary to purchase U.S. exports: The high tariffs imposed in 1922 (Fordney–McCumber) and 1930 (Hawley–Smoot) made it more difficult for foreigners to sell to the United States and to earn the foreign exchange with which to buy U.S. goods. This conundrum gave rise to the "dollar shortage" or "dollar gap."[3] Concern about the insufficient purchasing power of foreigners was especially acute in the aftermath of World War I, when much of Europe was unable to service foreign debts, much less pay for new imports. Bankers and exporters pressed for measures to increase the dollar outflow to resolve this contradiction. At the urging of exporters and the American Bankers' Association (ABA), the Congress in 1919 passed the Edge Act, which permitted banks to circumvent antitrust restrictions and combine to form corporations specializing in international lending. The corporations could either discount short-term trade acceptances or make long-term loans.[4]

In 1920, more than 500 bankers and businessmen agreed to try to organize under the Edge Act a Foreign Trade Financing Corporation that would specialize in long-term trade credits.[5] The Corporation was to have a capital base of $100 million, with the capacity to lend ten times that amount. The organizing committee was composed of leading business and banking figures representing such major powers as Standard Oil of New Jersey, International Harvester, Westinghouse Electric, General Motors (GM), and many leading banks. The plan was endorsed by the ABA, the National Foreign Trade Council (NFTC), the National Association of Manufacturers, the American Exporters and Importers Association, and the American Farm Bureau Federation. Despite this impressive backing, the corporation was unable to find subscribers to its stock offers and had to be abandoned.

This effort on the part of private individuals and firms to assemble capital to finance U.S. exports failed for several reasons. Some bankers worried that the new corporation would diverge from its proposed concentration on long-term lending and enter into competition with the private banks in short-term discounting. Whereas some bankers felt that the corporation ought to lend to exporters holding "blocked accounts" (if the foreign buyer had deposited payments in local currency at his local bank but had been unable to obtain foreign exchange in return) to reopen trading channels, others saw such a maneuver as merely transferring bad debts to the new corporation. There was general concern that the corporation might favor particular interest groups. Some considered that the intended size of the corporation was imprudently large—although it would be necessary if risks were to be spread out sufficiently. The demand for long-term credits was deemed uncertain. The European market remained unsettled and burdened with war and reparation debts. United States foreign policy lacked direction.

Competitive rivalries, uncertainties, scale, diplomatic issues: The private sector could not organize itself by itself to meet a systemic need. Slightly more than a decade later, the government would create an institution—the Export-Import Bank—which, because of its public-sector nature, could overcome the roadblocks that had stood in the way of the ill-fated Foreign Trade Financing Corporation.

By the mid-1920s, U.S. international lending was substantial. With hindsight and in light of the widespread defaults of the 1930s, some observers have judged the creditors to have been reckless, whereas others have argued that the system required an even higher level of credit.[6] Regardless of the volume of international credit, the U.S. banking system preferred to make short-term loans rather than perform the role intended for the Foreign Trade Financing Corporation—the provision of long-term credits required to finance capital goods exports.[7] This time-preference of the banks (which will be examined more thoroughly in Chapter 3) could be explained in terms of the immaturity of their international offices, the banks' desire to balance their short-term liability structure with short-term assets, and the avoidance of uncertainties inherent in long-term investment.

With the collapse in 1929, the dollar gap became a chasm, as the net flow of American capital reversed and flowed toward the United States. (Indeed, the flow reversal, which began in 1928, may have been a cause of the collapse.) Thus, although from 1925–7 the average annual net outflow of private American capital from the United States exceeded $1 billion, in 1931–3 the average annual net inflow was $400 million.[8] The resulting contraction of international liquidity contributed to the sharp decline in U.S. exports that fell from $5.1 billion in 1928 to $2.6 billion by 1932. Machinery and transport equipment exports were hard hit especially, falling from $1.1 billion to $209 million. During his chairmanship at the Eximbank, the future governor of the Federal Reserve, W. McChesney Martin, Jr., remarked that "It has been the relative shortage of dollars abroad and not the lack of demand for American goods which has operated since the late '20's to restrict the vigor and growth of our natural export industries."[9]

The shortage of trade credit was exacerbated but not created by the worldwide depression. Moreover, even if the United States had not been running such substantial trade surpluses, the changing composition of its export trade—the growing emphasis on capital goods—was generating a credit problem that the private commercial banks, with their preference for short-term assets, were unable or unwilling to resolve on their own. Even after the passage of a special law allowing them to act in combination, the banks were unable to construct an institution that would meet the needs of the maturing U.S. economy.

Eximbank and the New Deal

In Executive Order 6581 (February 2, 1934) Roosevelt declared that he was establishing the Export-Import Bank as a logical and necessary extension of three acts central to the early New Deal: the Reconstruction Finance Corporation (RFC), the National Industrial Recovery Act (NIRA), and the Bank Conservation Act. Exim was a child of the RFC, because it would use government credits to stimulate essentially private economic activity. Exim's ability to guarantee private credits implied a regulator role consistent with the designs of the Bank Conservation Act, whereas Exim's potential role as a coordinator of trade groups engaged in external commerce fit into NIRA ideology. As with other New Deal programs, Exim was meant to work harmoniously with—not to displace—private capital. Some New Dealers who believed that the government should not only subsidize but also direct the economy saw in Exim an instrument to manage foreign commerce. Exim would only fulfill partially such visions.

The capital for the Eximbank would come primarily from the RFC. This use of RFC monies was consistent with the Corporation's charter "to provide emergency financing facilities for financial institutions, to aid in financing agriculture, commerce and industry . . ." Roosevelt's Executive Order creating Exim emphasized that the Exim-supported exports would stimulate American industry and employment, thereby facilitating the reconstruction being pursued by the RFC. Improving the financial health of the U.S. capital goods industry was given special priority by a number of Roosevelt's aides, including Adolphe Berle and Bernard Baruch;[10] because Exim would concentrate on this sector, its contribution to reconstruction had particular potential.

Despite the worry of conservatives that the RFC was another example of Roosevelt's strategy of "creeping socialism," under Jesse Jones the RFC devoted the bulk of its $60 billion toward regenerating private enterprise.[11] To some, like Cordell Hull, who were worried about government encroachment upon the free enterprise system, Exim, at first glance, appeared a threat. Such worries were unfounded. Exim immediately offered assurance in its "General Policy Statement" that it "expect[ed] to supplement rather than to compete with existing sources of export and import credit," and credit would be granted only when "circumstances indicated that commercial banks cannot handle the business." Exim worked closely with advisory committees of the ABA and NFTC in developing its programs. The President of the ABA, R. S. Hecht, wrote the members at the end of 1934:

The officials [of the Eximbank] made it plain to us that there was no thought of competing with our commercial banks, but simply to work out a plan of cooperation in respect to special lines of business outside the scope of ordinary commercial banking.

The Committee [of bankers] met in Washington with [Exim] President George N. Peek and other officials of the Export-Import Bank on November 22 and 23, and following a careful interchange of views, formulated a detailed plan of procedure to bring about a maximum of cooperation between the commerical banks and the government institutions. This was found to be wholly satisfactory by Mr. Peek and his associates.[12]

The ABA's Advisory Committee to Exim laid out a five-point "plan of cooperation" with Exim in 1934; even today these suggestions are a good explanation of basic Exim policy. Exim was to:

1. Help to finance transactions of a tenure beyond the length of a commerical bank transaction, up to five years;
2. Join in the extension of credit with commercial banks to handle for a concern a sizeable business where the amount of the risk might not be prudent for commerical banks to handle alone, or where the concern is unable to obtain commercial banking facilities for the amount required;
3. In approved transactions, assume a part of the risk;
4. Assist in solving the problems of doing business with countries where there exists difficulty in obtaining foreign exchange;
5. Be the focal point of all the governmental activities in assisting in providing the markets for American commodities and goods.[13]

These functions, enthusiastically endorsed by the bankers as serving to "augment the facilities of the commercial banks," would provide the necessary trade finance, with long-term maturities and in amounts large enough to cover investment projects—when and only when the private banks did not want to lend. Exim would also offer insurance for private credits against commercial and possibly political risks (as inferred in point 4).

Only point 5—the hope that Exim would coordinate all official trade promotion activities—has not been realized. The desire to coordinate, or at least remove some of the "anarchy" from the competitive capitalist system, surfaced in various New Deal programs, including two that Roosevelt referred to in the Executive Order establishing Exim: the NIRA and the Bank Conservation Act. The NIRA gave business immunity from the antitrust laws allowing firms to get together and "rationalize" their own behavior. Business and labor were encouraged to set wages, profits, and production targets on an industrywide basis. (The NIRA floundered amidst ideological dispute, uncertain procedures, and insufficient bite, and finally was declared unconstitutional by the Supreme Court in 1935.)

The bankers' vision of Exim as a coordinating agency for foreign trade was echoed by other actors, including Exim's first President, George N. Peek. Exim was created initially to deal with the planned Soviet economy,[14] and Peek believed that government intervention in trade was here to stay. Peek, who was also Roosevelt's Special Adviser to the President on Foreign Trade, favored the establishment of a "federal trade board" that would "coordinate all our foreign trade activities under a unified agency."[15] Exim represented a step in that direction. Peek stated:

One fact should be clearly understood. On the Board of Trustees [of the Eximbank] the Department of State . . . has an influential position. The Department of Agriculture, the Treasury Department, the Reconstruction Finance Corporation, the Federal

Trade Commission, the Tariff Commission, and the Department of Commerce all collaborate in the person of specially delegated trustees. The operations of the Bank are, therefore, not conducted by a small bureau with private notions of its own, but by a central clearing house of the Administration, representing all the government entities intimately concerned with our foreign trade.[16]

Others, including Exim executive vice-president Charles Stuart, and Eugene Thomas, chairman of NFTC, suggested that Exim could collect and make available information on the exchange positions of countries. When excessive lending had occurred already, Exim should step in and unblock foreign accounts to reopen trade channels. But Exim might refuse to do business in a market—and by implication, discourage private lending for lack of Exim guarantees—if a nation were refusing to grant generalized trade concessions.[17] Stuart, who had been a consulting engineer in the Soviet Union from 1926–31, was an advocate of the NIRA and government planning generally.[18] He spoke approvingly of two attempts before Congress then—the Lewis and Sheppard bills—whose purposes were to increase government coordination and support for foreign trade.[19]

Exim has managed to perform some coordinating activities. It has provided credit information on many foreign buyers, has "unblocked" foreign accounts, and has coordinated its activities in line with diplomatic objectives. The Bank has worked to fill important gaps left by the private market, namely, the provision of export credit insurance, and long-term trade credits. Exim has not, however, evolved into a centralizing "trade board," nor has it regulated successfully bank lending overseas.

Exim and the Reciprocal Trade Act

Roosevelt's Executive Order establishing Exim made no mention of the trade policy Exim was to foster. Proponents of two of the contending schools, that is, bilateralism and multilateral reciprocity, thought the Bank would play a useful—an essential—role in their schemes. The first chairman of the Bank, George N. Peek, was a stalwart advocate of bilateral and even barter agreements. In late 1934, he attempted to arrange an agreement with fascist Germany—whose bilateral trade approach Peek admired—whereby Germany would purchase U.S. cotton and Exim would handle the exchange transactions, including the sale of reichsmarks to Americans wishing to purchase German products. The Bank truly would act as an export and import agency and coordinate the entire deal. Opponents to bilateralism within the administration convinced Roosevelt, however, to scotch the transaction.[20]

Peek was not alone in seeing the usefulness of Exim for bilateral trade agreements. Recommendations sent to Exim by the advisory committee of the ABA and the Committee of Exporters and Importers informed Bank officials that Exim aid would be "especially" appropriate where preferential quotas for U.S. goods had been established. The advisors did caution, however, that barter agreements should be concluded only after clearance by the State Department.[21]

Those who supported the principle of unconditional most-favored nation (MFN) treatment, as enshrined in the Reciprocal Trade Act of 1934, also saw a role for the Export-Import Bank. Having overcome his initial fears about Exim's "planning" schemes, Secretary of State Cordell Hull, whose name is associated with the MFN principle, saw the Bank performing several useful functions that included providing credit for the increased trade flows to result from tariff reductions; augmenting demand for surplus U.S. production; dealing with the "sovereign" problems of government controls or other actions; and countering competition from foreign eximbanks. In 1939, Hull wrote the following apologia for the state bank:

Several features of the existing situation increase the necessity of having some institution as the Export-Import Bank to carry out these (credit) operations among which I may mention the following: (1) the existing unemployment and agricultural surpluses in this country; (2) the widespread existence of various types of controls over trade and delays in payment for trade which create conditions unusually hard for the exporter or commercial banker to handle by himself; (3) the virtual cessation of private capital investments to which other countries—especially the growing ones of Latin America—could ordinarily look for the credit facilities to carry them through their ordinary trade fluctuations and help to finance their development; and (4) the fact that other governments are in many ways giving credit and financial assistance to their commerce and the complete lack of it would mean that American producers would lose substantial business available to them with some measure of credit assistance.[22]

Although the advocates of "free trade" tended to equate their economic design with a utopian vision of world peace, the realm of trade was actually one of intense competition and nationalist frictions. To the extent that increased trade, rather than domestic planning, was seen as the route to recovery, the struggle over markets was especially likely to become severe.[23] An official export credit and insurance agency was needed, it was repeatedly argued, because other major trading nations had been establishing their own agencies.

Charles Stuart toured Europe in 1935 to acquaint himself directly with the competition. He reported back to the White House that, since the war, Great Britain, Germany, France, and Italy had each established an official export credit agency, which, however, were operating at generally modest levels. Stuart was convinced that U.S. exporters had lost sales to British suppliers for an electrification project in Poland and a second project in Brazil because the British firms had been underwritten by their official credit agency.[24] Hull, arguing for Exim's continuation, agreed that the U.S. Government had to give its exporters equal backing.

One region of increasing competition between the United States and Germany in the late 1930s was Latin America. Exim concentrated its energies there to prevent Germany from penetrating traditional U.S. markets and from making political inroads in the historical "sphere of influence"[25] of the United States. Exim's exponents considered that the state bank would be useful not only in protecting old markets but in prying open new ones. Charles Stuart stated: "The Bank will grant credit on the merits of cases brought before it, but it will not ignore the factor presented by the desirability of doing business with those countries where definite assurance for the sound increase of American business exists."[26] Exim credits and guarantees could be withheld from governments resisting Secretary Hull's initiatives for more open borders, whereas Exim would be forthcoming to support commerce with nations agreeing with the State Department's designs for reducing the barriers to trade.

Conclusion

The New Deal, with its greater willingness to use the state to solve systemic problems, created an export credit and insurance agency to fill certain gaps in the trade sector that private actors had been unable to close. The depression, with its idle capacity and collapse of international trade and capital markets, heightened the need for an eximbank. It would be a mistake, however, to view Exim as purely a product of the depression. Just as other New Deal initiatives, it was a long time brewing, and met needs that preceded and continued after the Crash.

Although it was a state agency, Exim was never meant to displace private initiative and was not seen as a threat by private interests. Quite the contrary: Exporters and the transnational banks approved of Roosevelt's creation, and worked successfully to mold Exim so that it would complement and not compete with private capital.

The exponents of two contradictory strategies for reviving foreign trade, bilateralism and the MFN principle, saw Exim as a relevant tool for their approaches. Even in Cordell Hull's advocacy of the return to the "open door," the state had important functions to perform. Exim would provide the financial underpinnings for expanding trade through its own credits and by stimulating the international activities of the commercial banks through its guarantees. By extending generous terms, Exim could generate a demand for surplus U.S. production. Its long-term credits would become increasingly useful in spreading American technology around the globe, and Exim would soon undertake the financing of huge investment projects, including steel mills and copper mines.

But Exim's usefulness was not limited to being a mere source of credit, as Cordell Hull and others understood. Nations that failed to recognize that increased foreign trade was in their own interests might be convinced by Exim concessions, or by the refusal of Exim support in times of crisis. Even though the Soviet model would not be adopted by most trading partners of the United States, governments would become increasingly active in economic affairs. The United States would need its own state credit agency to support its traders and creditors in their dealings with foreign governments and to help U.S. exporters in their struggles against government-backed competitors in third markets. These functions would still have to be performed in the postwar period, and Exim would develop and expand accordingly.

The historical evolution of the Bank: a brief sketch

The following brief summary of Eximbank's history provides a chronological outline, which shall be filled in by the more detailed analyses of specific functions and policies made in subsequent chapters. Unfortunately, no complete history of the Eximbank has been written, and this sketch, covering forty-five years of intense activity, stresses only the major topics of the Bank's evolution.

The early years: global depression and war[27]

Exim's first major project was aborted when the United States conditioned Soviet access to Exim facilities on Soviet payment of U.S. debt claims. The immediate purpose for establishing Exim had been to create a state trading corporation to do business with the Soviet Union; Moscow had requested a $200 million credit, including $100 million on twenty-year terms, to import machinery and industrial equipment, especially for railroad construction.[28] Not until the era of East–West detente in the early 1970s would Moscow agree to pay the debt in greatly depreciated dollars and Exim—although only for a brief period—would finally open its windows to the Soviet Union.[29] In the intervening years, Exim had become thoroughly accustomed to doing business with the state agencies that had become commonplace in mixed economies.

In the 1930s, Exim authorized credits tied to specific agricultural and heavy industrial products, and extended balance-of-payments loans to countries suffering a foreign-exchange crisis. Exim credits to China and various European countries, on terms beyond the ninety-day maturities available from commercial banks, helped dispose of surplus cotton, tobacco, and wheat. Long-term credits facilitated the export of such capital goods as locomotives, road-building equipment, and cotton gins. Exim also authorized loans to assist several countries to liquidate arrearages on dollar-denominated debts. For example, in 1935, Exim offered to discount Brazilian notes held by U.S. exporters. These notes had been issued to U.S. exporters awaiting payment in dollars on overdue accounts, and Exim's loan was intended to facilitate the liquidation of these arrearages and stabilize U.S.-Brazilian trade. In 1939, a second loan was extended to the Banco do Brazil to permit direct liquidation of outstanding dollar claims of U.S. exporters.

As U.S.–German relations deteriorated, Exim focused on improving relations with Latin America and excluding German influence from the Western Hemisphere. In 1938, Exim authorized its first "development loan" of $5 million to Haiti to finance U.S. exports of equipment, materials, and engineering services, as well as local costs, for the completion—under the direction of a

U.S. engineering firm—of over 100 separate infrastructure projects, including port facilities, roads, and sewer systems. Other Latin countries received general-purpose lines of credit. In 1939, Exim demonstrated its willingness to cooperate with a state development agency controlled by a Popular Front government, by allocating $5 million for the discounting of notes received by U.S. exporters from the Chilean government's Fomento Corporation.

With the advent of war, Exim was integrated firmly into the countries' strategic policies. Credits were extended quickly to the threatened Scandinavian states, but the Nazi sweep through Europe forced Exim to confine its activities to Latin America and, to a lesser extent, China. President Roosevelt and Congress sharply raised Exim's lending power from $200 million to $700 million, to enable the Bank to participate with other U.S. Government agencies—including lend–lease, the Rubber Reserve Corporation, and the Metal Reserve Company—in increasing U.S. trade with Latin America, especially in raw materials. The most celebrated credits, totaling $45 million, were authorized in 1940–3 to Brazil's national steel corporation, Companhia Siderurgica Nacional. United States Steel Corporation had helped design a steel plant for Brazil but was unwilling to provide the financing for the U.S.-made equipment. Exim's decision to finance the Volta Redonda steel mill resulted in its first direct involvement in an industrial project and in a long-standing relationship with the Brazilian steel industry. Similarly, Exim extended the first of a series of loans to what eventually became the world's largest iron-ore exporting company, Companhia Vale do Rio Doce. Exim's first credit served to develop the iron ores and to rehabilitate the railroad and port facilities needed to ship the ore to England, which was then cut off from its traditional sources of supply. Other war-related credits were extended, for example, to Mexico to build a refinery to produce gasoline for aviation; to the Aluminum Company of Canada (Alcan) for the production of ingots; and to Argentina and Bolivia for the purchase of equipment to mine tungsten ores, with output from all of these ventures earmarked for the United States. In 1943, Exim was placed formally under the jurisdiction of the Office of Economic Warfare.

By the close of the war, Exim already had tested many of the instruments it would continue to use to expand U.S. exports, while simultaneously pursuing the foreign policy objectives of the moment. Exim quickly had developed close working relations with the commercial banks. Exim was discounting their claims, sharing loans by taking the longer maturities, and substituting for the banks when they judged the risk too great, the credit too large, or the terms too extended. All this had been done, with Exim being careful not to crowd out the private banks from profitable business. Demonstrating considerable flexibility, the Bank had ventured to extend lines of credit to central banks, "program loans" for infrastructure and public works, and "project" loans for particular firms in agriculture, industry, and raw materials. Public agencies and corporations, as well as private firms, were eligible for credits. Exim at times resisted pressures from other U.S. government agencies, especially the State

Department, and was often accused of being too conservative and bankerlike for a state agency; nevertheless, the Bank's activities generally were consistent with broader U.S. foreign policy objectives, especially in times of national crisis.

The postwar period

The Export-Import Bank Act of 1945 codified Exim's structure and purposes, and remains in force today, albeit with numerous amendments. The 1945 act made Exim an independent government agency presided over by a five-person bipartisan Board of Directors appointed by the President. The Bretton Wood Agreements Act of 1945 established the National Advisory Council on International Monetary and Financial Problems, composed of the departments of Treasury, State, and Commerce; the Federal Reserve; and Eximbank, and gave it authority to coordinate the policies of U.S. international lending agencies, including Exim. The Eximbank Act also imposes a ceiling on outstanding Eximbank commitments, and the act must be amended periodically to raise the ceiling. Congress and the executive branch (now, through the Office of Management and Budget [OMB]) set annual limitations within the statutory ceiling (see Table A.1 for actual annual authorization levels). The 1945 act also authorized the Treasury to purchase $1 billion in Eximbank capital stock, and increased the Bank's lending ceiling from $700 million to $3.5 billion to help Europe finance its postwar reconstruction.

Eximbank Board Chairman, Leo Crowley, argued that with lend–lease terminating and the International Bank for Reconstruction and Development (IBRD) not yet functioning, Exim had a crucial role to play in the interim. Testifying before the House Banking and Currency Committee, Crowley stated:

The United States has before it an unusually favorable opportunity to maintain its foreign trade at high levels and at the same time ease the problems of reconversion at home and assist in the reconstruction and further development of the economies of foreign countries . . . If private and government financing is available on appropriate terms, large exports of these products (of heavy industry) can be carried out to mutual advantage. It is to be hoped that most of this financing can be arranged through private channels, but it is certain that a considerable amount of Government assistance will be required especially in financing exports of capital equipment, which must be sold on terms which take into account the time required for installing it and getting it into operation.

Substantial lines of credit, including one for $650 million to France, were opened to dollar-short European governments for the purchase of a wide variety of surplus U.S. agricultural and industrial products. These loans were part of a broader flow of U.S. funds, including a separate $3.75 billion Treasury Department long-term credit to Great Britain, and a large appropriation to the UN Relief and Rehabilitation Administration.

Exim refused to lend to certain countries, such as Greece, for lack of the necessary "reasonable assurance of repayment," despite the State Department's fear of the communist insurgency. Partly at Exim's urging, Congress, in 1948, created the first in a series of foreign assistance agencies more suited than Exim was to handling riskier loans at concessional rates. Exim did serve as administrator of over $1.5 billion in foreign assistance credits bearing softer terms, but did not have to carry the risk.

From its inception Exim had worked closely with U.S. investors overseas and in 1948 became the agent for political guarantees issued by the Economic Cooperation Administration to U.S. industrial investments abroad. Exim continued to extend its own credits to U.S. subsidiaries,[30] but Congress denied the power to Exim itself to insure U.S. overseas investment.

With the initiation of the Cold War, Exim increased its standing interest in "strategic" raw materials.[31] In the early 1950s, equipment was financed— sometimes to a U.S.-owned mining firm—to produce iron ore, manganese, nickel, tungsten, uranium, zinc, copper, and cobalt. In many cases the output was reserved for the U.S. market. The Atomic Energy Commission (AEC) stimulated the loans for mining uranium in South Africa,[32] whereas other loans were issued under the authority of the Defense Production Act. In 1953, Exim acceded to State and Defense Department recommendations and authorized a $100 million credit to France to import U.S. military equipment.

The mid-1950s were a less exciting time than the war years for Exim. The Marshall Plan took the lead in reconstructing Europe, while the World Bank and new bilateral agencies created additional competition by offering development assistance and agricultural credits. Exim's activity level stagnated, and the Bank contented itself with the boast "all these agencies are following in the path pioneered by the Bank."[33]

The last twenty years

As the private financial markets recovered from depression and war, Exim followed its statutory mandate to supplement and encourage but not compete with private capital and gave increasing emphasis to its guarantee and insurance authority. In 1961, Exim created an affiliate, the Foreign Credit Insurance Association (FCIA), composed of the larger U.S. marine, casualty, and insurance companies. The FCIA, on behalf of itself and the Eximbank, was empowered to insure export credit extended by U.S. suppliers or their banks, for both commercial and political risk. Exim phased out medium-term lending (one to five years), while expanding and refining its own guarantee programs to cover medium and long-term bank loans.[34] By the early 1970s, Exim was fully integrating commercial banks into virtually all of its loans, allowing the banks to take the earlier maturities, often covered by an Exim guarantee. At the same time, Exim waited for the longer-term maturities to repay its direct credit participation.

During the 1960s, Exim's rhetoric, and to some degree its lending philosophy, shifted from concern about countries' development and international financial stability to a more intense concentration on promotion of U.S. exports in an increasingly competitive world. In the early 1960s, Exim still had referred to its loans as "development project credits," and many loans to Latin America were issued under the aegis of the Alliance for Progress. The Bank also extended sizable "emergency trade credits" to ease foreign-exchange crises in Brazil, Venezuela, Chile, Mexico (twice), Canada (twice), Italy, and Great Britain. By the end of the decade, as the U.S. trade balance worsened, Exim was overwhelmingly emphasizing export promotion and "meeting the competition" from the export credit agencies of other industrial nations. In the 1970s, Exim phased out "emergency trade credits" as other international institutions—the International Monetary Fund and the private banks—handled the task of balance-of-payments financing, and development projects not directly productive were left to the World Bank and the regional banks, including the IDB. Nevertheless, Exim's essential characteristic—the financing of heavy capital goods—remained constant, and kept pace with technological change as Exim devoted increasing funds to such products as commercial jumbo jets, nuclear power stations, and advanced telecommunications facilities.

Commercial competition with our industrial "allies" increased in tempo, and in 1971, Congress mandated Exim to offer conditions "competitive with the government-supported rates and terms and other conditions available for the financing of exports from the principal countries whose exporters compete with United States exporters." In the mid- and late 1970s, Exim joined the other Organization for Economic Cooperation and Development (OECD) export credit agencies in negotiating "International Agreements on Officially Supported Export Credits," which attempted, with very limited success, to prevent official export credit wars by setting minimum interest rates and maximum maturities for different markets.[35] At the same time, Exim maintained its interest rate on its direct credits at below the market rates, and the widening subsidy adversely affected Exim's profit rate.

Throughout the 1970s, Exim remained an instrument of U.S. foreign policy. For example, military base agreements with Spain, Turkey, Greece, and Portugal involved promises of future Exim loans, as did the Panama Canal Treaties. In the case of Chile, Exim followed Henry Kissinger's directives and publicly refused loans to the reformist government of Salvador Allende[36] but extended a $21 million credit to the subsequent Pinochet regime during its first year. Exim sought to increase U.S. and loosen Soviet influence in those relatively open Eastern European countries (Yugoslavia, Poland, and Rumania), while assisting U.S. exporters and banks to penetrate new markets. In 1980, the Carter Administration promised the People's Republic of China $2 billion in Exim credits over a five-year period.

This short introduction to Exim's history suggests the Bank has adapted its policies in response to a changing domestic and international environment.

New technologies and the creation of competing official lending institutions like the World Bank have altered the types of products and projects Exim supports; shifting trends in foreign policy have affected the geographical directions of Exim activity; and the mix of credits and guarantees has responded to the needs and capabilities of private finance. Most identifiable however, is Exim's constancy of basic purpose, as first proposed by the ABA Advisory Committee in its five-point "plan of cooperation" in 1934.

Chapter 2

Eximbank's mainstay: the direct loan program

Background details

The most important of the activities of the Export-Import Bank is its "direct loan program," which authorizes credits to importers of U.S. goods and services. The credits are made in dollars, generally bear maturities of over five years (measured from date of authorization), are normally in excess of $1 million and sometimes $100 million or more, and support capital goods exports. The loan may be in support of the sale of a single, large-ticket item, such as an aircraft; may support several of the same item, such as locomotives or tractors; or may encompass thousands of separate items that will be used in a single investment project. The former aircraft-type loan is referred to as a "product loan," whereas the open account extended to a broader-based supply operation, including whole turnkey plants, is referred to as a "project" loan.

Exim calls the backbone of its operations the "direct loan program" because the Bank makes the loan directly to the foreign importer. The actual applicant, however, may be any of several parties in the export transaction.[1] First, the U.S. supplier who is hoping to win the bid, or who may have already signed the contract, may approach Exim itself; this is a likely procedure when the exporter has had frequent experience with Exim and has an established banker–client relationship, or when the importer lacks the experience or the capacity, as is sometimes the case with the poorer developing countries. Second, and alternatively, a subsidiary of the importer based in the United States may be the applicant, and may later handle procurement. A third possibility is for a financial intermediary to approach Exim. The commercial bank may be acting on behalf of the U.S. firm or the foreign importer. In either case, its job is to line up the necessary finance; the largest international banks dominating trade finance are very familiar with Exim. At times, although the initial applicant is the prospective buyer, the detailed negotiations with Exim will be carried on by a more proximate and better-connected firm, either the U.S. manufacturer or the financial intermediary.

In the case of a project loan, Exim may provide the "creditworthy" borrower enough support to cover all potential U.S. sales. The borrower must pay an annual commitment fee, equal to 0.5 percent of the authorized credit that has not yet been disbursed. Should the borrower decide not to purchase a quantity of U.S. goods equal to the original authorization, the excess may be canceled. Occasionally the entire transaction may fail to materialize, and the whole loan would be canceled. Approximately 12 percent of the amounts authorized are never disbursed. If, however, the project's management decides to purchase more U.S. goods than contemplated at the time of the first authorization, or if costs of the U.S. exports escalate, Exim may decide to grant a supplementary loan; the adjustment for inflation is termed "cost-overrun finance."

Loans bear an expiration date, which is set to allow for full disbursement if the project proceeds as scheduled, with some additional leeway. If necessary, the borrower may request an extension beyond the original expiry date. Exim will accede usually to such a request, unless the creditworthiness of the project has deteriorated. In that case, the Bank might proceed to assure the completion of the project, but may ask in the revised loan agreement for additional covenants that will increase the likelihood of repayment.

There are two basic procedures for disbursement of Exim direct credits. First, the borrower may purchase the U.S. goods, pay the U.S. suppliers directly, and then request reimbursement from Eximbank. A second approach is a "letter-of-credit" procedure. The borrower authorizes the establishment of a commercial letter of credit, subject to Exim approval, at a commercial bank chosen by the borrower. The commercial bank will pay the U.S. supplier upon presentation of required documents. Exim will then reimburse the commercial bank. A variation on the letter-of-credit procedure occurs when "progress payments" are made during the manufacturing process; such progress payments are made typically for large-ticket items, like aircraft or nuclear power plants. Exim, acting through a commercial bank, will make disbursements while construction is in progress, before shipment.

In the letter-of-credit procedure, although the borrower is formally the buyer, Exim is dealing primarily with the U.S. supplier and the financial intermediary. The foreign buyer never receives the Exim funds. The whole process need not leave New York. The commercial bank deposits the payments in the supplier's account, and Exim, in turn, writes out a check to the U.S. bank. In the case of progress payments, Exim's advance disbursements are providing the U.S. supplier with working capital. When repayments begin, Exim then deals directly with the buyer, who must repay in dollars. The job of collection falls on the Bank's shoulders.

In 1969, Exim ceased to bear the entire financial burden of a transaction as a matter of routine. A major portion of the finance now generally comes from a private source, usually a commercial bank, but sometimes from the supplier or his finance or leasing subsidiary, very occasionally from an insurance company, or from the Private Export Funding Corporation (PEFCO),[2] an Exim offshoot. Until 1977, Exim was willing to cover only 30 to 55 percent of total U.S. costs. With a down payment by the buyer of 10 to 20 percent being required, that left the commercial lenders with 25 to 60 percent. In 1978, Exim agreed in certain instances to finance a higher percentage of the contract cost. Exim may guarantee, for a fee, all or a portion of the commercial finance.

A typical financial package was the one anticipated by the preliminary commitment granted to the Brazilian National Steel Company (CSN), in December 1975:

Financing	$ (millions)
10% cash payment	18
45% Exim loan	81
30% private source loan, with Exim guarantee	54
15% private source loan, unguaranteed	27
Total cost of U.S. goods and services	180

The commercial financial burden actually may be greater, because the buyer is likely to try to finance the downpayment as well. Also, interest fees during construction may be capitalized and financial coverage sought, but not from Exim. Exim, of course, will not cover any costs the project may incur from purchasing goods from third countries, and generally refrains from directly covering the costs of local materials and labor, although it might guarantee offshore lenders that will.

Exim and the commercial banks may disburse in either one of two patterns. Disbursement may be *pari passu,* in which case the borrower draws down against all lenders simultaneously, in proportion to their coverage of the financed portion of the transaction. Or alternatively, Exim may disburse its loan first, with the commercial lenders following later. Similarly, with repayment, all lenders may be repaid at the same pace, or Exim may wait and let the commercial lenders be repaid first. In the case where the loan maturities are very long, and the commercial banks are unwilling to accept such a long-term asset, Exim may agree to disburse first and get out last, thereby generating the pattern shown in Table 2.1, which for purposes of illustration assumes a 10:45:45 financial package with repayment in 16 equal semiannual installments. Since the late 1970s, however, Exim has preferred *pari passu* disbursement.

Eximbank charges an interest rate on the outstanding portions of its loans. The rate held at a steady 5.5 to 6 percent from the mid-1950s through 1966, when the rate was raised to 6 percent, where it stayed until 1974. In early 1974, Exim raised its rate to 7 percent, and then in July, 1974, it adopted a completely new policy of charging different rates on different loans, the charges rising from 7 to 8.5 percent depending on maturation. Since then Exim has adjusted periodically its interest rates to accomodate, at least partially, for changing market conditions, at times maintaining slightly higher rates for the longer maturities.

Table 2.1. *A pattern of disbursements and repayments with Exim "in first and out last"*

	Disbursements	Repayments
By Exim	———	
	———	
	———	
By private bank	———	
	———	
	———	
To private bank	———	
		———
		———
		———
		———
		———
		———
		———
To Exim		———
		———
		———
		———
		———
		———
		———

Although interest charges normally are constant for all borrowers, the Bank has reserved the right, which it has exercised, to adjust rates in consideration of special factors; notably, rates have been lowered when U.S. exporters were judged to be facing intense foreign competition.

In every case, however, once Exim has quoted a rate it remains fixed throughout the lifetime of the loan. Exim believes that borrowers prefer the certainty of a fixed cost on their liabilities. This fixed-rate policy distinguishes Exim from most commercial lenders, which, when lending over such long maturity ranges, generally charge a variable rate. The variable rate normally is adjusted every six months, and is set at a certain predetermined margin (usually $\frac{1}{2}$ to $2\frac{1}{2}$ percent) above a base-market rate, either the U.S. "prime" rate, or above the London-Inter-Bank Offer rate (LIBOR), normally understood in long-term international lending as being the six-month dollar deposit rate in London.

The overall cost to the borrower can be determined by combining with appropriate weights the interest charges of Exim and the initial quote of the private finance, although the costs of the private finance remain uncertain and will fluctuate with market conditions. The fee on each Exim dollar weighs more heavily if Exim is "out" longer, that is, when disbursement is not *pari passu,* and/or when Exim waits for the later maturities.

Eximbank often requires that both interest fees and principal repayments be secured by one or various guarantors. Frequently guarantors are governments, their monetary authorities or development banks, although sometimes Exim will accept the guarantee of one or several private firms or banks judged to be strong financially.

The discussion of the authorization and disbursement procedures of the direct loan program, and commercial bank participation, repayment patterns, and interest-rate schedules leads to an examination of the raison d'être of the program: What manner of traded goods are financed by Exim's direct credits?

The allocation of loans by sector, with examples

The sectoral division of Exim's direct credit authorizations (committed and disbursed) that were outstanding as of December 31, 1975, and July 31, 1979, are displayed in Table A.2.

Exim classifies its loans according to the economic sector where the product will be used. Loan officers, who assign the classifications, do not disaggregate the items covered in any one loan, but rather assign a single Exim code number to the entire loan. Thus, if the loan is for a copper processing plant, regardless of which inputs are being exported, the whole authorization will be classified under the sector of "mining and refining." When a loan is authorized, it is classified into 1 of 329 product codes, which are subsumed under one of the eight economic sectors (Table A.2). The following text offers examples of loans authorized in the 1970s, or if authorized earlier, still active at the end of 1975. Authorization dates are in parentheses.

Agriculture

$2.5 million loan for a sugar-growing and -refining complex in the Ivory Coast (April 24, 1972)

$75 million loan for cotton sales to Japan (authorized annually from the early 1950s until 1978)

$1.6 million loan for sugar mill expansion in the Dominican Republic (August 24, 1972)

$18 million loan for an irrigation dam project in Afghanistan (April 29, 1954)

$705 thousand loan for fruit-processing equipment for the Philippines (December 9, 1971)

$6.2 million loan for shrimp trawlers to Korea (September 19, 1974)

Communication

This category, like the remainder, primarily falls in the Commerce Department, Schedule B, grouping 7, for machinery and transportation equipment, but also includes commodities from other groupings, especially code 8, miscellaneous manufactures: aircraft navigational equipment, earth–satellite ground stations, microwave equipment, broadcasting and telephone equipment, computers, films, musical instruments, toys, watches, printed matter, arts, antiques, and other cultural artifacts.

$2.9 million loan for offset presses for Canada (January 6, 1975)
$1.5 million loan for expansion of a microwave relay and tropospheric system in Peru (FY 1977)
$2.2 million loan for an earth–satellite ground station in Zaire (September 28, 1970)
$2.6 million and $4.5 million loans for expansions of microwave systems in South Korea (May 8, 1969 and November 21, 1975)
$1.1 million loan for cyber 72–14 computer system for Poland (March 15, 1973)
$4.0 million loan for telephone installations in Trinidad and Tobago (December 2, 1965)
$9.2 million loan for frequency modulation and television broadcasting equipment for Indonesia (July 31, 1975)

Construction

This category is defined broadly to include building materials (Schedule B 6600), earth-moving equipment (Schedule B 7184), such manufactures as pipes and tubing, pumps, as well as entire constructions such as hotels, office buildings, educational and public facilities, sewage systems, and urban development projects.

$800 thousand loan for hotel expansion in Kenya (January 24, 1973)
$157 thousand loan for scrapers and tractors for Brazil (January 10, 1975)
$440 thousand loan for a power shovel for Mexico (June 24, 1971)
$3.2 million loan for road-building equipment for Nicaragua (FY 1977)
$1.9 million loan for a 400-room hotel in Tehran, Iran (July 31, 1969)
$9.9 million loan for hospital and health facilities in Korea (April 30, 1975)
$1.9 million loan for prefab schools and facilities in the Bahamas (January 4, 1973)
$1.8 million loan for motor graders for Turkey (April 24, 1972)
$1.9 million loan for water supply system in Uruguay (August 31, 1961)

Electric power

This category primarily corresponds to Schedule B 71 and 72—electrical and nonelectrical machinery—but it also encompasses portions of a power plant not included in "construction," as well as power distribution and transmission facilities: electrical power switches; diesel, gas, and turbine generators; electric motors; hydro- and nuclear power equipment and plants; nuclear fuel, nuclear research and training; and thermal and oil-fired power plants and equipment.

$102.2 million loan for hydroelectric power transmission line in Zaire (November 21, 1973)
$141.5 million loan for 2 nuclear power plants for Spain (January 27, 1972)
$732.1 million loan for 2 nuclear power plants for South Korea (FY 1978)
$9.0 million loan for nuclear fuel for Sweden (June 22, 1967)
$2.7 million loan for 15 gas turbine units for Argentina (October 16, 1971)
$2.5 million loan for 2 mobile power generator units for Mexico (June, 1975)

Manufacturing

Limited primarily to nonelectrical machinery (Schedule B 71), to include manufacturing equipment for aircraft, automobiles, cement, computers, fertilizers, pipe and tubing, steel foundry (7152), textiles and petrochemicals. Where an entire plant is so classified, construction materials could be included.

$1.8 million loan for a cement plant in Brazil (May 11, 1972)
$35.0 million loan for expansion of an automotive plant in Brazil (June 8, 1972)
$12.0 million loan for a wire and cable plant in Chile (March 16, 1967)
$6.9 million loan for tire plant expansion in Mexico (FY 1978)
$1.3 million loan for spinning frames for weaving for Taiwan (February 12, 1973)
$1.3 million loan for agricultural chemicals plant in India (November 13, 1975)
$3.1 million loan for expansion of polyester yarn plant in Korea (January 3, 1973)
$16.0 million loan for a pulp and paper mill in Thailand (June 23, 1966)
$12.2 million loan for expansion of fertilizer facilities in Canada (September 5, 1974)
$60.0 million loan for petrochemical plant in Iran (April 6, 1967)
$2.0 million loan for fertilizer plant in Japan (June 23, 1966)

Mining and refining

Subsumed mostly under nonelectrical machinery (Schedule B 71) is equipment for mining, as well as processing, of zinc, lead, copper, bauxite, gold, and so forth, as well as oil and gas drilling equipment and steel mill plant and equipment. The inclusion of steel, considered as part of a vertically integrated mining and refining process, deprives the "manufacturing" category of an important item. Inputs such as coal, coke, metal scrap, rubber, chemicals, and petroleum are also encompassed.

$13.5 million loan for development of nickel deposits in Indonesia (December 13, 1972)
$68.0 million loan for oil and gas field development for Norway (October 1, 1973)
$1.7 million loan for bauxite mining equipment for Guyana (January 14, 1974)
$5.7 million loan for expansion of iron ore mining complex in Australia (November 19, 1970)
$50.0 million loan for integrated steel mill in France (June 29, 1971)
$15.0 million loan for integrated steel mill in Japan (December 17, 1964)
$13.5 million loan for expansion of oil refineries in Israel (November 20, 1975)
$240 million loan for natural gas liquefaction facility in Algeria (FY 1978)
$11.3 million loan for oil refinery in Taiwan (April 2, 1973)

$3.5 million loan for phosphate mining and processing in Israel (May 31, 1962)
$10.0 million loan for coal mining in Canada (November 6, 1969)
$43.2 million loan for expansion of iron-ore mining facility in Canada (December 30, 1970)
$33.4 million loan for copper mining and processing in Trust Territory of New Guinea (now Papau–New Guinea) (March 5, 1970)
$13.6 and $9 million loans for copper mining in Zambia (January 13, 1972 and January 27, 1972)
$56.3 million loan for copper mining and processing in Zaire (August 15, 1974)
$2.8 million loan for oil drilling rigs for Burma (March 11, 1971)

Transportation

The means of air, land and sea transport as well as portions of the related infrastructure not included in construction comprise the transportation sector. Items covered include aircraft engines and parts, diesel engines, helicopters, commercial aircraft, railroad locomotives, ships, motor vehicles, highway and railroad development projects and maintenance, harbor and port construction, and subway systems.

$31.6 million loan for six DC–8 commercial jets for Sweden (January 23, 1967)
$10.9 million loan for one DC–10 jumbo jet for Cayman Islands (May 13, 1974)
$808 thousand loan for one executive jet aircraft for Brazil (December 23, 1975)
$6.1 million loan for six helicopters for the United Kingdom (January 21, 1974)
$2.7 million loan for airport design and construction in El Salvador (June 1, 1961)
$25.5 million loan for one 747 jumbo jet for Pakistan (FY 1978)
$2.6 million loan for diesel locomotives for Tunisia (June 11, 1964)
$14.7 million loan for components for 195 locomotives for Brazil (November 20, 1974)
$4.6 million loan for harbor and port construction in Guatemala (June 11, 1964)
$41.9 million loan for highway development in Bolivia (March 6, 1942)
$18.7 million loan for a suspension bridge in Venezuela (August 23, 1963)
$6.8 million loan for subway car components for Brazil (FY 1978)

Table A.2 shows that three sectors accounted for three-quarters of the authorizations: transportation, electric power, and mining and refining. Commercial jet aircraft and nuclear power, subsectors of transportation and electric power, respectively, accounted for at least 40 percent of loan authorizations. Although these products have been sold with Exim financing all around the world, and would account for a sizable percentage of the number of loans, they owe their predominance in loan volume to the size of each item. Loans in support of nuclear plants can easily exceed $100 million. A single jumbo jet can cost as much as $40 million.

Mining and refining are evidently a major aspect of Exim's activity. The Bank has been involved in small and very large projects, in the industrial as well as the underdeveloped countries. Support has been extended for both the mining as well as the processing stage (which would normally fall under "primary metals" or perhaps "chemicals"). Exim has been especially active in copper, nickel, iron and steel, and petroleum.

Exim has devoted a surprisingly small share—not more than 10 percent—of its authorizations to manufacturing. In part, this volume is understated because of the inclusion in "mining and refining" of processes normally thought of as manufacturing. Otherwise, the type of manufacturing supported has tended to be of the "traditional" or "light" sort, namely, textiles, cement, and tires, but Exim has also lent for the more "modern" processes, like automotive and chemicals. The Bank has not lent much, if any, support for the establishment of plants to produce capital goods abroad.

Agriculture largely has been neglected by Exim. A sizable portion of the existing exposure represents cotton and tobacco exports, which are holdovers from long-standing lines of credit for industrial countries begun in the postwar period, before the Commodity Credit Corporation (CCC) opened its Export Credit Sales Program in 1956. They are exceptions to Exim's concentration on capital equipment. Sugar, which has attracted loans in various countries, is the main foreign crop of interest to Exim. Despite the inclusion of irrigation projects, exposure in agriculture is small. Power generation equipment, classified under its own heading, could generate electricity for the countryside and could somewhat mitigate the neglect of rural areas.

The low loan volume in communications understates Exim's involvement. Because such credits tend to be modest in size, several hundred million in exposure has allowed Exim to play an active role in communications programs in many countries, especially in lesser developed countries (LDCs). Earth–satellite ground stations have been an Exim speciality; the Bank has also supported numerous communications networks using the microwave system. Telephone systems are another frequent Exim borrower.

Because road development, as well as port facilities, are categorized under transportation, construction is somewhat understated. Exim occasionally has supported schools and hospitals, but loans for large international hotels have been more frequent. Earth-moving and other construction equipment, which could easily fall into the transportation category, are often backed by Exim. Nevertheless, construction has not been a dominant Exim concern (partly because most components in construction work are local materials).

Exim loans as a percentage of U.S. exports by product group

International trade data are not classified by sector but by product group. Therefore the Exim authorizations cannot be compared to the general pattern of U.S. exports by using the eight sectors. Fortunately, Exim has regrouped its loans to compare them to U.S. exports as ordered in the Standard International Trade Classifications (SITC). Table A.3 shows the breakdown by product groups, for disbursements in 1974. Table A.4 gives the corresponding SITC codes. Also shown, as a percentage share of total U.S. exports and by product type, are exports shipped in 1974 that benefited from these Exim loans disbursements. Although the level of disaggregation is not very great, several interesting details are revealed.

It is immediately clear from columns 1 and 2 of Table A.3 that most agricultural produce and industrial intermediary inputs, such as chemicals, are traded without the assistance of Exim credits. (The U.S. Government has other export promotion credit programs specializing in agriculture, namely, the CCC and Public Law (PL) 480.) Nearly $2 billion of the $2.24 billion in Exim disbursements are classified as machinery and transportation equipment, with most of the remainder being armaments ($157 million), followed by miscellaneous manufacturing, with only $8 million. Aircraft, primarily commercial jets, is the single largest category, with $727 million or 32 percent of total loan disbursements. In close competition for second largest grouping are chemical processing plants and equipment ($417 million) and power-generating machinery ($389 million).

Column 3 of Table A.3 gives some indication of the weight of Exim's lending efforts in U.S. exports. In 1974, Exim loans participated in U.S. exports whose value was 5 percent of total exports. Focused on capital goods, Exim loans supported some 12 percent of machinery and transport equipment. Exim appears to have supported several times the amount of nuclear and hydropower plants and equipment than actually were exported. There are two explanations for this. First, Exim may disburse to cover progress payments that are made while the item is in construction and before the actual shipment; second, items that Exim includes in the "plant" may be classified elsewhere in the SITC. Despite these serious and evidently gross imperfections, it can be concluded safely that Exim is involved in a major proportion of such exports. Discussion in Chapter 9 reveals that most nuclear plants that leave the United States enjoy Exim involvement.

Table A.3 places Exim loan support for commercial jet aircraft at 40 percent of shipments, and of railroad vehicles at 32 percent. Although the problem of progress payments may hold for these items, leads and lags should wash out. Because ancillary plant equipment is not involved for planes or locomotives, these measures are more exact. The high percentages give a clear indication of heavy Exim involvement in select sectors.

When viewed from the perspective of all U.S. exports, Exim direct lending appears to be of reduced impact, just as many programs and many economic variables, when viewed in a macrosweep, appear marginal. But looking more acutely, first at investment goods, and then at specific sectors, notably aircraft, nuclear power, and certain specialized machinery (such as offshore drilling rigs and copper mining equipment), it is apparent that Exim covers a healthy portion of the total.

Table 2.2 gives an indication of the percentage of capital goods exports covered by all of Exim's loan and guarantee programs. Because Exim's guarantees are medium and long term, they are assumed to involve capital goods. The data on the Foreign Credit Insurance Association (FCIA)—Exim's affiliate, which is reinsured and closely scrutinized by its parent—as presented in Chapter 4, suggest that about 60 percent of FCIA insurance covers machinery and trans-

Table 2.2. *All Exim programs as a percentage of U.S. merchandise and capital goods exports*

Export value ($ billions)	1973	1974	1975
Loans	6.558	8.795	7.362
Guarantees	.524	.431	.613
FCIA insurance (60%)	2.078	2.119	2.716
Total	9.160	11.345	10.691
U.S. merchandise exports	71.4 (13%)[b]	98.3 (12%)	107.1 (10%)
U.S. capital goods exports[a]	27.8 (33%)	38.2 (30%)	45.7 (23%)

Note: Exim figures are for fiscal years, U.S. export figures for calendar years.
[a]Capital goods figures are from section 7, "Machinery and Transport Equipment" of Schedule B groupings of commodities, Commerce Department, *U.S. Exports: World Area by Commodity Groupings,* 1973–6.
[b]Figures in parentheses show the export value of all Exim programs as a percentage of exports.

portation equipment. Table 2.2 compares Exim loan, guarantee, and insurance authorizations (rather than disbursements) to U.S. merchandise exports and also to machinery and transportation exports, during 1973, 1974, and 1975. The figures suggest that Exim programs were supporting roughly one-quarter of U.S. capital goods exports. If automobiles, which accounted for one-quarter of machinery and transport exports in 1975, are excluded, the percentage of investment goods exported that were supported by Exim would be appreciably greater.[3]

Repayment terms

Capital goods are sold on credit with lengthy maturities for two reasons. First, because the amounts are often great, and second, because the payoff period is extended, as the machinery must be installed or the plant constructed before the buyer even begins gradually to make the return on the investment that will allow for repayment of debts. It follows from Exim's selection of exports that its loan portfolio will be weighted heavily toward the long-term end of the maturity spectrum.

Table A.5 shows this to be so. On loans being disbursed in 1974, for example, only 5 percent bore maturities of less than five years and most of these were agricultural products. Vestiges of the postwar period—and maintained by pressure from agricultural interest groups—Exim was still making these loans for cotton shipments to Japan and tobacco to the United Kingdom and Canada. (In Table A.5, "term" is measured from the date of disbursement, as it is commercial bank practice, rather than from the date of authorization, which is the definition used by Exim in its interest-rate schedule.) A full 69 percent of dis-

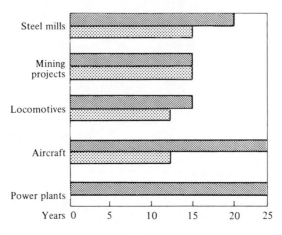

Figure 2.1. A comparison of maturities in domestic capital goods financing and those available to foreign purchasers of comparable U.S. goods. Top bar (dark) indicates maturities for the domestic capital market, the bottom bar (light) for Exim. (*Source:* Eximbank, *Annual Report FY1975*, p. 7.)

bursements had maturities of over ten years; aircraft, locomotives, and chemical plants tended to place in the ten-to-twelve-year range, whereas power-generating equipment and petroleum refineries stretched beyond twelve years. As will be discussed in Chapter 3 where Exim is compared to other financial intermediaries, this maturity structure differs sharply from commercial banks, most of whose claims mature within one year. Only a development lending institution such as the World Bank, or perhaps an institutional investor, carries a portfolio whose assets are frozen into a future so distant.

Eximbank argues that U.S. investors have been willing to provide even more futuristic maturities for comparable capital goods sold domestically, as the graph in Figure 2.1 illustrates. However, that portion of the capital market that provides such long-term finance—the bond and equity markets and other instruments purchased by institutional investors—are generally not accessible to foreigners seeking trade finance.

The suppliers

The preceding discussion, although it is a thorough treatment of sectors and products, does not provide an answer to the question of which U.S. corporations have been the production sites for the commodities that Exim has helped finance. In all of Exim's publications, as well as internal reports, there is no known attempt to answer this question. Exim's "Statement of Active Loans," however, does mention the name of the supplier with each loan, except when, as occurs frequently, there are several, and then the listing is "various." For large projects, although the number of U.S. suppliers would be great, Exim sometimes names the prime contractor. Military suppliers are also excluded. Despite these obstacles, an analysis of loans authorized during two time frames—calendar years 1972–3 and the second semester of 1975—is revealing.

The 1972–3 sample finds that the twenty-five leading corporations[4] accounted for 83 percent of the loans where suppliers were identified, which totaled $2.9 billion. The four principal recipients—Boeing, McDonnell Douglas, Westinghouse, and GE—received over 60 percent of the nearly $3 billion in classifiable authorizations. This trend is confirmed in the later, 1975 sample, where the same four firms captured an even more impressive 84 percent of the $849 million in loans where the supplier could be identified (for calendar years (CY) 1974–5, they captured 53 percent).

For the 1972–3 sample, 13 of the 25 were rated among the 300 largest industrial corporations, as ranked by *Fortune* in its May 1974 survey of the "Fortune 500": These included, in addition to the top four (Boeing, GE, McDonnell Douglas, and Westinghouse), General Motors (GM), Ford, Bethlehem Steel, Lockheed, General Tire and Rubber, Allis Chalmers, Koppers, Foster Wheeler, and Fuller (a subsidiary of Northrop). Seven of the others are major construction firms, which would have provided engineering and procurement services for large overseas projects, themselves subcontracting to other U.S. suppliers unidentified by Exim. In the 1975 sample of 15 firms, in addition to the top 4, GM, Lockheed, and Allis Chalmers (a capital goods producer), reappear from the earlier sample. Of the remaining 8, 5 also made the top 300 in *Fortune*'s 1976 ratings. The remaining 3, Lipe-Rollway, Gensco, and Colorado Fuel, made the list by capturing one sizable loan each. (In a list that covers a longer time span, such one-shot victories are edged out by those able to maintain access to Exim funds.)

Not surprisingly, there is a strong overlap between Exim's distribution of loans by product and its concentration of loans among producers. Exim leans heavily toward supporting power-generation equipment and commercial aircraft: Westinghouse and GE dominate the former market, whereas Boeing, McDonnell Douglas, and to a lesser extent Lockheed, dominate the latter. The appearance of GM on both lists partially reflects its strong position as a producer of locomotives.

The buyers by geographical region

Exim finances the sale of products of U.S. corporations on a global scale. Table A.6 shows the geographical distribution of outstanding Exim loans as of 1975 and 1979. A majority and rising proportion of loans have been made to the

LDCs. In 1975, approximately one-third of existing loans were in Europe, with nearly 5 percent being to Eastern Europe (the USSR, Poland, and Rumania), but the 1974 congressional restriction on loans to the Soviet Union contributed to a reduction in the European share to 25 percent by 1979. Loans to most of the European countries have been primarily for aircraft and power equipment, which will be discussed in Chapter 10. Chapter 6 will discuss the determinants of Exim lending to LDCs.

Chapter 3

Eximbank and the U.S. capital market

The unknown bank

For even the most well-informed Americans the U.S. Export–Import Bank is no more than a name that recalls some glancing mention in a mostly forgotten newspaper story. More than one Congressperson has proved to be unaware that the Eximbank was a wholly U.S. institution. Many people, should they hear mention of Exim, associate it with the World Bank, a much better known institution. The Eximbank, seemingly, has kept a low public profile—although it has not failed to court carefully those whose support has mattered.

Commercial banking institutions still are inhabited by dark-suited, secretive figures, but their public affairs officers have not shied away from using the modern mass media to place their banks' names before the public. New Yorkers have been promised a quick "chemical reaction" at Chemical Bank, and everyone has a friend at Chase Manhattan. Part of the media push of commercial banks is a facet of their competitive struggle to capture the public's savings, and part of it is to create "good will."

Eximbank does not have to compete for the public's deposits. When the Bank needs money, it either borrows from large investors, or, as is now the practice, has the U.S. Government borrow money for it. So long as Exim retains the good will of the Office of Management and Budget (OMB) and Congress, it retains access to Treasury funds.

Scholars have written extensively on the activities of the commercial banks, not as individual corporate institutions but as "private capital markets." The Eximbank, both as institution and function, has been almost completely neglected by academic writers, whether historians or social scientists.

The discussion of this chapter will try to exhibit Exim in its proper place in the international capital markets. To begin, the volume of Exim activity will be compared with that of the multilateral development institutions, whose main function is also to provide long-term capital to finance the international movement of investment goods. Attention will then shift to another major source of lending to foreign borrowers, namely, U.S. financial intermediaries, especially the commercial banks, but also nonbank financial institutions. The volume of their international lending, as individual banks and in the aggregate, will be compared to Exim's, after which the discussion will focus on the provision of credit tied to export trade. Special attention will be given to comparing activity levels at the long-term end of the maturity spectrum.

Exim and the international development banks

At first glance, Exim and the World Bank, the largest of the international development banks, might appear to be two completely different species. The World Bank, although located in Washington, is a multilateral institution, whereas Exim is a parochially national agency. The World Bank addresses human suffering in Asia and Africa, but Exim today makes no pretenses about its strictly business-oriented concerns regarding U.S. corporate competitiveness and export promotion.

Stylistic differences should not blind one to the tremendous similarities in purpose between Exim and the World Bank. Both provide long-term capital to allow the borrower to import investment goods. The World Bank lends exclusively to LDCs, but most of Exim's commitments are also to the developing world. Both institutions have devoted significant resources to electrical-power generation, mineral extraction, and capital-intensive transportation construction. The World Bank and Exim have a long, conflictive history over which should finance disputed projects.[1] Sometimes they have jointly supported projects.

The understated Exim has had, in fact, a career that even the energetic and growth-oriented president of the World Bank during the 1970s, Robert McNamara, might respect. Over its lifetime, Exim has committed $47 billion in credits to foreign borrowers (as of September 30, 1978), whereas the three divisions of the World Bank Group, International Bank for Reconstruction and Development (IBRD), International Development Agency (IDA), and International Finance Corporation (IFC), have promised their clients $59 billion. The figure for Exim does not include the $50 billion in additional guarantees, insurance, and discount options that Exim has authorized to U.S. clients who in turn were granting credit to foreign customers. Exim, it is true, is an older institution, having been founded in 1934, whereas the World Bank is a postwar creation, but Exim's activity before 1945 was very limited.

In the 1965–74 decade, the lending activity of the two bodies was comparable. Exim authorized over $25 billion in loans, the World Bank $22 billion, with Exim surpassing or equalizing the more famous development agency in all but three years. Although the World Bank had the legal power to insure loans, it did not do so; thus, if annual authorizations for insurance and guarantees in support of international credit are added in, Exim totals excelled in every year by safe margins. Also, as Exim loans cover only a portion, generally under 50 percent, of a transaction (while the World Bank had just begun to venture into cofinancing with private creditors), the export value supported by each Exim loan was greater. Thus, in FY1974, the total value of goods supported by Exim loan commitments was $8.8 billion, and of loan plus guarantee commitments $12.8 billion, both of which surpass the World Bank's FY1974 $4.5 billion commitment level.

In the second half of the 1970s, while Exim loan levels slumped, the World Bank expanded rapidly, such that by FY1978 World Bank lending more than doubled Exim's. Nevertheless, Exim's total activity levels—including loans and guarantees—still rivaled the World Bank's, and the export value of products supported by Exim continued to surpass the lending levels of the World Bank Group (see Table 3.1).

The World Bank Group is larger than the combined strength of the three regional banks—the Inter-American Development Bank (IDB), the Asian Development Bank (ADB), and the fledgling African Development Fund (ADF). The IDB had its origins in the Alliance for Progress of the Kennedy era, and attained the billion-dollar authorization level only in 1974, whereas the ADB did not reach that goal until four years later. None of the three regional banks approaches the financial scope of Exim. Until 1976, Exim's annual loan and guarantee activities even surpassed the combined annual commitments of all the international development institutions (Table 3.1).

A size comparison with the commercial banks

If Exim can more than hold its own against the much-vaunted multilateral lending agencies, how does it compare to a second major source of international credit, the U.S. commercial banks? Before examining aggregate data, it will be instructive to see how Exim matches against individual financial corporations. Table 3.2 displays the lending levels of five of the nation's largest banks.[2]

Despite the extraordinary growth of private bank lending in the 1970s, at the end of 1978 Exim's activity levels exceeded the outstanding loan levels attained by two of the five largest U.S. banks, J. P. Morgan and Company, and Manufacturers Hanover Trust. Only the top three giants of finance—Citicorp, the Bank of America, and Chase Manhattan—show higher levels of exposure.

The loan balances of the commercial banks include credits to domestic as well as international customers. Table 3.2 breaks out loans made to foreign borrowers by the largest private banks. All of Exim's loans, although written in Washington, are extended to foreign borrowers. When foreign activities are compared, only Citicorp had a level of exposure, at $35 billion, surpassing that of the Eximbank.

The overwhelming majority of Exim's loans ($17 billion at the end of FY1978) bear maturities of over five years. Of its $35 billion in overseas loans, Citicorp categorized only $2.8 billion as being foreign-currency loans (i.e., not in local currency, many of which are consumer loans) not guaranteed by an industrial country institution, with maturities over five years.[3] Alternatively, of the $30.9 billion in loans charged to overseas offices, $4.8 billion had such long-term maturities.[4] These figures suggest that Exim is, by far, the most important source of long-term international finance among U.S. banking institutions.

Table 3.1. *A comparison of international development bank and Eximbank commitments*

Fiscal year	World Bank group	Inter-American Development Bank	Asian Development Bank	Total Development Banks	Eximbank commitments		
					Loans	Loans and guarantees	Export values
1973	3.6	0.7	0.4	4.7	4.1	8.5	10.5
1974	4.5	1.0	0.4	5.9	4.9	9.1	12.8
1975	6.1	1.1	0.6	7.8	3.8	8.3	12.5
1976	6.9	1.2	0.9	9.0	3.9[a]	10.1[a]	14.0[a]
1977	7.3	1.2	0.5	9.0	1.2	5.6	8.5
1978	8.7	1.5	1.0	11.2	3.4	7.4	10.6

[a]Includes the transition quarter resulting from the redefinition of the fiscal year.

Source: World Bank, *Annual Reports* (Washington, D.C.: World Bank, 1973–9); Inter-American Development Bank, *Annual Reports* (Washington, D.C.: Inter-American Development Bank, 1973–8); and the U.S. Treasury Department, *Annual Reports of the National Advisory Council on International Monetary and Financial Affairs* (Washington, D.C.: GPO, 1973–9).

Table 3.2. *A comparison between activity levels of Eximbank and the five largest private U.S. banks*

Bank	Total loans	International loans[b] (loans, year-end, 1978, $billions)
Citicorp	52.3	35.0
Bank of America NT & SA	49.3	20.9
Chase Manhattan Bank	38.5	21.7
Manufacturers Hanover Trust	23.4	12.5
Morgan Guaranty Trust	19.0	11.5
Eximbank[a]	26.4	26.4

[a]Includes committed loans and contingent liabilities at end of FY1978.
[b]In their respective annual reports for 1978, Citicorp, Chase Manhattan and Morgan Guaranty listed loans by domicile of the borrowers; the Bank of America listed "loans to foreign customers," and Manufacturers Hanover simply listed "foreign loans." These last two categories should correspond closely, although not necessarily exactly, to the "domicile" category.

Exim's specialty: the long-term loan market

The U.S. Treasury Department publishes aggregate data on claims on foreigners[5] reported by banks, whether U.S.- or foreign-owned, located in the United States. As of September 30, 1978, such claims on foreigners totaled $107.3 billion.[6] Leaving aside intrabank claims and foreign customer liabilities, the remaining bank claims on foreigners totaled $59.5 billion. Of these, only $12.8 billion had remaining maturities of more than one year. The Treasury fails further to disaggregate outstanding loans by maturity, but data published by individual banks indicate that a substantial majority of these medium- and longer-term claims would fall due within five years. In any case, Exim, with $17 billion in loan commitments, the large majority with maturities in excess of five years, had a greater volume of long-term international loans than all the banks in the United States combined.

The U.S. Treasury also publishes data on international claims of nonbank financial institutions in the United States.[7] As of September 30, 1978, such institutions reported $18.3 billion in outstanding short-term claims and $5 billion in claims with maturities over one year. The combination of these long-term claims with those of financial institutions yields a total figure of $17.8 billion, approximating Exim's loan commitments. The majority of such claims, however, would bear maturities under five years, and be classified by Exim as "medium term." Most of Exim's loans are committed for over five years, as required by the type of heavy capital goods Exim finances.

These statistics illustrate the surprising weight of Eximbank in the financial markets for internationally mobile long-term capital. Clearly, any study of U.S. financial intermediaries as sources of this important type of finance that fails to consider the impact of Exim is omitting an important variable.

Trade credits

Exim's energies are focused on trade. Commercial lending institutions, however, extend credit to foreigners for a gamut of reasons, including relative interest rates and exchange-rate movements not necessarily directly related to the international flow of goods and services. Unfortunately, banks are not required to break out export credit as a separate category in their international claims reports. An indication of the relative weight of export credit in international bank lending, however, can be surmised from statistics gathered by the Federal Reserve while it was monitoring the Voluntary Foreign Credit Restraint Program (VFCR). Because the VFCR guidelines allowed exemptions for export credit, the Federal Reserve required all U.S. commercial banks and U.S. branches and agencies of foreign banks to report their level of export finance. Whatever the success of the VFCR as a control mechanism, this attempt at government regulation typically did make available some interesting economic data.

Tables A.7 and A.8 reproduce the data as released by the Federal Reserve. Table A.7 shows assets of the 226 VFCR-reporting U.S. banks, whereas Table A.8 covers 71 reporting agencies and branches of foreign banks located in the United States. Table 3.3 aggregates portions of these two tables. Line 2 of Table 3.3 has been constructed by summing lines 2(C) from the two Federal Reserve tables, to yield the total of outstanding export credits.[8] Similarly, line 1 sums lines 1(A) of the two tables in the Appendix to show total claims.[9]

In a survey of 1970 VFCR-reported data, the Federal Reserve found that 30 percent of the export credits had original maturities of over one year (most of which, incidentally, were held by the seventeen largest banks).[10] Line 3(B) on Table 3.3 extrapolates this finding to the later data (which failed to include their own maturity schedules), to show the quantity of long-term claims outstanding against foreigners that were classified as trade credits.

Three observations can be made about this statistic, which had reached only $2.8 billion by June, 1974: 1) Banks in the United States had not been anxious to supply long-term trade finance; 2) trade support weighed more heavily among total long-term claims (in the neighborhood of 30–40 percent) than among short-term claims, which accords with an a priori judgment recognizing the more varied functions of short-term flows; and 3) Eximbank had been a much more fertile source of long-term direct trade credits than all the commercial banks in the United States, whether domestic or foreign owned, summed together.

Line 2(A) indicates that of those export credits U.S. banks were willing to extend, a considerable portion—50 percent in November, 1971, 31 percent in

Table 3.3. *Foreign claims and export credits of U.S. and foreign branches of banks reporting under the VFCR guidelines ($ millions)*

Category	Nov. 1971	Dec. 1971	Nov. 1973
1. Claims, including loans, acceptances and deposits held for own account	13,532	14,687	22,273
(A) U.S. banks	10,515	11,700	14,438
(B) Agencies and branches of foreign banks	2,817	2,987	7,835
2. Export credits other than to residents of Canada	3,503	4,092	8,143
(A) U.S. banks	2,789	3,299	5,860
Participated in or guaranteed by Exim/FCIA	1,388	1,429	1,837
(B) Agencies and branches of foreign banks	714	793	2,283
Participated in or guaranteed by Exim/FCIA			43
3. (A) 2 as percent of 1	25.9	27.9	36.6
(B) 30 percent of 2	1,052	1,228	2,443

Source: From Tables A.7 and A.8.

November, 1973—were guaranteed by Exim/Foreign Credit Insurance Association (FCIA). The decline resulted from an alteration of the VFCR guidelines exempting all export credits, not just those covered by Exim/FCIA. Because Exim/FCIA guarantees and insurance failed to keep pace with U.S. exports in subsequent years, the degree of coverage may have fallen somewhat further.

During the time the VFCR guidelines were in effect, the Federal Reserve also collected trade credit data from U.S. nonbank financial institutions. Their involvement in trade finance was shown to be nominal: For example, as of December, 1972, of $16.7 billion in assets held for their own account, nonbank financial institutions reported only $97 million in export credits.[11] (The bulk of their assets was invested in Canada.) Their $1.2 billion in direct obligations of international institutions suggests, however, some indirect support for long-term trade finance.

Financial guarantees: cofinancing with the private banks

Just as Exim at its inception was responsive to the needs of the private sector for capital, so have its programs adapted to the changing abilities and requirements of the private capital markets. As the capacity of the commercial banks to extend medium- and long-term loans has grown, Exim has taken them on as co-workers in export finance. Rather than supply 100 percent of the credit itself, Exim now divides the financial package between itself and commercial lenders. The magnitudes have varied over time, yet during the 1970s the private sector generally covered between 30 and 70 percent of the financed portion of a transaction; this excluded the downpayment, which commercial intermediaries also may have financed.

The private sector, mainly the commercial banks, now fully participate in Exim's business, but they do not necessarily share the risks. Exim stands ready to cover the participating private finance with a financial guarantee that covers all commercial and political risks, and guarantees full repayment of principal and most of interest charges. (The guaranteed interest will be 1 percent above the Treasury's borrowing rate for comparable maturities and will be fixed at time of authorization.)[12]

For its financial guarantee Exim used to charge 0.5 percent per annum on the outstanding balance of the guaranteed loan, but because of increasing losses on its various guarantee and insurance programs, Exim raised the rates in 1975, to between 0.75 percent and $1\frac{1}{2}$ percent, depending on market credit ratings: the riskier the market, the higher the charge. In FY1978 rates were lowered to the 0.5 to 1.0 percent range, as part of an attempt to coax the banks to increase their support for U.S. exports.

Exim offers three justifications for the financial guarantee program:[13]

1. To assure that Exim supplements and encourages, rather than competes with private sources of export finance, as its legislative act mandates
2. To assure that private financial institutions will continue to provide export credits and
3. To spread Exim's limited cash resources to the largest possible number of purchases and projects

The financial guarantee program became increasingly active in the 1970s (see Table A.9). In the 1960s, the U.S. commercial banks were expanding rapidly their overseas business and increasing their interest in lending long-term maturities. The following figures show the long-term claims on foreigners reported by banks in the United States:

Year	$ (millions)
1957	1,174
1960	1,698
1965	4,517
1967	3,925
1970	3,075

Source: U.S. Treasury Department, "Financial Operations of Governments and Funds," *Treasury Bulletin* (Washington, D.C.: Government Printing Office), Table CM-II-4.

At the same time, U.S.-owned banks literally were moving overseas, such that by 1971 the assets of their foreign branches had reached $60 billion,[14] a portion of which was available for long-term trade finance. The banks would and could argue that, should Exim take them out of overseas financing entirely, it would be competing with private capital. This would contradict a basic tenet of business philosophy, which is imbedded firmly in the Eximbank Act of 1945, as amended: "In the exercise of its functions [the Bank] should supplement and encourage, and not compete with, private capital." For Exim to provide 100 percent of the financing clearly was competing. To provide only a portion, while insuring the privately financed fraction, was to supplement and support.

The decline in long-term loans after 1965 was caused in part by the ceilings placed on international lending by the VFCR program to halt the outflow of capital. The especially restrictive ceiling was placed on long-term loans, because their delayed payback was seen as detrimental to the balance of payments and the strength of the dollar. The VFCR, however, contained an important exemption: An export credit that was guaranteed by Eximbank or its affiliate FCIA was excluded from the lending ceilings.[15] The banks, therefore, could benefit from an Exim guarantee program that would cover their long-term maturities as a mean of circumventing government regulations. After 1970, when Exim's financial guarantee program began its rapid growth, long-term overseas bank lending did resume its growth, although the gradual removal of the VFCR in the 1970–4 period makes it impossible to isolate the impact of Exim's financial guarantees.

The financial guarantee program thus allowed Exim to encourage rather than compete with private capital, at the same time allowing the commercial banks to circumvent distasteful controls on international capital movements. The appointment by Richard Nixon in 1969 of Henry Kearns as chairman of Exim also contributed to the development of the guarantee program. Kearns, a former used-car dealer from the Los Angeles area, was a dynamic salesman who had a mandate from the Administration and Congress to increase substantially Exim's volume of business. This mandate, reflected in the removal of Exim's outlays from the budget, was part of the general export promotion thrust to shore up the weakening dollar. Kearns understood quickly that Exim could get a greater return for each dollar lent by covering only a portion of each export. The number and volume of exports supported by each Exim dollar could be increased by splitting the financing burden with the private sector.

Financial guarantees, moreover, weighed less heavily against Exim's activity levels as set by Congress and OMB, because insurance and guarantees are charged on a fractional basis (25 percent) against activity ceilings.

To Exim's credit, the concept of "cofinance," in which public and private capital mix in a single transaction, was only just beginning to catch on at the World Bank and the IDB by 1975. The IBRD put together its first such financial package in late 1975 in a loan (to the Companhia Siderurgica Nacional) to Brazil for steel manufacturing, a sector that Exim had been extending mixed direct credits and financial guarantees to for several years.

Table 3.4. *The ratio of financial
guarantees to direct credits, as of
December 31, 1975*

Risk group	Ratio
A	13%
B	48%
C	67%
D	19%

Source: Unpublished Eximbank memoranda and author's calculations.

Exim used to give each country a credit rating: A was the best, B and C intermediate, and D the worst except for those countries "off cover." In 1977, Exim ceased to label countries A, B, C, or D, switching instead to an insurance-fee ranking that was very similar to the ratings, but less explicit. Table 3.4 compares Exim's exposure, as of December 31, 1975, by type of risk, for financial guarantees and for direct credits.

Notable is the much lower ratio of financial guarantees to direct credit for the A countries, mainly the European Economic Community (EEC), Canada, and Japan. It is unlikely that Exim's percentage of participation in exports to Western Europe is generally greater than to the LDCs. Assuming, therefore, that the participation of private finance stands in a similar ratio for at least A, B, and C countries, it follows, not surprisingly, that the banks have been more willing to carry the risk when lending to industrial nations.

(The explanation for the low ratio for the D countries derives from the special circumstances of those few D countries where Exim has much exposure. In the case of the then D-rated Chile, for example, when Exim rescheduled $303 million in loans between 1973 and 1975, it paid claims on guaranteed loans, some of which then became oustanding Exim "loans" to Chile. Consequently, as of the end of 1975, Exim had only $17 million in financial guarantees out in Chile, whereas it had $319 million in direct credits.)

The richest countries have the best access to private finance without having to be covered by Exim. The C countries, which are generally the poorest, are evidently also considered less creditworthy by the commerical banks, which frequently seek Exim's guarantee when lending to them. At the same time, the less creditworthy and usually poorer countries must pay higher fees for Exim's guarantee. The commercial banks formally pay the guarantee fee, but it is agreed generally that the banks successfully pass on most, if not all, of the fee to the borrower.[16] The poorer borrowers are doubly penalized: They need guarantee coverage more frequently, and they pay more for it.

Commercial bank behavior and the role of the state

Commercial banks prefer short-term risks for several reasons relating to their liability structure, interest-rate fluctuations, uncertainty, flexibility, government regulations, and custom. Because bank liabilities primarily are short-term deposits, sudden withdrawals could cause a liquidity crunch if the bank's assets were frozen in long-term investments. Also, should interest rates on deposits rise, while the rate of return on assets was fixed by long-term arrangements, a bank could find its costs exceeding its earnings. If interest rates should rise, a portfolio dominated by short-term claims can promptly relend funds at higher rates when receivables are canceled. Another reason for bank preference for short-term loans is that rapid turnover allows for frequent collection of profitable "front-end" fees, such as "administrative" charges. Finally, because bank examiners tend to rate long-term loans as riskier than short-term, they reinforce bankers' psychological aversion to the increased uncertainty associated with long-range projects. Keynes attributed the preference for short-term assets to psychological motives: "Of the maxims of orthodox finance none, surely is more anti-social than the fetish of liquidity, the doctrine that it is a positive virtue on the part of investment institutions to concentrate their resources upon the holding of 'liquid' securities."[17]

In bankers these psychological traits can affect lending when they are "played out" through the interest rate. Bankers argue that often they will not supply long-term funds *at any price* (i.e., the supply curve becomes vertical). The reasoning is either that no interest rate is considered high enough to offset the perceived risk or, when lending to corporate clients (the group generally involved in capital goods trade), the rate above prime that can be asked is circumscribed by bank–customer relations. A loan officer would rather inform the clients that the bank is unwilling to increase its exposure with them than insult clients by quoting an extraordinarily high interest rate. Such is the traditional gentlemanly behavior of the banking community, and its relation to corporate customers produces an upwardly sticky interest rate.[18]

Citibank, in its *1975 Annual Report,* offers this explanation for its maturity scheduling:

Since risk increases with the length of the obligation, determination of maturity scheduling is an integral part of Citicorp's asset management. The majority of Citicorp's loans outside the United States mature in less than one year; longer maturities are specifically and closely controlled and limited to stronger borrowers. Short maturities permit relatively rapid reduction in exposure as conditions change (p. 19).

This preference of important financial intermediaries for short-term lending is disfunctional from the point of view of U.S. manufacturing firms interested in overseas markets. The United States has developed a "comparative advantage" in heavy capital goods, which cannot be shipped bit by bit, as would be appropriate for routine 180-day lines of credit. United States investment goods are lumpy and expensive, require massive front-end finance, and because they earn returns only gradually over many years, they must be sold under slow and lengthy payment schedules. To complement the U.S. industrial structure, an institution was needed that would provide international credits in very large amounts with generous repayment terms. Because the private U.S. capital market appeared unwilling to play this role, the job fell to the State (see the argument in Chapter 1 on Exim's origins).

The preceding discussion demonstrated that Eximbank, at the end of 1978, had committed more long-term maturities than all the U.S. commercial banks combined, and three times as many as all nonbank U.S. financial institutions. A sizable portion of those long-term maturities that the commerical banks had extended, moreover, were guaranteed by Exim or Exim's affiliate, the FCIA. Exim's bank and financial guarantee programs are intended to coax the commercial banks to provide the type of credit the U.S. industrial sector needs to sell its capital goods abroad. (Chapter 8 traces Exim's historical support for the international activities of the private banks. Chapter 4 discusses how Exim, through its insurance affiliate, the FCIA, has continued to encourage private capital to increase its participation in export finance.) To the extent that Exim succeeds in restructuring the U.S. capital market and its international lending practices, the private financial market would then complement the "real" sector and the State could gradually withdraw. In the absence of sufficient private zeal, the task of meeting the international credit needs of U.S. capital goods' exporters has remained with the State, in the form of the Eximbank.

Chapter 4

The Foreign Credit Insurance Association

The Foreign Credit Insurance Association (FCIA) was founded in 1961 as an affiliate of Eximbank, to offer insurance to U.S. exporters. The FCIA is an amalgam of over fifty "of the nation's leading marine, property and casualty insurance companies"[1] whose combined assets exceeded $40 billion in 1978.

The FCIA was founded on two basic principles. First, the risks involved in export insurance could be spread among the numerous affiliated companies, and by increasing the total volume of business the pooled portfolio would be diversified. Second, the private firms would act with the backing of the State, as the Eximbank was to be involved intimately both in a managerial and financial capacity. The main justification for government involvement was the need of U.S. exporters to neutralize the competitive edge foreign competition enjoyed by having their own national export insurance agencies.[2] The insurance companies were being called on to serve U.S. exporters but not, however, to enter a new field for their own profit.

Theoretically, export credit insurance stimulates exports by acting both on the supply and demand sides of the transaction. The suppliers are encouraged to sell overseas because the risk has been reduced, and because the insured export paper is a nearly risk-free asset, which can be discounted readily by a financial institution. These two conditions assure prompt liquidity for the supplier. At the same time, the buyer is stimulated to purchase U.S. exports because of the greater willingness of the supplier to extend credit. To the extent that FCIA insurance causes a reduction in interest charges, the price-elastic buyer also is encouraged. (In practice the premium charges, which are passed on to the buyer, generally exceed any reduction in interest costs.)

Description of programs

The numerous variants on FCIA policies[3] essentially break down into short-term (up to 180 days) or medium-term (181 days to 5 years), with coverage being either for political risks only, or for both political and commercial risks. The comprehensive Master Policy unites all the separate policies, to cover both types of risk for both short- and medium-term sales. In each case the eligible applicants include manufacturers, commerical banks,[4] and other financial institutions, and export merchants. Applications may be made through any insurance agent or broker, to an FCIA regional office, or to FCIA headquarters in New York's World Trade Center.

Commercial risks are those arising either from insolvency of the buyer or failure of the buyer to pay the insured within six months after maturity of the obligations, that is, "protracted default." Political risks are defined as "transfer risks" and "other." The transfer risk results when the buyer is unable to obtain U.S. dollars in a lawful market, despite having deposited the U.S. dollar equivalent in local currency with the proper exchange authority. This could occur when a solvent firm finds its country to be bereft of foreign exchange, or when foreign-exchange controls result in an allocation that excludes the buyer.

Other political causes for nonpayment include requisition or expropriation by a governmental authority of the buyer's business, as well as "war, hostilities, civil war, rebellion, revolution, insurrection, commotion or other like disturbance." Valid causes for indemnity under political coverage include the cancellation of an import license, or any other new official law or regulation that, through no fault of the buyer, prevents the import of the insured shipments. The exchange-rate risk, although it may result from official action, is not covered. Default by a firm affected adversely by exchange-rate movements would be covered under commercial risk.[5]

The FCIA often relies heavily on the lender's opinion as to the creditworthiness of the buyer. To stimulate some caution on the part of the lender, the FCIA generally requires that the policyholder retain a portion of the risk, normally 10 percent. In riskier markets, the FCIA may agree to cover only 70 percent or 80 percent of the risk. For certain agricultural commodities, coverage may be increased to 98 percent. Some FCIA policies contain a deductible provision, whereby the insured absorbs first losses. Other policies set the policyholder's losses as a percentage of retained risk on each defaulted payment. The deductible policies, such as the Master, are considered "catastrophic," as the insured is covered completely, after the initial deductible, in the event of massive losses.

Under short-term policies, interest payments are not insured, but partially covered by a medium-term policy. In neither case does FCIA place restrictions on the interest charged to the buyer.

For short-term insurance, the FCIA issues a policy that covers the "whole turnover," that is, all export shipments of the insured, although exceptions are allowed, for example, on exports to Canada or exports covered by a confirmed letter of credit. Medium-term insurance is extended on a buyer-by-buyer basis; it may be for a single transaction, or for repetitive sales under a revolving line of credit. A Master Policy, however, which covers medium-term transactions, allows for coverage for multiple buyers. When a policy covers more than one buyer, it carries an aggregate limit (which may be in the tens of millions of dollars), as well as a "discretionary credit limit," which is a dollar limit (often well under $100,000) within which the insured may grant credit to any single buyer without prior FCIA approval. To be insured for a larger amount to a single buyer, a "Special Buyer Credit Limit" must be requested.

Table A.10 shows the breakdown of annual authorizations among short-term, medium-term, and master policies. When the FCIA was founded it initially offered only short-term policies, and short-term insurance continues to account for more than half of its annual authorizations. Short-term policies cover a wide range of products, including food, chemicals, partially processed goods, and some nonelectrical machinery (approximately 20 percent of shipments). In contrast, medium-term coverage is reserved primarily for machinery and transportation equipment, reflecting the longer repayment period required for capital goods or expensive consumer durables such as automobiles.

As Table A.10 shows, FCIA business began to grow rapidly in FY1970, as did Eximbank generally, such that, from FY1969 to FY1973, FCIA insurance authorizations increased from $842 million to $2.5 billion. In FY1974, although Exim loan authorizations grew 21 percent, FCIA activity stabilized. The association's *Report of Operations 1974* attributed the difference to a consciously conservative policy adopted because of the recession: "The FCIA Board of Governors and management recognized these upcoming . . . financial and credit problems among foreign importers . . . early in 1974 and decided to pursue a cautious underwriting policy during the year" (p. 2). This approach is opposite to that a public agency would take if it were pursuing a counter-cyclical policy. Rather than retrenching along with the private market in times of adverse financial conditions, it would act boldly to absorb the heightened risk into the public sector, thereby stimulating private business.

One frequent user of the FCIA attributed the association's slowed growth to its greater concern with profitability, an opinion reinforced by the sharp hike in premium costs announced in 1975. The association had suffered losses in the early 1970s—especially in Chile[6]—and, moreover, had begun to pay its shareholders dividends. The FCIA client complained that the increased concern with profitability had caused the association to adopt a more conservative evaluation of a buyer's creditworthiness.

Determination of creditworthiness

To determine the commercial creditworthiness of a buyer the FCIA requests that its statement of financial condition be submitted, generally as approved and audited by an accounting firm—the FCIA itself will not go to the firm to do an in-depth study of its books. (When granting discretionary authority, the FCIA will visit the firm's credit rating department to judge its competency.) The FCIA will examine the buyer's financial statement in the traditional manner, checking profit and liquidity trends, and will perform the usual "ratio" analysis, which is intended to reveal the firm's financial soundness. The FCIA will also solicit opinions from such agencies as Dun and Bradstreet, and from commercial banks, generally the largest ones, that have had previous experience with the buyer. Local references may also be included. The FCIA together with Exim keeps computerized files on over 100,000 foreign buyers, recording their past transactions with the two agencies. Finally, the FCIA may consult the records of the Berne Union, an international association of issuers of export credit.

Buyers are often guaranteed, by individuals, banks, public agencies, or, in the case of subsidiaries, by the parent company. The financial statement of the guarantor is also examined, as are credit references. A strong guarantor sometimes will offset sufficiently a poor rating for the buyer, and thereby offer the required "reasonable assurance of repayment." In some cases even a strong guarantor will not warrant taking a risk with a financially weak buyer. Considerable leeway for judgment exists.

The FCIA relies heavily on the opinion of other institutions in determining its credit rating of buyers. (When discretionary authority is granted, the FCIA depends completely on outside opinion.) Most sources of information are private firms. It is not surprising that the opinions of private firms would be valued highly, as the FCIA itself is simply an amalgam of private insurance companies. Most of FCIA's underwriters come from the world of commercial banking. The confidence of FCIA in the opinions of the private sector suggests that its credit ratings will mirror those of the private market. As one veteran FCIA officer concluded, "FCIA uses the same criteria as the private banks." But, because it is backed by a government agency (Exim), and because it will take into account political consideratons, the FCIA's portfolio might not strictly reflect the credit ratings as gleaned from the private market. For example, an insurance officer from an international credit and marketing firm, a repeated user of FCIA, stated that it should be "obvious" that an exporter can ask his congressional representative to pressure Exim to grant insurance coverage for his market. Exim itself provides the coverage for political-risk insurance and determines the credit rating of each country; the FCIA acts only as the agent.

Premium cost

Premium costs for an FCIA policy are a function of the type and length of coverage, the credit rating of the buyer, and whether the credit is guaranteed. For medium-term and master policies, buyers are categorized, in descending order of quality, as "sovereign" (e.g., Ministry of Finance or Central Bank), "nonsovereign public" (semiautonomous government agencies or firms), and "private," with a subcategory of "private guaranteed" buyers that fare somewhat better. Premiums for medium-term coverage can add several percentage points to the cost of a transaction: Coverage for political and commercial risk can cost, per $100 of financed shipments, $2.45 for a "sovereign" buyer, $2.80 for a "nonsovereign public" agency or a guaranteed private firm, and $3.50 for an unsecured private firm. Short-term coverage costs in the $0.15 to $1.00 range.

Shipments to riskier buyers not only may demand higher premiums, but also might bear the burden of various restrictive conditions, such as the mandatory presence of an acceptable guarantor and the removal of discretionary authority from policyholders. Before November, 1979, higher levels of downpayment and exporter risk retention could be required, but the 1979 reforms made the normal cash payment of 15 percent and the exporter commercial risk retention of 10 percent standard for all markets.

Before 1977, the country of the buyer weighed heavily in determining premium fees. Shipments to firms with good credit ratings were several times more expensive to insure in weak countries than in A countries. The FCIA found that the country distribution of losses did not justify this approach, which prejudiced firms in the lower-rated countries—frequently the poorer LDCs—and worked against U.S. exporters seeking to penetrate these newer markets. The 1977 reforms also simplified greatly the FCIA fee structure.

As was the case for financial guarantees, the consensus is that the buyer bears the cost of the FCIA premium.[7] The charge is passed on as a cost, either in the price of the item, or as a cost of shipment and packaging, or, overtly, as insurance. Thus, those buyers already in shaky financial straits must pay considerably more for FCIA coverage. Because FCIA insurance can add several cents on the dollar to the cost of imports, the extra financial burden is very real. The burden of the premium would be mitigated if the insured lender lowered the interest charge. An Exim director has remarked that, for reasons never clear to him, banks have not dropped their rates despite FCIA/Exim coverage.[8] An official of an East coast international credit corporation opined that lenders may be willing to reduce interest charges that had been set abnormally high because of the buyer's weak creditworthiness, but would not reduce the already relatively low rates charged to prime borrowers. If this is correct, then FCIA insurance, by lowering interest costs to weaker markets, induces changes in market prices that offset, at least partially, its premium charges. It is unlikely, however, that interest rates would fall sufficiently to compensate completely for the stiff premiums levied against high-risk buyers.

FCIA and Eximbank

The FCIA has very close institutional ties with its parent, Exim. Moreover, the policies of the two institutions nicely complement each other in their support of U.S. exports.

Exim's control over the FCIA is complete. An Eximbank officer is one of the ten members of FCIA's Board of Governors (the other represent nine different insurance companies). More important, all major policy decisions must be submitted to the Exim Board for approval. Even individual insurance policies, if large enough, are subject to Exim's veto; as of 1976, under the reinsurance agreement between FCIA and the Bank, FCIA's Delegated Authority to commit insurance of whatever type, without prior approval by Exim, was limited to an aggregate of $2,125,000 per buyer.

Exim logically can exert this authority because it reinsures FCIA policies for 100 percent of the political risk, and because it is Exim that offers political insurance, with the FCIA acting as agent. Exim also absorbs commercial losses on any claim when it passes a certain amount. This "stop-loss" provision limits the FCIA's potential liabilities.

When the FCIA was first set up in 1961, it represented Exim's response to a 1961 amendment to its legislative act allowing the Bank to "charge against the limitations imposed by Section 7 of this act, not less than 25 per centum of the related contractual liability which the Bank incurs for guarantees, insurance, coinsurance and reinsurance against political and credit risks of loss." The amendment, like its offspring, the FCIA, was an objective of the Kennedy Administration.

The FCIA was the natural complement to Exim's direct loan program. By offering insurance, Exim could involve itself in exports moving on short and medium-term credit. The entire range of exports, from agricultural goods and other consumables to heavy capital equipment, could thereby benefit from official backing, either through insurance, credits, or both.

The FCIA and Exim are complementary especially in large overseas projects. Exim may finance the heavier and more costly equipment through its direct credits. At the same time, smaller components may be covered by FCIA insurance.

With the development of its medium-term discount and bank guarantee programs, Exim entered into direct competition with the FCIA's own medium-term insurance. These programs offered basically the same services of reducing the risk while facilitating liquidity. The FCIA made its policies, as did Exim, available to financial intermediaries. Exim argued that this duplication produced a healthy competition among programs. The FCIA believed that its parent had unnecessarily created medium-term programs that were usurping the insurance association's natural function.

Exim used to have a short-term discount program that competed with FCIA's own short-term policies. With the development of the bankers' acceptance market,[9] however, Exim considered that its own short-term discount program was unnecessary and competed with the private market, so it was dropped.

Conclusions

This brief sketch of the FCIA has highlighted some of its behavioral characteristics and the fundamental principles behind its creation. While the private U.S. market was unwilling to offer systematically export insurance, foreign governments were providing such services to their own exporters. To fill this gap in the private market, to foster U.S. exports, and to match the activity of other governments, the FCIA was created. The guiding principles are risk pooling and diversification. The actors are private insurance companies, but the public sector stands ready to absorb any large losses. (For Exim to offer the short- and medium-term credits is forbidden by the commandment that it is better for the Bank to supplement and encourage private capital than to compete with it.) Being an amalgam of private firms, peopled with analysts whose experience lies in the private market, the FCIA tends to apply the only criteria it knows in credit analysis, although it may not be immune to political pressures channeled perhaps through its parent, Exim. The members of the association, being private firms, have come to believe that the FCIA ought to be profitable. Fees were raised sharply in the mid-1970s; according to some users credit ratings have stiffened; and more cautious policies are adopted during uncertain economic conditions. This profit-seeking, risk-reducing behavior has conflicted in several instances with the public goal of export promotion; caution during cyclical downswings abroad has deprived exporters of credit insurance at the very time when export demand is weak; and, because premiums are generally passed on as costs to the buyer, the price-elastic purchaser may look elsewhere. Actuarial logic—just as much as a view of the proper role of a state-supported institution as risk taker and promotor—motivated the reforms of 1977, after which the FCIA ceased to emphasize country conditions in setting premiums. The FCIA premium structure no longer inhibits systematically U.S. creditors and exporters from penetrating newer, lesser-known markets.

Part II

The selection and distribution of loans

Chapter 5

Determinants of loan authorizations to developing countries

Exim pays close attention to the country of the borrower when analyzing loan applications. "Country conditions" are a factor in determining commercial risk, and define the degree of political risk. Exim monitors closely its level of exposure in each country, quantifying it in each major loan document presented to the board of directors. Country conditions are especially important when—as occurs in the majority of cases—an official institution is either the borrower or guarantor. In addition, before a major transaction is approved, the State Department can express its attitude toward the government of the country in question.

Exim credits to most of the industrial countries are concentrated heavily in aircraft and nuclear power stations. These transactions, which will be analyzed in Chapter 9, are more reflective of sectoral rather than country policies; actually all the industrial countries carry an automatic A credit rating at Exim. Therefore, in examining the distribution of loans across countries, this chapter will concentrate exclusively on lesser developed countries (LDCs).[1]

Exim has lent to well over 100 countries, but many LDCs have received relatively insignificant amounts. Table 5.1 lists the leading thirty LDCs, by amount of outstanding credits authorized as of the end of FY1974. The level of commitment ranged from $1.1 billion for most-favored Brazil to Egypt's $36 million. Not shown is the bunching of the remaining nations who have had less access to Exim's treasury. The thirty countries displayed accounted for 62 percent of all Exim loan activity, and the large portion of LDC activity.

Exim's business is trade finance. The following discussion examines how the trade and financial patterns of the thirty largest of Exim's LDC clients relate to Exim loan activity. Shown on Table 5.1 is a measure of a country's participation in international capital markets: Listed are outstanding (including undisbursed) credits authorized by private sources that had maturities of one year or more, and that had been made to, or guaranteed by, the recipient country's government. This measure of foreign debt, which is the best available, is provided by the World Bank. Private sources include suppliers' credits, private banks, bonds, and obligations arising from nationalizations. Credits to private firms or individuals that are guaranteed publicly are captured; private non-guaranteed credits, such as those that might be made within a transnational corporation (TNC), are not recorded. Although the data therefore understate

Table 5.1. *Thirty LDCs: levels of Exim lending compared to other economic indicators*

Country	Rank	Exim loans[a] ($ millions)	Debt[b] ($ millions)	Schedule B-7[c] U.S. exports ($ millions)	GNP[d] ($ billions)	U.S. aid[e] ($ millions)
Brazil	001	1,120	4,670	823	52.0	2,972
Spain	002	942	733	449	41.5	1,858
Iran	003	864	2,096	328	15.2	2,356
Taiwan	004	733	389	398	7.4	6,718
Mexico	005	557	4,252	1,367	40.3	542
Yugoslavia	006	527	563	99	16.8	2,695
Chile	007	337	1,434	58	8.0	1,351
Argentina	008	293	2,250	133	31.0	469
Algeria	009	280	3,309	73	6.1	242
South Korea	010	273	1,702	282	9.9	11,425
Indonesia	011	204	981	162	10.9	1,812
India	012	171	443	86	61.9	9,037
Zaire	013	168	947	90	1.9	440
Philippines	014	155	281	180	8.6	2,183
Venezuela	015	148	938	484	13.8	307
Turkey	016	147	241	129	13.7	6,557
Israel	017	146	2,425	246	8.1	2,047

Ivory Coast	018	102	455	53	1.8	79
Pakistan	019	98	603	29	8.8	5,072
Portugal	020	97	408	69	7.6	499
Peru	021	88	977	163	7.4	600
Singapore	022	79	165	449	2.8	37
Colombia	023	79	616	156	9.3	1,253
Panama	024	78	359	104	1.3	266
Jamaica	025	60	260	82	1.6	91
Dominican Republic	026	58	224	67	2.0	497
Liberia	027	46	21	21	0.4	251
Thailand	028	37	85	74	8.3	1,883
Malaysia	029	37	320	83	4.9	93
Egypt	030	36	279	80	8.3	1,206

a Outstanding (including undisbursed) Eximbank credits, as of June 30, 1974. *Source:* Eximbank, *Cumulative Records*, 1974.

b Outstanding (including undisbursed) external public debt (including publicly guaranteed private) from private sources, including suppliers, banks, and "other." Calculated from World Bank, *World Debt Tables* (Washington, D.C., 1975) (EC-167/75), vol. 1, Table 4 (annex).

c Purchases of U.S. exports of machinery and transport equipment, Section 7 of the Schedule B groupings of commodities. *Source:* Commerce Department, *U.S. Exports: World Area by Commodity Groupings* (Washington, D.C.: Government Printing Office) FT455/ Annual 1973, 16–19.

d GNP as of mid-1972. *Source:* World Bank, *World Bank Atlas* (Washington, D.C.: World Bank, 1974).

e United States government foreign assistance, military and other, net of repayments, July 1, 1945 to December 31, 1973. *Source:* The National Advisory Council, *International Finance: Annual Report for Fiscal Year 1975* (Washington, D. C.: Government Printing Office) Table B-1, 206–11.

the true level of indebtedness, they should give an indication of relative levels of foreign borrowing.

Column 4 of Table 5.1 shows each country's purchases of U.S. machinery and equipment in 1973; this subset of all U.S. exports is more relevant for Exim business, as Chapter 2 demonstrated. Also shown is each country's gross national product (GNP) as of mid-1972, as well as the total net U.S. aid received from 1945 to 1973, including military grants and (net) credits.

The figures for foreign debt, U.S. aid, and Exim loans are accumulated stocks, whereas U.S. exports are a one-year flow. The justification for mixing stocks and flows in the same table is that each series was chosen as the best indication of true activity level: Private credits, U.S. aid, and Exim loan authorizations, as yearly *flows,* are very erratic for many countries, a problem that is avoided by employing a stock accumulated over time; export flows, on the other hand, tend relatively to be stable.

The thirty countries listed account for 81 percent of the aggregate GNP of the developing countries, and 84 percent of their accumulated external debt. They accounted for 24 percent of U.S. equipment and machinery exports (hereafter referred to as capital goods) in 1973, and had received 42 percent of all outstanding postwar aid.

Countries with higher levels of international borrowing and capital goods imports from the United States have also ranked among the larger uses of Exim (Table 5.1). For example, Brazil, the top-ranking Exim borrower, had the highest foreign debt and was the second largest importer of U.S. capital equipment. Although the ordinal rankings of Exim borrowers do not correspond perfectly to the country rankings for debt and trade, the top ten Exim users generally were much more active in these two areas than were the second group of ten, which, in turn, showed higher levels of financial and trade activity than the third group of ten. Appendix B contains the regression analysis that substantiated the view that a country's level of foreign debt and imports of capital goods do "explain" some reasonable portion of the distribution of Exim loans.

The statistical analysis also revealed that, as a country's importation of capital goods from the United States increased, Exim's attention to that country increased disproportionately. Exim's disproportionate favoritism of the larger borrowers was an interesting result; the central conclusion of an analysis of Table 5.1, however, is that the Eximbank has moved squarely within the overall matrix of U.S. trade and world capital flows. Exim has concentrated its lending in those same LDCs that are the major purchasers of U.S. capital goods, and frequent borrowers on the international (as well as the U.S.) private capital markets.

Table 5.1 shows correlation but not causation, and the statistics do not reveal whether Exim has been following or leading decisions made by private actors. Perhaps the process can best be viewed as simultaneous, with Exim, exports, and private capital intertwined with all moving together. Chapter 6 on credit-

Table 5.2 *The leading LDC Exim customers: measures of GNP and external growth*

Country	Trade sector growth, 1968–73[a]	Per capita, annual GNP growth, 1965–72[b]	Debt-service ratio, 1973[c]
Brazil	229%	5.6%	14%
Spain	192	5.0	4
Iran	218	7.2	11
Taiwan	382	6.9	4
Mexico	111	2.8	25
Yugoslavia	155	5.5	7
Chile	45	2.2	11
Argentina	117	2.8	18
Algeria	151	3.5	13
South Korea	289	8.5	14

[a]Growth in the trade sector is the percentage increase in exports and imports in 1973 as against 1968. Growth in the world trade sector was 141 percent. *Source:* IMF, *International Financial Statistics.*
[b]Source: World Bank, *World Bank Atlas,* 1974.
[c]Debt-service ratio is defined as the service on public (including publicly guaranteed private) debt as a percentage of the exports of goods and non-factor services. For all LDCs, the debt service ratio was 9.4. *Source:* World Bank, *World Debt Tables* (EC-167/75), vol. 1, table G and table 6 (annex).

worthiness criteria will expand on this observed similarity between Exim and private-sector behavior, as will Chapter 8, which examines the relation between Exim and the transnational corporations.

The most-favored nations

The top ten LDC recipients of Exim loans accounted for 46 percent of outstanding authorizations to all countries, developed and underdeveloped (see Table 5.1). The regression analysis has explained Exim lending levels to LDCs in terms of select variables, yet more information emerges by taking a closer look at the most-favored ten, examining movements in their foreign trade sector, GNP growth rates, and their debt-service ratios.[2] These variables are displayed, by country, in Table 5.2.

Seven of the ten countries experienced rapid growth in foreign trade (exports and imports) and gross domestic product; The remaining three, Mexico, Argentina, and Chile, are Exim's traditional Hispanic-American clients. (From 1935 through the 1950s, Exim was oriented primarily toward Latin America, except for a brief period after the war when Exim gave loans for reconstruction in Western Europe.) In foreign trade, in the years 1968–73, the sum of exports and imports for five of the countries grew much more rapidly than the world average of 141 percent. Algeria and Yugoslavia also surpassed this average rate but by a lesser margin; however, Yugoslavia's trade sector has been expanding much more rapidly in previous years, and Algeria's growth speeded up in 1974.

In domestic product, the performance of Exim's non-Hispanic-American clients is even more impressive. Six of the seven achieved per capita growth rates of 5 percent or more over the 1965–72 period; again, Algeria's growth was somewhat slower, but would catch up in 1974–5.

Thus, seven of Exim's most-favored clients have demonstrated dynamic growth with special emphasis on international commerce, that is, their expansion has been accompanied by a growing openness to foreign trade.

Most of Exim's major clients were becoming more integrated into world trade, but simultaneously they were borrowing heavily from both public and private sources. Seven of the ten reappear in the list of the 10 largest LDC borrowers in private capital markets. By 1973, these seven countries were devoting a considerable percentage of their resources, despite rapid export growth, toward repaying the accumulated foreign debt; more than 10 percent of each nation's receipts from the export of goods and services was being eaten up by debt service. The highest debt-service ratios were experienced by Mexico, Argentina, and Chile, whose debt payments in 1973 would have been much higher than listed in Table 5.2 except for a multilateral debt relief exercise. Of the remaining less heavily burdened countries, Yugoslavia's 7 percent debt-service ratio was still considerable and growing. Only Spain and Taiwan had escaped.[3] Of course, among the major creditors of these ten countries was Eximbank.

A high debt-service ratio, by itself, is neither good nor bad. If indicative of creditor confidence and based on an intelligent intertemporal allocation of resources, a high level of foreign borrowing may boost growth. Such a capital influx is often seen as relieving a major bottleneck to growth in a capital-short economy. The debtor country, however, makes an important compromise: To be able to repay its creditors, it must insert itself further into the international economy by increasing its exports (although reducing imports is possible theoretically, this low-growth option is unattractive, especially for most LDCs with their rigid structure of "essential" imports). Alternatively, the debtor country can seek to repay old debts by borrowing anew; but creditors are likely to exact a commitment that the refinancing be accompanied by a pledge to increase exports, and so the integration of the debtor country into the international economy proceeds apace.

Substantial accumulated foreign debt and rapid growth in the trade sector are two good indicators that Exim's major clients, by and large, were well integrated already into both the U.S. and international trade and financial markets, and becoming more so. Exim, by facilitating the flow of goods and capital, was playing its part in this increased integration.

Of Exim's top ten LDCs, seven fell into the World Bank classification "high-income" developing country (per capita income exceeding $375); of the remaining three, two—Iran and Algeria—enjoyed the status of being "oil exporters," while South Korea stood at the top of the list of "middle-income" LDCs, as of the end of 1973.[4] This group of higher-income LDCs, with their rapid growth and openness to foreign trade and, generally, to foreign capital, are now of paramount interest to U.S. firms, banks, and the U.S. Government. Robert Hormats, while serving as Deputy for International Economic Affairs on the National Security Council, explained this interest from a historical perspective:

If you take a look at the last thirty years of history of the international economy, perhaps the two most significant elements are the fact that Japan and West Germany have been brought into the system as cooperating and participating members . . . As a result, they have been two of the most dynamic countries in the international economy over the last thirty years, in terms of export markets for the United States and in terms of financial relationships with other countries . . . This has obviously benefited the United States enormously. The task over the next 10 to 20 years is to try to do the same thing for many of the key developing countries . . . Saudi Arabia is obvious. Iran, Brazil, Korea, Mexico, Venezuela, Indonesia.[5]

By placing the State firmly behind the outward thrust of U.S. firms and banks, Exim has been reinforcing this outward movement, and aligning the U.S. Government with it. Exim's lending patterns fit well into Hormat's prescription for U.S. foreign economic policy.

Political variables

Aid flows are an indication of political support, or at least interest in, the recipient country by the grantor. The correlation between Exim authorizations and U.S. aid was found to be low (see Table B.1), despite the inclusion of Exim credits in the official aid figures. Certain countries that are generally "strategically" located have received aid, including military, in amounts that are disproportionate to their economic ties to the United States, for example, Thailand, Turkey, Israel, Taiwan, and South Korea (see Table 5.1). Other countries, such as Egypt, India, and Pakistan, have been important target countries in the Cold War.

The relationship between Exim and concessional aid is complex. Sometimes Exim substitutes for other forms of aid, and sometimes Exim loans are part of an overall assistance package. Exim's more nearly commercial-rate loans gradually can replace concessional grants and loans as a country graduates from aid. It is noticeable, however, that seven of the ten LDC nations most favored by Exim have received $1 billion or more in net aid flows (excluding Exim credits). Aid at such levels is a clear sign of political support.

Of the three remaining, Mexico and Argentina were considered too wealthy to receive bilateral aid, although Mexico has been a favorite of the U.S.-influ-

:d multilateral lending agencies. The United States has maintained gen-
y good relations with both countries. Only Algeria among Exim's top ten
⊃ clients cannot be classified so readily. After its independence, the relations of Algeria's socialist government with the United States were cool. By
the time they began to improve, the U.S. bilateral aid program was winding
down, so that nearly all U.S. "aid" credits to Algeria have come from the
Eximbank.

The first and second Exim credits to Algiers, authorized in 1970–1, financed
traditional Exim products—two Boeing 727s and GM locomotives—but two
other early loans (totaling $23 million) were earmarked for irrigation, a
"developmental-type" project. By 1976, the Bank was concentrating its business in Algeria on extracting and refining natural gas for export to U.S. ports.
Together, these different types of loans composed a three-pronged attempt to
warm Algiers toward the United States and to increase U.S.–Algerian economic ties. The jet planes were prestige items, and together with the locomotives, made Algeria's transport system dependent on U.S. technology and spare
parts. The irrigation loans demonstrated U.S. sympathy for Algeria's ambition
to make its desert bloom. The very large loans for the natural gas extraction
and refinery complex served several purposes: They showed U.S. Government
support for Algeria's most important development project; helped U.S. firms
gain a foothold in a formerly French-dominated market; and secured supplies
of natural gas for the U.S. market and for the El Paso Gas Company of Texas.
The increased two-way trade flows were intended to create mutual interests
between the trading partners. In sum, Exim loans were a major vehicle in the
U.S. Government's efforts to improve relations, diplomatic and economic, with
an oil-rich and influential third-world nation.

This examination of U.S. aid levels and intentions indicates that a high level
of Exim lending often runs parallel to strong official political support for, or at
least hopeful interest in, the government of the borrowing country. In no case
was Exim found to be lending heavily to a "hostile" regime. Countries such as
Cuba, Iraq, and Syria have had little or no access to Exim programs. Congress
has proscribed lending to communist countries in the Eximbank Act (Section
2.(2)(B), as amended and approved January 4, 1975), unless the president
makes a special determination. Although Exim has been allowed to lend to
Yugoslavia, Poland, and to a lesser degree to Rumania, no loans have been
made to the rest of Eastern Europe, Albania, or North Korea, and in 1975,
Congress specifically had limited Exim exposure in the USSR to $300 million
(Section 7.(a), as amended and approved January 4, 1975).

Some "hostile" countries have been "off cover" for many years, yet in other
cases Exim has been willing to lend to certain governments but not to others.
The relatively low level of outstanding Exim loans in Peru as of FY1975
reflected the closing of Exim's window after 1968 when a nationalist military
grouping seized power and expropriated U.S. companies. In the example of
Chile, the accumulated level of Exim loans exceeded that predicted by the low

level of U.S. exports. Chile had been a favored Exim customer before 1970, but upon the election of the leftist President Salvador Allende, Exim withdrew. This withdrawal combined with a general credit blockade (see note 36, Ch. 1) to reduce sharply Chile's imports from the United States by 1973 (see Table 5.1).

The denial of loans to hostile socialist regimes in the postwar period, or the turning of the spigot on and off for political purposes, as in the examples of Chile, Peru, and Algeria (loans were withheld from Algiers until its moderation in 1970) are the continuation of tactics Exim has employed from its beginnings. Innumerable historical cases exist where Exim refused to do business with one party in power, only to undertake lending to a more acceptable successor regime, or after the existing party had altered sufficiently its policies. In Exim's very first initiative, in its attempt to open business with the USSR, the loan was conditioned on the Soviets agreeing to an accord on debts claimed by U.S. firms and citizens; the recognition of U.S. claims would have been seen as an important concession to the U.S. concept of property rights, but no agreement was reached and the Exim loan was scotched.[6] Eximbank did not return to Moscow until Secretary of State Kissinger convinced a much moderated Soviet leadership to agree to make the required debt payments in return for access to Eximbank credits.

Exim's second initiative—its first fruitful one—was to lend $4 million to Cuba, the first in a series of five loans made between 1934–8.[7] The loans provided budgetary support for the new pro-American government of Fulgencio Batista. Batista had seized power from President Ramon Grau San Martin, whose government was perceived as being radical and anti-American: the United States' refusal to recognize San Martin's government "meant that Cuba could not receive economic assistance or negotiate a new trade agreement with America."[8] According to Hawthorne Arey, the official biographer of Exim during its early period, the purpose of the Batista loans was to "assist Cuba to reestablish its economy on a sound basis."

China offers another historical example of Exim favoring one political regime over another. In the late 1930s Exim extended loans to assist the nationalist Chinese regime of Chiang Kai-shek, but the Bank made no loans to the communist government of Mao Tse-tung. Similarly, Exim lent to Batista in Cuba, but no business has been done with his successor, Fidel Castro.

On the other side of the political spectrum, a 1964 presidential ruling had rendered South Africa ineligible for Exim loans. This overt closure of a once active Exim program for political purposes was meant as a public display of U.S. displeasure with apartheid, and especially with South Africa's colonization of Namibia. In 1978, Congress amended Exim's legislative act to prohibit it from extending insurance as well as credit to the Government of South Africa, to its public agencies, and to private firms unless "the purchaser had endorsed and had proceeded toward the implementation of" the fair employment, antisegregation "Sullivan" principles.

After having received some loans in 1974, shortly after the military coup against Salvador Allende, Chile again lost access to Exim credits for political reasons. In 1977, Exim's legislation was amended to instruct the Bank to "take into account, in consultation with the Secretary of State, the observance and respect for human rights," and the State Department requested Exim not to make loans to the government of General Augusto Pinochet, although Exim did continue to permit insurance of up to $750,000 per buyer.[9] The "human rights" language was altered ("Chafee Amendment") in 1978 to require a presidential determination to deny Exim facilities to countries on the grounds of violating human rights or engaging in international terrorism. In response to the refusal of the Chilean Supreme Court to extradite or order the trial of three Chileans, including the former head of Pinochet's secret police—who was accused of assassinating in Washington Allende's Ambassador to the United States, Orlando Letelier—President Carter decided to deny Chile access to Exim. This decision was part of a package of measures designed to reduce further the already very limited official U.S. economic, diplomatic, and military presence in Chile. Although the State Department's determination under the 1977 amendments had been based on Pinochet's poor human rights record, President Carter's determination was designed to demonstrate U.S. condemnation of Chile's harboring of international terrorists. As in the earlier cutoff of Exim credits to Allende, the Bank was but one of several instruments used to implement administration foreign policy toward Chile. Similarly, the decision by the Reagan Administration early in 1981 to allow Exim to renew lending to Chile was intended to signal a normalization of relations with an authoritarian but friendly government. This decision reflected the new administration's concentration on perceived security, rather than human rights issues.

Chapter 6

Creditworthiness

For an individual, his credit rating is second in importance only to his wife.
 —Ranking official at Citibank
I just call them the way I see them.
 —John Pfeiffer, Chairman of Standard and Poor[1]

The first task of this chapter is to dispell any notion that "creditworthiness" is an objective determination. Commercial as well as government bankers do gather hard facts to reduce the margin of error in their credit ratings. Evidence is examined on the past payment performance of the applicants, their financial status, the present standing of the firms' industry, the conditions of the economy of the borrowers' country, as well as projections on these same variables. Electronic communications and computer data banks are making more information available with greater speed. But bankers cannot be considered obsessive number crunchers. They are too aware of the imperfections in data—especially in the international area, where data are often unreliable and out of date. And bankers still place great importance on personal, face-to-face contact with the borrower.

Once the data are gathered, each bank officer attaches his or her own weights to each variable. This final, subjective assessment stymied three researchers, Kalman Cohen, Tom Gilmore, and Frank Singer, who developed a heuristic computer model with elaborate subroutines to try to explain commercial bank lending patterns, only to find that the final creditworthiness ruling on a loan application still depend on the weights assigned to the crucial variables by management.[2]

Macroeconomic projections are laden with imperfections. Econometric models rely heavily on historical trends, which are sufficient guides to the future in a linear world only. Investors may glance at such models, but ultimately "animal spirits" determine their course of action. As Keynes concluded in his classic discussion of investment patterns:

A large proportion of our positive activities depend on spontaneous optimism rather than on a mathematical expectation, whether moral or hedonistic or economic. Most, probably, of our decisions to do something positive, the full consequences of which will be drawn out over many days to come, can only be taken as a result of animal spirits— of a spontaneous urge to action rather than inaction, and not as the outcome of a weighted average of quantitative benefits multiplied by quantitative probabilities. Enterprise only pretends to itself to be mainly actuated by the statements in its own prospectus, however candid and sincere. Only a little more than an expedition to the South Pole, is it based on an exact calculation of benefits to come.[3]

Bankers as a group have specific prejudices resulting from their work environment.[4] Exim, of course, is a bank, and many of its directors have come from the private banking community.[5] Bankers appreciate certain forms of economic behavior—approvingly labeled "prudent"—and look askance at others. They also relate well to some forms of human behavior, and much less well to others. In the world of banking, where deals ultimately are made face-to-face, the personal element can be extremely important. Without delving into a lengthy sociological discourse, it should be easy to understand that most U.S. bankers feel more at ease doing business with British conservatives than with Tanzanian socialists.

Personal prejudices are important especially when the decision makers have little in-depth knowledge of the potential borrowers, as is often true in government agencies. The State Department has desk officers for most countries, but their level of economic expertise varies greatly.[6] Other agencies, such as the National Security Council (NSC), Central Intelligence Agency (CIA), Treasury, and the division of bank examiners in the Comptroller of the Currency are spread very thin, and each economist (generally not a Ph.D.) will be responsible for several or more countries, at least outside of the most important ones. Frequently the analysts will never have visited their countries and will not speak their languages. Exim is no exception.

Where knowledge is sparce, prejudice flowers. Even if objective social judgments were a theoretical possibility, they hardly can occur in the atmosphere of ignorance in which decisions about a country's creditworthiness are made in Washington.

Sovereign risk

As pointed out in Chapter 4 on the Foreign Credit Insurance Association (FCIA), there are two types of risk in international lending: the "sovereign" or political risk and the commercial risk. If all currencies were convertible, and that nasty barrier to the free movement of goods and capital—the nation–state—did not exist, lending over long distances would be complicated by only the potential ignorance introduced by greater spatial and perhaps cultural separation. The division of the globe into sovereign entities introduces a "political" risk into lending across national barriers.

Political default, as defined by Exim, can result from the transfer risk, or from interventions by the borrower's government that prevent repayment. The failure of a government to provide the borrowing firm with the foreign currency to repay debts (transfer risk) may arise because the central bank has run out of international reserves ("involuntary" default) or because it refuses to release reserves despite their existence ("voluntary" default). Similarly, rescinding of an import license can be out of "moral" degeneracy or malicious intent (voluntary), or because reserves have run out (a sort of political *force majeure*).

The determination of a nation's creditworthiness must take into account the likelihood of default because of voluntary or involuntary motives. Political instability poses the threat of voluntary default, should an unfriendly party assume power; a government that puts a low priority on maintaining its international obligations also represents a greater likelihood of eventual voluntary default.

There is a gray area: A government willfully pursuing fiscal and monetary policies that deplete its reserves would appear to classify as an involuntary default, but it could be argued that it voluntarily let itself slide into arrears. The situation becomes even more complex when trying to determine whether a given government had sufficient political control to enact the sort of austerity measures generally necessary to halt a drainage of reserves.

The cases of Chile and Zaire illustrate the importance of a government's priorities by their different responses to a precipitous fall in export earnings caused by a drop in the price of copper (the main export commodity) in 1974–5. Chile placed extreme emphasis on meeting its heavy debt service, restricting imports and creating massive unemployment, but Zaire preferred to slip into de facto default.

The political element in commercial risk

For Eximbank loans, the distinction between political and commercial risk is to a considerable degree artificial and misleading because the financial health of firms likely to borrow from Exim is conditioned by decisions made by the State. Many of Exim's borrowers are either public corporations, or firms whose output, prices, and costs are determined at least partially by administrative decisions. Approximately half of Exim's loan authorizations supports either aircraft or power (nuclear or conventional) generators; the purchasing firm is most often a government corporation, and even when not, its rates for flight fares or power usage will be determined by official bureaucrats. In addition, many other Exim borrowers, especially in lesser-developed countries (LDCs), are fully aware that their financial health may be determined by the central administration, if not by pricing, then by licenses, tax policies, or by the granting or denial of access to central bank borrowings: In many countries credit allocation is influenced heavily by political, as well as personal ties.

Exim will sometimes seek assurances from a government that the borrower will receive preferential treatment. DuPont, for example, was planning a joint venture with private Iranian interests to construct a $400 million synthetic fiber plant in Iran near Isfahan. In issuing a preliminary commitment in April,

1976, Exim conditioned its $40 million loan on the government agreeing to the following assistance for the new enterprise:[7]

1. $130 million government loan at subsidized interest rates
2. Assurance of adequate protection of selling price
3. A monopoly charter at least until the Iranian market would support a second supplier
4. An assured supply of vital raw materials to producers of intermediate products
5. Exemption from import tariffs on imported inputs for production as well as for "finished goods used for market development"
6. Tax concessions

The Iranian government also indicated that it would prohibit imports on competing synthetic fibers and fabrics. An Exim vice-president explained that such conditions, although in violation of principles of free trade, are nevertheless "everyday affairs."

Many of the firms Exim lends to command an important if not dominant position in their domestic markets. They are most likely to suffer severe financial strain in the event of a general economic crisis. Such a crisis is apt to be related to a balance-of-payments disequilibrium and a shortage of foreign exchange. It is academic whether the firm defaults because it cannot make the deposits at the central bank, or the deposits having been made, the central bank is out of hard currency. The root cause of the default lies in the economic condition of the country.

When the government of a borrower guarantees an Exim loan, the link between political conditions and the loan's safety is then made entirely explicit. The absence of such official guarantees, however, should not obscure the realities that in any case render the borrower's capacity to repay subject to governmental influence. The distinction between commercial risk and political risk is much less sharp than Exim would have it.

Case studies of denied loans

Some understanding of Exim's creditworthiness criteria can be gained by looking at loan applications that were denied. In reality most denials are given informally, before the application actually is considered by the board at their regular meeting. Loan officers, vice-presidents, or perhaps board members normally would indicate, politely, that Exim prefers not to consider the request. The board generally would need to deny formally a loan only if the applicant were insistent. The insistent supplicant is unlikely to be rewarded, for the recommendation of the loan officers and regional vice-presidents—who usually have been in contact with that board member who specializes in their area—rarely is overruled in the board meeting (the five board members are full-time employees at the Bank). Similarly, the board rarely will deny a loan that the staff recommends approving. Of course this has varied somewhat under different chairmen, with Kearns noted for quick and routine approvals,[8] whereas DuBrul was more cirumspect. Carter appointee John Moore, Jr., adopted a more positive attitude toward loan applications.

Of the following examples of denied loans (a few eventually returning to the board for approval) most were denied formally by the board during FY1976.

Pakistan

1. FMC Corporation requested Exim assistance to finance $16.5 million in U.S. costs for a conveyor belt system to carry iron ore to a steel mill to be built and financed by the Soviets (January, 1976). Although the Soviet involvement may have been a factor, denial was primarily because of country conditions that did not offer reasonable assurance of repayment. Exim had been involved in Pakistan's repeated reschedulings of official debt. The country's ability to service additional, even nonconcessional debt was judged to be limited, and Pakistan was off cover (i.e., ineligible) for long-term debt for several Berne Union members (the Berne Union is an international association of credit insurers). Country conditions of "poor" rendered irrelevant the prospect of the borrower, the government-owned Pakistan Steel Mill Corporation.

2. Dresser Industries requested support for $17 million in U.S. costs for drilling rigs—the buyer again was a Pakistani government corporation (April, 1976). Country conditions rated poor were important once more, and the project was considered speculative because of the very uncertain prospects for finding gas and oil. The fuels would be for import substitution.

3. General Motors requested assistance in financing $45 million in U.S. costs for locomotives and spare parts (April, 1976). Pakistan's inability to service new nonconcessional debt meant that the transaction would not earn foreign exchange, making the request even less attractive. Moreover, a recent World Bank report had argued that Pakistan Railways needed revised pricing policies.

4. Loan of $13.4 million for a McDonnell Douglas DC-10-30, for PIA, the national Pakistani airlines (May, 1976). The board previously had held up this loan pending the promise of the Government of Pakistan to inject $10.7 million in equity into PIA before disbursement. The promise having been made, Exim decided to *approve* the loan, to be guaranteed by the government and by a first mortgage on the plane. Despite country conditions of poor, the airline was termed profitable and a foreign-exchange saver.

Sudan

1. Request by Pullman–Swindell to assist in financing $7 million in U.S. exports for a clay factory (April, 1976). Sudan was facing balance-of-payment difficulties, and foreign-exchange shortages, and the project's projected contribution to Sudan's foreign-exchange earnings capacity was judged insignificant.

The proposed guarantor, a Sudanese commercial bank, did not offer suffi-ciently strong security. Also, Sudan had a record of slow payments to Exim in direct credits.

2. Request by Hartford National Bank and Trust for a $3.5 million special buyer credit limit under its short-term FCIA policy for wheat sales to the Sudanese ministry of finance. In April, 1975, Exim had resumed cover of renewals and moderate-sized new insurance and guarantee transactions (up to $2 million) to Sudan, such that short- and medium-term exposure had risen from $3 million to $14.5 million. This rapid increase in exposure; delays in some repayments; the Sudanese heavy balance-of-payments deficit; and the fact that the transaction exceeded the $2 million maximum guideline led the board to uphold the staff's denial recommendation. The board noted that such agricultural exports would not contribute to the Sudan's development, and, in any event, would be handled more appropriately by PL480 concessional assistance.

Algeria

Exim analysts thought that Algeria's headlong rush to develop was resulting in a too-rapid accumulation of foreign debt, which could produce near-term, balance-of-payments problems, but the country's natural resources, and its rel-atively competent and strong central government made Algeria, in the long run, basically creditworthy. The Bank adopted a policy of selectivity, empha-sizing projects in the energy sector, which would have a direct, positive impact on Algeria's export earnings. In 1973, Exim had begun lending heavily to Son-atrach, the Algerian hydrocarbon agency, for the development of its natural gas fields, a portion of whose output was scheduled to be delivered to the United States by El Paso Gas of Texas. Among those loan requests that were not selected were:

1. Bechtel's request for assistance in financing a $7 million feasibility study for a massive steel complex (April, 1976).

2. A second Bechtel request was denied by the board on the same date for financing the engineering design and related services for an irrigation project. The Exim staff had concluded that concessional financing would be more appropriate for such an agricultural infrastructure project.

3. Science Management Corporation's requested financing to cover $100 million in U.S. equipment and services for a training center that would educate Algerian labor from the semiskilled to the professional level (April, 1976). The Bank believed that the policy emphasis on foreign-exchange earnings pre-cluded such a project. Moreover, training not related directly to a project should be better paid for in cash.

4. General Electric and Westinghouse, bidding against each other, both requested assistance in financing U.S. exports for a 640 megawatt gas-fired steam power plant to provide energy for a proposed industrial complex (Jan-

uary, 1976). The U.S. firms alleged that they faced competition from foreign suppliers. Other U.S. firms were interested in contributing to the complex. Nevertheless, Exim denied the request because of the additional exposure involved, and for lack of sufficient information on what promised to be yet another ambitious development project for overheated Algeria.

5. Pullman–Kellogg requested help to finance the approximately $500 million in U.S. costs for a one billion cubic foot per day liquid natural gas (LNG) plant, for which the firm had been awarded the engineering and procurement contract (May, 1976). The Bank recognized that a denial could halt the project and/or prejudice U.S. suppliers. Nevertheless, to avoid a very large addition to the Bank's exposure in Algeria, Pullman–Kellogg was turned away.

Argentina

In the closing days of the last Peronist regime (finally overthrown in March, 1976), Exim judged that the chaotic political and economic situation rendered country conditions "poor"; to avoid political irritation, Argentina was not placed off cover, but loan requests were denied routinely, and FCIA and commercial bank discretionary and delegated authorities were revoked. Exim continued to deny loans in the face of repeated requests by the embassy in Buenos Aires that the Bank approve select applications. Among the denials were:

1. The Argentine government's steel company, Somisa, requested credits to help finance $5 million of principally replacement items (January, 1976). Despite Exim's satisfactory twenty-year experience with the borrower, Somisa's necessary dependence on the government for foreign exchange to service external debt was reason for denial.

2. Petroquimica General Mosconi, a government-owned petrochemicals company, requested an increase to a $5.5 million loan authorized in 1972 by $360,000, for additional nitrogen facilities (November, 1975). Although the plant was operating successfully already, any improvement in the poor rating for country conditions was judged to be remote, and the loan was denied.

3. The First Wisconsin National Bank of Milwaukee requested guarantee coverage on the sale of a machine tool with a contract price of $51,294 (December, 1975). Adverse country conditions overrode Exim's satisfactory experience with the guarantor, and the existence of a reasonably satisfactory obligor with solidly favorable credit information.

Kenya

Morrison–Knudsen requested finance to help cover $57 million in U.S. costs for a water supply project in Nairobi (April, 1976). Because of the weakening of the Kenyan economy and the persistence of balance-of-payments problems, the Bank was restricting itself to projects of a "self-liquidating" nature, that is foreign-exchange earners. Moreover, the Exim staff considered this water supply project as the sort of social infrastructure appropriate for concessional financing, and noted that the IBRD had financed Phase 1 of the same system.

Yugoslavia

1. General Electric (GE) requested an Exim commitment to help finance $185 million in U.S. exports of two 600-megawatt steam turbine engines (March, 1976). The country analysis noted that: Yugoslavia had been struggling with balance-of-payments problems; its debt burden was considerable; its growth plans were dependent heavily on continued foreign capital inflows; and that the skepticism of private lenders regarding the country's medium-term prospects would not facilitate foreign borrowing. Thus, country conditions and Exim's already large exposure ($909 million) had led the Bank to adopt a policy of selectivity. Exim currently had a preliminary commitment to U.S. suppliers for another $180 million for power generation; only if they were to lose these bids might the Bank reconsider this new GE request, which was denied.

2. Yugoslavia, combined with expressions of interest from U.S. suppliers, requested aid in financing $50 million in exports for three hospitals (March, 1976). The loan was denied peremptorily because of country conditions and Exim's heavy existing exposure.

Philippines

An Exim loan of $1.4 million was requested for Spicer Philippine Manufacturing Company for equipment for a plant to make auto parts (April, 1976). The guarantor was to be the Dana Corporation, the parent company of Spicer. The staff recommended *approval,* noting good performance of the Philippine economy, the strength of the Dana guarantee, and potential competition from foreign suppliers. It was decided, however, that Spicer would probably procure in the United States even without Exim, and that Dana could raise the money on the private capital markets, but was looking at Exim's relatively cheap $8\frac{1}{2}$% interest rate on the six-year loan. Chairman Dubrul's board insisted on overriding the staff's recommendation and denied the credit for this subsidiary of a U.S. multinational.

Mexico

Union Carbide Mexicana, a majority-owned subsidiary of Union Carbide Corporation, requested a Exim loan of $2.3 million for plant expansion. The borrower was certainly creditworthy, and Exim had lent it $1.8 million in 1971. The proposed six-year loan, however, was of shorter duration than a $23-million loan obtained from the Bank of America, and the firm maintained access to the U.S. capital market. No foreign competition existed. Therefore, because the sale was assured, Exim denied the credit to avoid competing with private sources of finance.

Costa Rica

The National Central Bank of Lancaster, Pennsylvania requested a $3.6-million-loan for the export of eighty tractors and earthmovers from Caterpillar for rural road development (March, 1976). Costa Rica was still creditworthy, but a cautious approach was considered necessary because the economy was deteriorating, and export earnings were dependent heavily on two commodities (coffee and bananas), while a rising debt burden would be serviced only with difficulty in the medium term. Poor performance in repayment of previous loans for road equipment was also a factor. Associated FCIA insurance for the export of Ford, GM, and Mack trucks and earthmoving equipment were also denied.

Norway

A/S Mosvold Shipping Company requested assistance in financing the $10.2 million in U.S. costs for offshore-drilling equipment (January, 1976). At first the loan was denied in November, 1975, because of the company's high debt to net worth ratio, the lack of a guarantor, and the project design. However, Mosvold had redesigned the project, and a Norwegian insurance company had agreed to guarantee repayment. Although the company's debt burden remained high, the denial was reversed and the loan approved.

Tanzania

Continental Illinois and Bankers Trust requested Exim support in financing up to $85 million in the U.S. costs for textile equipment (October, 1974). Denial was based on country conditions. Although the balance of payments had been in surplus in 1972–3, a large deficit resulted in 1974. Growth rates were slowing, and the agricultural sector especially was experiencing difficulties. A portion of the textile output would be for export, but the staff argued that any Exim financing should be for projects that would be clearly self-liquidating. Exim's existing exposure in Tanzania consisted only of a small amount of short-term insurance and no direct credits.

It should be noted that if any applications came in during FY1976 for the following countries they were denied either formally by the board or informally, for they were off cover for everything except short-term FCIA insurance: Syria, the People's Democratic Republic of Yemen, Congo (Brazzaville), Benin, Bangladesh, and Haiti (in addition to the congressionally proscribed socialist countries). The first four could be labeled politically radical, whereas Bangladesh's poverty could absorb only highly concessional assistance. The reason for the exclusion of Haiti is unclear.

Explaining the denials

In the wake of the New York City bond default, Edward Gramlich tried econometric analysis to determine the creditworthiness criteria of the rating agencies.[9] Gramlich found that the ratio of gross outstanding debt to the assessed value of property in a district appeared important (its coefficient had a t-statistic of 1.6, whereas the R^2 was equal to .03); this ratio has a parallel in a nation's debt-service ratio. But Gramlich's main conclusion was: "The rating services are private agencies, and though they publish voluminous information on the budget of borrowing governments (which Exim does not do on its borrowers), it is impossible to tell exactly how they arrive at their ratings. A statistical attempt to explain their ratings . . . left a large random component to the ratings." These findings were corroborated by other studies, and are a warning to those who would hope to pinpoint statistically the measures of creditworthiness. Senior government and private banking officials, including those at Exim, are increasingly willing to look at quantitative formulas as one input in determining credit ratings, but they have resisted subjecting management decisions to econometrics.

A nonstatistical analysis of the twenty-one loans just discussed can reveal certain patterns in Exim behavior. Most salient is the importance of country conditions in denials. The overriding importance of country conditions supports the earlier discussion that emphasized the political component underlying the commercial risk. A financially troubled government not only cannot assure foreign-exchange availability (political transfer risk), but it also cannot be counted on to provide the proper support, via direct and indirect subsidies, that guarantee a firm's health. Of course, poor country conditions are likely to affect adversely, and directly, a firm's profitability.

Country conditions are especially important for those large numbers of Exim loans to utilities for power generation and to airlines. Both types of entities frequently have rate structures precluding profitability; moreover, too often the indivisible nature of the imported capital good results in underutilized capacity. Official subsidies are necessary. Also, it deserves repeating, most Exim loans are either to public agencies or else carry a government guarantee. The guarantee is only as good as the condition of the country's economy.

No attempt will be made here to offer a detailed critique of the judgments regarding the various countries' economic conditions and prospects. Very briefly: First, although numerous variables were considered, Exim, just as commercial banks, essentially was assessing a country as it would a firm, judging it creditworthy if its prospective cash flow looked sufficient to meet debt service, and if its management appeared to be of "good character."[10]

A second observation made from the denials is that certain countries, as well as some projects, are considered more appropriate for official aid agencies. Pakistan is an example of a poor country with an accumulated foreign debt; Exim believed that Pakistan would have difficulty repaying all but highly concessional loans, which have very low interest rates and very extended repayment terms. Referral to an aid agency could also occur because of the nature of a project: The Kenyan water supply system was labeled "social infrastructure" and regarded as more appropriate for official assistance. The Algerian training center and the Costa Rican rural road development also probably were considered aid-type projects. The Algerian irrigation scheme was so labeled.

The sample of denied loans also indicates the preference for projects that are "self-liquidating," that is, earn foreign exchange. Such export earnings insulate the project somewhat from the country's overall reserve position, and lessen dependence on government-exchange allocation. In a general economic crisis, however, a central bank can still refuse foreign exchange to a firm, even if it is an export earner. Creditors such as Exim sometimes try to circumvent this requisitioning by lending on the condition that an escrow account be set up outside the exporting nation, into which the firm's foreign-exchange earnings are placed in sufficient quantity to meet debt service. The exporter's central bank never sees the money. In 1976, for example, Exim approved additional financing to cover cost overruns incurred during the construction of the long transmission line designed to carry power from the Inga dam complex to the Shaba copper belt in Zaire. Zaire's protracted economic crisis motivated Exim to demand that debt service on the loan be extracted from the proceeds of Zaire's mineral exports before the proceeds were remitted to Kinshasa.

For many lesser developed countries (LDCs), the big foreign-exchange earners are raw materials; consequently, Exim's preference for self-liquidating projects reinforces traditional trading patterns. In numerous cases, Exim has lent to expand already large export centers, as, for example, in the case of copper in Chile, Peru, Zaire, and Zambia. These countries were increasing their reliance on a single commodity whose price has a highly volatile history. Exim's willingness to contribute to their effort is inconsistent with the faulting of Costa Rica for dependency on two (unstable) commodity exports.

Exim's preference for self-liquidating projects introduces—or rather exacerbates—a tendency in international capital markets[11] toward favoring export industries in LDCs over industries producing for the domestic market, even though the latter's rate of return may be just as high or higher. Because the LDC must supplement the foreign capital with local resources to complete the project—resources in the form of labor, infrastructure, and even capital—the preferences of Exim and other international creditors have a distorting impact on resource allocation within the borrowing countries.

From Exim's perspective, export-earning projects have other advantages beyond greater assurance of repayment. By increasing the foreign country's export receipts, its capacity to purchase more U.S. exports has been increased.

In the broader sense, the export-oriented project helps to insert the foreign nation into the international marketplace.

Exim looks with favor on projects exporting raw-material, but it would be a mistake to understand Exim as obstinately opposing the industrialization of LDCs. Exim has, for example, heavily supported chemical and steel complexes in LDCs, and power generators that can be used by industry. Even in the case of primary commodity projects, Exim has often been willing to finance equipment for mineral processing, as in the Algerian hydrocarbon case, which allows the LDC to export with more "value added."

Exim's penchant for power-generation equipment and aircraft and locomotives is not easy to reconcile with the emphasis on self-liquidation, although international airlines and railroads do earn some foreign exchange. In the Yugoslav case, Exim was willing to reconsider the request for a loan for power equipment if outstanding preliminary commitments to that sector should expire, despite the concern with Belgrade's debt burden.

A significant debt-service burden was reason to deny loans for industrial projects designed to serve primarily the domestic market. Yet Exim has financed such equipment to countries that have heavy debt service, for example, Brazil, Argentina, Chile, South Korea, and Israel. Rather, as shown in Chapter 5 on the country distribution of Exim loans, Exim's largest borrowers are countries with high debt-service ratios. The existence of a debt ratio of 20 percent or even higher is not in itself a cause for concern. It becomes so only in the context of a generally gloomy projection of a country's balance of payments.

Another observation is the absence of explicit attention to the impact of a project on development. Foreign-exchange earnings and debt service capacities are important indicators of a borrower's financial health. If by development, however, is meant the broader impact of a project, backward and forward linkages, the relevance of shadow prices, the impact on human-capital formation, and so forth (not to mention income distribution or balanced growth), then these concerns are only incidental to Exim. Exim, of course, does not claim to be a development agency, although, ultimately, many of its loans do support projects similar to those of the official development institutions.

The denial for the training facility in Algeria shows the low priority attached to the development of human capital. Such training could be supported only when directly tied to a capital investment using U.S. machinery, that is, when the transaction demands it. The general Exim policy that training be paid for in cash does not acknowledge that return to education, just as return to a machine, is realized only gradually over time. An educated labor force, moreover, is as necessary a component to development as is electric power. In its broadest influence, Exim's preference for capital over human investment contributes to a capital-intensive development process.

By choosing some projects over others, Exim helps to mold a country's development pattern. An astute and well-organized country could try to limit this influence by presenting Exim with a single list of priority projects. A country can also alter Exim's preferences by offering stronger guarantees on favored projects. To coax Exim into financing agricultural production for the local market, it may be necessary to lobby the U.S. Embassy, to emphasize the high-priority nature of the endeavor, to assure the project official subsidies, and to promise extensive press coverage when the Exim loan is announced. Even then the Exim Board may decide to refer the project to the Agency for International Development (AID).

Exim can be pressured by U.S. suppliers. Undoubtedly the decision to grant the loan to the Pakistani airline was influenced by McDonnell Douglas.[12] Nevertheless, as in the Yugoslav power-generation case or the Pullman-Kellogg request for loans for a second gas project in Algeria, Exim, despite allegations of intense foreign competition and lost exports, will try to hold the line if it feels it lacks reasonable assurance of repayment. Exim has its own institutional welfare to protect.

Exim will not hesitate to use its leverage as an important lender to demand that the borrower alter its behavior as a condition for a loan. Conditions ("restrictive covenants") may be placed on debt to equity ratios, or some other indication of financial health, as Exim tried to do in the example of the Norwegian drilling equipment and as it succeeded in doing in the Pakistani Airlines case. Electricity rates in more than one country have been influenced by Eximbank (as well as by another financier of power generation, the IBRD). Tax rates, import allowances, market protection, government subsidies, and dividend policy are among those areas that Exim feels justified in discussing while negotiating a loan.

An institution with its own history, Exim takes into account a borrower's track record. In the case of the denial to an old friend, the Argentinian steel company, one senses true regret. Costa Rica's past sins—slow repayment on road maintenance equipment—contributed to its defeat. The outcasts—Cuba, China (until 1980)—who have defaulted against Exim are, of course, ineligible, although foreign policy concerns are relevant. In the Chilean case, the defaults of the early 1970s severely hurt Exim, and the Bank responded very reluctantly and only partially to State Department pressures to resume business in Chile, following the 1973 coup.

Exim is also concerned with its country exposure levels, because it seeks to diversify risk. The intention to hold down the growth in loan levels in Algeria reflected this concern to a degree. Exim, however, flatly denies having internal country exposure ceilings, and the concentration of loans in select countries indicates considerable flexibility in determining safe exposure levels.

Only one loan denial dealt with each of the two important policy issues of not competing with private capital and with financing the subsidiaries of multinationals. It may be that many more such denials occurred informally, but the record of approved loans suggests that denial is not the pattern. Other government agencies, notably the Federal Reserve, long have complained that borrowers were seeking Exim's subsidized interest rate, and that Exim was displacing private capital. The American Federation of Labor and Congress of Industrial Organizations (AFL-CIO) repeatedly has denounced Exim support for the flight of "run-away" shops. In the case of the denial to the Dana Corporation subsidiary in the Philippines, the staff, who had recommended approval, were especially surprised at the position of DuBrul's board. It should be noted, however, that DuBrul was not opposed to financing subsidiaries per se; in this instance his real objection was that Dana could raise the money itself, and that Exim would be displacing private capital. DuBrul, who came to Exim in early 1976 from Lazard Freres, made the enforcement of Exim's legislative mandate to complement rather than compete with private finance perhaps his major policy objective.[13] In both the Dana and Union Carbide cases the proposed Exim loans were for only six years, which is within the range commercial banks will handle.

Creditworthiness and loan distribution by country and sector

The previous discussion dissected faulty loans to determine on what bases Exim makes denials. Chapter 5 examined the country distribution of approved loans to comment on Exim's lending patterns and preferences, and Chapter 2 described the distribution of loans by economic sectors. It is now possible to merge the three findings. First, what does the understanding of creditworthiness criteria explain about the distribution of loans across countries? Second, what do the characteristics of the denied loans explain about the sectoral dispersion?

The previous analysis of the country distribution of Exim loans showed that loan authorizations are correlated positively to the level of importation of U.S. capital goods, and to the apparent judgments of creditworthiness made by private lenders. Exim borrowers must also be in the good graces of the U.S. Government, as demonstrated by their receipt of aid flows. The major Exim borrowers—who have concentrated successfully Exim's resources—generally evinced (with some exceptions) these economic characteristics: rapid growth of GNP and especially of their trade sectors, and high external borrowings that had resulted in relatively high debt-service ratios. The arguments that follow will attempt to show how creditworthiness criteria explain the dominance of these characteristics among Exim's most important borrowers.

Concentration

The examination of creditworthiness criteria showed the crucial importance of the evaluation of country conditions. Those countries considered either off cover or poor risks (Argentina) received no loans, whereas those requiring careful scrutiny (Pakistan, Algeria) chalked up numerous denials. The other side of the story is that, for countries considered solidly creditworthy, Exim is wide open for business. Loans will not be denied on country conditions, and because commercial risk is to such a great extent a reflection of political risk conditions, only firms that are grievously unsound would be turned away; even then, if the firm could come up with a sound guarantor its application might sail through.

There are, of course, limitations to concentration. Exim is subject to innumerable pressures to bestow its limited resources on different markets. The Bank strives, moreover, to maintain risk diversification by containing exposure in any one country. The Bank is also constrained from lending too much to the most creditworthy countries—including the industrial nations—if it wants to avoid competition with available private capital. I will return to this constraint later in this chapter.

In the capital stream

The preference of private lenders and Exim for the same LDCs argues strongly that Exim's appraisals of creditworthiness do not generally differ from those of the international banking community. Recall the fluidity of movement between Exim's board and the private financial sector. Recall the statement by the official at the FCIA that most of their analysts came from private banks, and that his association used the same criteria as the banks. To a great degree, Exim's values are those of the private marketplace.

In the beginning of this chapter it was pointed out that Exim analysts rely heavily on opinions of others, including commercial bankers, the financial press, and the orthodox International Monetary Fund (IMF) for information. Only very occasionally, if at all, do they get a firsthand look at an economy, be it in person or just through the subject government's own publications or other local materials. With a similar pool of selective information, screened by people with like conceptions, Exim loan officers quite naturally produce decisions similar to those of their private counterparts.

This tightly knit circle of interdependent opinions raises the problem of the "herd effect" in capital markets, as noted by Keynes.[14] Caution, for example, can become contagious and terminate in a general panic. Prophecies of gloom become self-fulfilling, as the borrower without a credit rating is forced into bankruptcy by the very fact of not being able to borrow. The preference of bankers for the closeness of the herd is one factor that contributes to concentration in capital flows, be the direction bullish or bearish.

An example of the herd instinct is the denial of the Yugoslav loans, which noted that because private lenders were skeptical of the country's medium-term prospects, private loans might not be forthcoming and so balance-of-payments problems could develop. Exim's own restraint could help turn this opinion into a self-fulfilling prophecy.

Finally on the issue of bank and Exim parallels: Because Exim splits a financial package with the commercial banks, a certain similarity necessarily exists between Exim and commercial bank lending patterns.

The discussion that has related Exim loan distribution to private lending has considered credit but not equity investment. The ready acceptance by Exim of the value of the guarantee of the U.S.-based Dana Corporation suggests possible parallel movements between Exim loans and U.S. equity. This issue will be discussed in depth in Chapter 8 on transnationals.

Openness and debt

The preference for self-liquidating projects that serve the export market would lead Exim to favor countries oriented toward foreign trade. The projects may be minerals, but can also be export-oriented industry. Rapid export growth is often a sign of rapid overall GNP growth, and several of Exim's major customers have followed export-led growth strategies. Rapid export growth holds the promise of foreign-exchange availability, even for projects or products that are not, in themselves, export earners; the main political worry—the transfer risk—is thereby alleviated.

The high debt-service ratios of Exim's major clients reflect the import demands that have been a by-product of trade-oriented development strategies. Some debt accumulation can be a sign of good financial management, but the high debt-service levels of a number of Exim clients, which have been compounded by the series of recent shocks—the sharp increases in the prices of internationally traded goods especially oil, and the 1974–5 recession and 1980–1 slowdown in the industrial countries—must be a cause for concern. It remains to be seen whether the debt-ridden countries can expand exports fast enough to service their liabilities. If not, the debt burden—to which Exim has made a substantial contribution—could become a fundamental contradiction in the foreign trade-oriented growth strategy.

Creditworthiness criteria and sectoral allocation

Mining and refining account for an impressive 20 percent of Exim loan authorizations. The emphasis on self-liquidation is one important explanatory variable. Large projects that export raw materials provide foreign exchange both to the firm and to the government, through taxation or exchange controls.[15] A second reason, however, accounts for Exim's dedication to commodities: pressure from the demand side. As Chapter 8 will show, U.S.-based transnational corporations (TNCs) are interested in Exim involvement in their overseas mining projects. Exim loans help cover the rising costs of mineral extraction and, of special importance, pull the U.S. Government into the project as a defense against perceived political risks.

At periods in Exim's history it has invested in commodity projects to increase their supply for the United States or the industrial world in general. This was especially true during World War II and the early days of the Cold War,[16] and supply considerations were again surfacing in the late 1970s. In other years, the supply issue was not paramount, and mining projects were favored primarily as good business. Exim's financial objectives and national commodities policies are generally congruent; a project gains acceptance at Exim if its output is assured of markets in industrial countries by a transnational firm that holds a marketing contract or equity share in the project.

Agriculture has received short shrift at Exim, for reasons which are now more apparent. The Algerian rural irrigation project was disparagingly labeled as appropriate for official aid. Little interest was shown in the Costa Rican rural road project. Agricultural projects are avoided partly because they are not sufficiently oriented to exports; the one area where Exim has been willing to lend is the exception that proves the rule, namely, agro-industrial sugar estates.

Exim may shy away from agricultural development because it lacks the straightforward balance sheet familiar to Exim's financial analysts. The Bank is also not comfortable with the unorthodox forms of rural organization some LDCs are experimenting with. The unsympathetic treatment given to the Tanzanian economy is a case in point.

Utilities and transport (mainly aircraft) account for at least half of Exim's loan volume. Would this result be anticipated from the findings about creditworthiness criteria? Utilities are not export oriented, and although some transport may produce foreign exchange, more often they are dependent heavily on official subsidies. Utilities and transport usually are government owned, so that they lack the advantage of U.S. equity participation or the guarantee of a strong private firm. The official aid agencies, moreover, have shown a readiness to lend for power-generating projects, as well as for transport (but not for commercial jets). Despite all these reasons for not lending to utilities and public transportation firms, in the Pakistani case the Bank selected the Pakistani airline above all the other denials; and in the Yugoslav case, the Bank showed sympathy toward the loan for power equipment.

Part of Exim's willingness to support these sectors is explained by its apparent preference for public borrowers, who should have the most direct access to foreign exchange. But this is not a wholly sufficient explanation for the heavy concentration of Exim attention on power and aircraft. The fundamental explanation lies in the nature of the items and the industries that supply them. The access that Boeing, McDonnell Douglas, GE, and Westinghouse have enjoyed at Exim has been demonstrated in Chapter 2. Chapter 9 will delve more deeply into the reasons behind the wide-reaching support the U.S. Government has granted these firms.

Finally, power stations, particularly nuclear ones, and commercial jet aircraft, are large-ticket items requiring especially long-term finance. The hesitation of the private U.S. capital market to supply these funds was shown earlier. Evidently, the fulfillment of this function—plugging the weak spots in the private market—takes precedence over normal credit judgments, at least when the applicant firm is one of the four dominant users of Exim funds.

Conclusion

The examination of rejected loans—coupled with the careful reading of over 100 approved loan memorandums—has revealed certain variables that stand out repeatedly in loan after loan and clearly dominate the loan selection process. The extraction of these variables explains a good deal about the Bank's values and the resultant loan portfolio.

Of central concern is the economic condition and outlook of the borrower's country. This finding is consistent with the earlier argument that the probability of default is a function of the priorities of a government: Voluntary default can occur only at the will of the debtor regime, and even involuntary default may be the result of previous economic decisions made by the ruling party. Country conditions must also weigh heavily, because the health of many firms borrowing from Exim is entwined closely with decisions made at the governmental level. Finally, Exim, by monitoring country exposure levels, can avoid overconcentration of risk in one market and can spread the Bank's limited largesse among the many "friendly" foreign governments.

Exim pays close attention to country conditions, but it does not show great concern with the impact of its loans on the borrowing country. The Bank does watch the loan's future addition to the country's debt-service burden, but this is a clear expression of vital self-interest. The broader developmental impact of loans goes unremarked, and Exim specifically shies away from programs that would train a labor force, except when such training is tied immediately to a U.S. export sale. Exim shows little worry over the themes that have come to dominate the literature of development economics: dual economies, capital to labor ratios, food production, and so forth. Exim's lack of attention to these issues mirrors similar attitudes in the private U.S. business sector.

Certain projects are more attractive to Exim than others. Export earners rank high, whereas rural development projects are given less status, and social infrastructure projects are ranked even lower, being considered more appropriate for an official aid agency. Exim generally examines the financial strength of the borrowing firm, and large, well-known firms, especially those with a track record at Exim, will rate high. If Exim has doubts about the particular project, it may recommend the borrower agree to special conditions, including restrictive covenants that, ipso facto, improve the credit rating. Some loans are approved because of the nature of the product, such as power generators and airplanes, despite the existence of otherwise unfavorable circumstances.

Certain loans can be decided on the basis of policy issues. The "scripture" may be invoked that the Bank, as a public agency, ought not to compete with private capital, causing a loan to be rejected or to be altered to reduce Exim's participation. The degree of foreign competition is also examined; especially where foreign eximbanks are reputed to be involved, the Bank's fervor is likely to be aroused.

This chapter has underlined elements relating to country, project, and policy that feed into Exim's decision-making process. Just as in the study cited by Cohen, Gilmore, and Singer, on commercial bank lending, it has been possible to extract from a large sample of loan decisions some insights into the thinking and evaluating underlying and comprising Exim's outlook. Similar to the Cohen study, however, is the finding that in any particular decision, the weight attached to each variable will vary, and depend on subjective factors at the staff or board level. Occasionally, decisions can even hang on the verbal interplay at the board meeting.

The factors dominating the Bank's decisions establish a spectrum: at one end, the Bank will not lend to a Tanzanian rural cooperative producing vegetables for the local market, whereas, at the other end, the Bank is very unlikely to refuse financing to a Brazilian iron-ore mine producing for export. Within these boundaries, the decision-making process is a complex nexus of subjective, political, and financial variables, and the elevation to a paramount position of some factors over others will depend on circumstances, as the board moves to assign implicitly weights to the various factors described.

The room for subjectivity in the decision-making process is increased by the contradictory nature of certain of the criteria. For example, a country is praised for being "open," which generally implies foreign borrowing—but a "high" debt service is considered dangerous; Exim should not compete with private capital—but where foreign competition is present, a matching subsidy may be required: The determination of the seriousness of the foreign competition is frequently subjective and is often dependent on sketchy information coming from self-interested sources. The Bank is torn constantly between its institutional concern to remain financially self-sustaining and its public mandate to take risks. Loan decisions will be influenced by which concern is weighing more heavily at the moment. The relative weight to attach to a guarantor is another vagary, which can cause Exim to go so far as to overlook the borrower's own financial position. Finally, the Bank's judgment may be contradicted by outside pressures, which have reversed more than one board decision.

Part III

Eximbank and the U.S. economy

Chapter 7

Export subsidies, business cycles, and nationalist rivalries

The Export-Import Bank can be studied as one among many state agencies using subsidies to alter the behavior of the economy away from the path that private actors, if left alone, would have taken. By offering subsidized loans, at rates and terms that differ from those of the market, the Bank induces economic actors to direct their energies toward the external sector.

The existence of these subsidies raises several interesting questions. What methodology should be used to measure the subsidies? How large have they been historically, and how does Exim finance them? Have these official subsidies been used as an instrument of macroeconomic stabilization? How efficient have they been in stimulating exports?

Measurements of Exim's subsidies

In an extensive study of federal subsidies, the Joint Economic Committee of Congress (JEC) defined "subsidy" as "the provision of federal economic assistance, at the expense of others in the economy, to the private-sector producers or consumers of a particular good, service or factor of production. The Government alters the price or cost of the good, service or factor as a *quid pro quo* for certain economic behavior by the recipient, either in the form of inducing the performance of economic activity or the forebearance of it."[1] This definition is consistent with one presented in a paper submitted for the JEC study by Carl Shoup, who wrote: "The economic theory of subsidy payments is the theory of how a government can induce changes in relative prices (either market price, or price to seller, or price to buyer) in the private sector, by offering rewards."[2] The introduction to the JEC study cites as one example of a subsidy, "implicit payments by means of loans at interest rates below the government borrowing rate or from loan guarantees." This example encompasses Eximbank.

A method for measuring quantitatively the subsidy element in a public-sector loan follows readily from the definition. A subsidy arises when the government's lending rate is less than that charged by the private market. The method involves the well-known technique of "present discounted value." The "present discounted value" (PDV) of a loan measures the value today of the expected

Table 7.1. *Estimates of subsidy values in annual loan authorizations ($ millions)*

	FY1970	FY1971	FY1972	FY1973	FY1974	FY1975
Office of Management and Budget						
New loan commitments	1,569	2,362	3,285	4,053	4,905	3,813
Subsidy	169	148	180	377	368	191
Discount rate	.095	.08		.095	.10	.10
Joint Economic Committee						
Subsidy	143	25[a]	139	179	404[b]	435[b]
Discount rate	.08	.085	.077	.076	.089	.089

[a]Appears erroneously small, and is probably a misprint.
[b]Based on projected loan authorizations that exceeded the actual.
Source: For Office of Management and Budget: Office of Management and Budget, "Series E," *Special Analyses* (Washington, D.C.: Government Printing Office), 1970–8. For Joint Economic Committee: U.S. Congress, Joint Economic Committee, *The Economics of Federal Subsidy Programs* (Washington, D.C.: Government Printing Office, 1972).

stream of interest and principal payments, discounted by the "opportunity cost of capital."[3]

If it is assumed that the opportunity cost of capital is reflected properly in the private market, then the appropriate "reference price" for the discount rate will be the interest rate quoted in the private market for a loan of comparable class and maturity (to be sure, the appropriate reference price may not always be obvious, and, may not even exist). When the interest rate on the public loan equals the chosen discount rate, the PDV will equal the face value of the loan. When the government's interest rate is subsidized, such that it is less than the market rate, the PDV becomes less than the loan's face value. The difference between the loan's face value and the PDV of the stream of subsidized repayments equals the "implicit subsidy."

Using the concept of PDV, various estimates have been made of the interest subsidy implicit in Exim's total authorizations in a given year. Table 7.1 shows those made by the Office of Management and Budget (OMB) and the JEC. The OMB has varied its discount rate in rough accordance with market trends, without apparently trying to choose precisely a market reference rate. The JEC chose different, generally lower discount rates, which were admittedly "very conservative" and therefore would underestimate the subsidy benefits. A comparison of the OMB and JEC estimates shows that the higher discount rates chosen by OMB predictably yield higher subsidy values, although the different results may also reflect the care chosen in estimating the average maturity and grace period of loans, and the sophistication of the statistical formulas employed. The JEC study fails to indicate any of this underlying information. The OMB assumed an average loan term of six years in 1973, eight years in 1974, and six years in 1975—but a Congressional Budget Office (CBO) study criticized OMB's 1975 figure, citing nine years as the proper term (defined as the period from the date of the first disbursement to the date of the final repayment).[4] The results of the OMB would, then, underestimate the true subsidy value.

Horvath has done a more careful, disaggregated calculation of the subsidy implicit in $2.3 billion in export credit granted in FY1973 (apparently excluding the discount and Cooperative Financing Facility (CFF) programs), based on a separate repayment term for each country, which was the weighted average of loans made to that country in FY1973.[5] Horvath chose a discount rate of $11\frac{3}{4}$ percent, which he considered to reflect more correctly the higher market interest-rates of the period. Although he calculated the subsidy for only $2.3 billion in credits, which was only 57 percent of the total authorization level used by OMB, his subsidy estimate of $307 million was 80 percent of OMB's calculation, reflecting his use of a higher discount rate and more appropriate maturity terms.

These various estimates measure the subsidy accruing to a set of loans authorized during a year. But the lag between authorization and disbursement means loans authorized in one year are, for the most part, only disbursed during the next one to three years. The CBO chose to estimate the subsidy element of disbursements made in FY1975. It selected a relatively high 12 percent discount rate, "as an arbitrary but defensible estimate of what Eximbank could have earned by lending domestically; it is only two points above the average prime rate charged by banks to their most creditworthy borrowers (in FY1975)."[6] Because most Exim disbursements in FY1975 were still at 6 percent, reflecting the rate in effect until early 1974, CBO felt it was justified to assume all disbursements bore a 6 percent rate, although in fact some would have been at the higher rates the Bank had been quoting more recently. On disbursements of $2,690,673,000 made in FY1975, CBO's 12 percent discount rate—double the 6 percent charged by Exim—yielded a subsidy value of $683 million. The CBO argued OMB had underestimated Exim's subsidy in FY1975 because of an insufficient discount rate and because of the assumption of an average maturity of six years, as opposed to the correct one of nine years.

The use of disbursed rather than authorized loans is somewhat arbitrary—and, in the CBO's case reflects its institutional concern with outlays—yet one advantage would be the ability to choose a discount rate appropriate at the time of the activation of the loan. But this advantage diminishes with the consideration that over the lifetime of the loan the opportunity cost of capital is fluctuating, perhaps radically. Commercial loans, with their variable rates, would float accordingly, but Exim's rate is fixed. The optimum strategy would be to calculate the stream of repayments resulting from one year's disbursements with the most appropriate discount rate for each repayment period. The CBO could not do this for FY1975 disbursements, because the opportunity cost of capital that will exist during the lifetime of these loans cannot yet be known.

To employ the methodology capturing the dynamics of the market price of capital, it is necessary to select a past year whose disbursements have, at least in their large majority, been repaid. The fiscal year 1964, when $398.4 million in disbursements were made is a good example. In the absence of good data on the maturity terms of these loans, it is necessary to extrapolate CBO's average repayment term of nine years; with the mean disbursement at January 1, 1964, the loans would have been terminated by December 31, 1972. According to the CBO method, repayment will be calculated in equal, semiannual install-ments—a proper assumption for Exim—with three grace periods, during which interest but no principal payments are required. Because Exim's interest rate on authorizations between 1960 and the third quarter of 1964 was fixed at 5.75 percent, disbursements in FY1964 should have been at that rate. It remains to choose a reference market interest rate. The CBO's decision to take "prime" plus 2 percent is justifiable on the basis that long-term international loans made on the euro-dollar market generally are made at roughly 1–3 per-cent above some comparable base rate. Using the PDV concept, the subsidy element in the disbursements made by Exim in FY1964 (under the above assumptions and with the discount rate varying for each repayment period in accordance with the opportunity cost of capital as reflected in the prime rate) was found to be $67 million, or 17 percent of the loans' face value.

One further improvement can be made to arrive at the best estimate of the subsidy in one year's disbursements. As Chapter 3 showed, U.S. financial insti-tutions have been reluctant to extend long-term international credit. Because bankers think that somewhat higher interest rates would not offset sufficiently the increased risk, and for other reasons, the banks have hesitated to make available longer-term export finance. Borrowers, however, would be willing presumably to pay higher rates to obtain the additional export finance; this should be especially true for developing countries. Consider that the high internal rates of return generally shown by World Bank cost–benefit studies are frequently for projects similar to those Exim finances. Because the supply curve for the banks vanishes for longer maturities, the demand curve cannot be observed either: how much more the borrowers would be willing to pay for long-term maturities remains indeterminate. Assume arbitrarily a willingness to pay an additional 2 percentage points on maturities to be repaid after six years. If the subsidy element for FY1964 disbursements is recalculated, with the discount rate on repayments made in the seventh, eighth, and ninth years being prime plus 4 percent, the subsidy comes to $80 million or 20 percent of the loans' face value.

The prime rates on which to base discount rates for FY1975 disbursements cannot be known yet, but CBO's estimate can be corrected to account for the market's hesitancy to provide long-term maturities. If the discount rate on the

Table 7.2. *Rates of return on loans, Exim and commercial banks*

	1970	1971	1972	1973	1974
Exim (FY) ($ millions)					
Interest and fees on loans	317.1	322.5	341.3	368.3	424.7
Loans outstanding (end of period)	5,714.0	5,665.0	5,956.0	6,586.0	7,902.0
Rate of return	.0555	.0569	.0573	.0559	.0537
Private banks					
Average rate of return	.085	.0678	.0623	.0830	.1092

Source: Eximbank, *Annual Reports* (Washington, D.C.: Government Printing Office, 1970–4); J. P. Morgan and Company, *Annual Reports,* New York, 1970–75; Manufacturers Hanover Corporation, *Annual Reports,* New York, 1970–5.

seven- to nine-year-repayment installments is increased to 14 percent, the subsidy value rises by 8 percent to $738 million.

So far, measurements have been presented for the subsidy value of the stream of repayments on loans authorized or disbursed in a given year. The alternative would be to calculate the subsidy value implicit in the sum of Exim loans outstanding (i.e., disbursed and not yet repaid) in any one year.

Table 7.2 shows Exim's rate of return during FY1970–1974 calculated as the ratio of interest and fees on loans to loans outstanding. Lacking a comparable aggregate data series for the private market, two large commercial banks were selected as exemplary—Manufacturers Hanover Trust and Morgan Guaranty Trust. As anticipated, their rates of return on loans outstanding were quite comparable, and Table 7.2 shows the average of the two. Most noticeable is the steadiness of Exim's rate of return—failing to vary by even as much as fifty basis points over the five-year period—testifying to the stability of Exim's rate during the years preceding 1974. On the other hand, the high turnover of the commercial banks' portfolio, and the floating rates attached to many of their longer-term assets, result in a more widely fluctuating rate of return.

If the holders of Exim's claims had to pay the rate of return being paid to the commercial banks, rather than what they actually paid to Exim, their interest costs would have been much higher during these years. For example, in 1974, after converting Exim's end-of-period figure on loans to a period average, the subsidy accruing to the holders of Exim's outstanding loans was a considerable $366 million. This is a static measurement of a single interest payment, rather than a stream of repayments, and no discounting is necessary. This most simple, one-period measurement calculates the difference between the cost of funds in the private market and the cost of outstanding funds that have been borrowed from a public agency.

The large interest subsidy on loans outstanding that benefited Exim clients in 1973 and 1974 was the result of the widening differential between the fixed rates on Exim's loans and the much more volatile market rates. (At the same time Exim's income suffered, falling from $140 million in FY1973 to $81 million in FY1975, because the Bank's cost of money rose with market rates, while its rate of return remained predetermined by past quotations.) It follows that, even if Exim's fixed lending rate were equal in every year to the current rates being asked by the commercial banks, some of Exim's borrowers could be beneficiaries eventually of a subsidy, that is, in those years when the market rate rises above the rate printed on Exim's receivable.[7]

This process could even out, if Exim raised its rate to reflect market conditions; should market rates then fall, holders of Exim's fixed-rate receivables would end up suffering a negative "subsidy," that is, a tax. (Exim's own income position would also recover handsomely.) The large subsidies realized, however, during the high market interest-rate periods of 1969–70 and 1973–4 will not be balanced, at least not fully, in the future, because of Exim's delayed and partial adjustment in its own rates, which did not reflect completely the leaps in market rates.

The subsidy impact of Exim's fixed interest rate requires one last comment. The interest cost on a fluctuating-rate loan is a function of two variables: the cost as quoted today, and the expected average cost—the latter some function of today's cost—over the life of the loan. The second variable, which cannot be known with certainty, introduces the element of risk the borrower on the private market must bear (no developed forward market for long-term commercial paper exists). For the risk-averse borrower, Exim's fixed rate offers an advantage generally not available in the private loan market. For this reason, the fixedness of Exim's interest rate constitutes a subsidy per se, over and above the subsidy resulting from interest-rate differentials or Exim's special willingness to extend long-term maturities.

How can Exim afford it?

Exim officials regularly testify before Congress, with great pride, that their Bank is a sound, businesslike financial institution. The proof offered for this assertion is that Exim has always been profitable. How is it possible Exim can dispense hundreds of millions of dollars in subsidies and still show a positive balance?

Some answers are found in Exim's sources of funds for FY1977, which are listed in that year's annual report (p. 23):

Source	$ (millions)
Net income	137.4
Borrowings from the FFB	3,917.5
Repayments and other credits to loans receivable	1,343.4
Other	133.8
Total funds provided	5,532.1

The two dominant sources of funds are reflows from old loans and borrowings from the U.S. Government. Exim used to borrow for short-term needs from the U.S. Treasury while meeting its medium- and long-term needs by issuing debentures and "participation certificates" on the private market; today it continues to dip into the U.S. Treasury for day-to-day needs, although its main source of funds is the Federal Financing Bank (FFB). The FFB is located in the Treasury and was established to centralize the financing of a number of federal agencies, including Exim. The FFB taps the private money markets and relends, for a tiny commission, to the various agencies. As of September 30, 1978, Exim owed notes payable to the FFB for $6.6 billion.

Whether borrowing as it used to on its own, or as it does today, through the FFB, Exim has had to pay an interest rate reflecting lenders' investments in assets backed by the "full faith and credit" of the U.S. Government. That is, Exim has always had access to funds at a privileged rate. In addition, Exim has been able to use its close relation to the Treasury to further reduce its costs. Chairman Kearns testified: " . . . The ability to borrow from the Treasury for short periods can very significantly reduce the cost of Eximbank money by freeing it from the vagaries and unpredictable fluctuations in the private money market."[8]

Exim has also been the beneficiary of "national interest" monies at special cut rates. Note 7 to the financial statements for the FY1973 *Annual Report* states:

The interest and other financial expenses reported by Eximbank include interest charges on certain borrowings ($332 million at June 30, 1973) from the U.S. Treasury at rates lower than the rate prevailing at the time the funds were borrowed.

These low-interest borrowings from the Treasury are tied-in directly to the rate, term and outstanding balances of certain concessionary loans the Bank has made in the national interest.

Exim completed repayment on these cut-rate loans, however, on June 30, 1978.

In addition to these subsidized borrowings, the Bank had $2.95 billion in monies that were interest free, as of 1978; $1 billion in capital stock held by the U.S. Treasury, which was paid-in when the Bank was reorganized in 1945; and $1.95 billion in reserves accumulated over the years from undistributed profits (undistributed because Exim has paid a dividend on its Treasury-held stock, in recent years at a rate of 3.5 to 5 percent, or $35 to $50 million). The existence of these funds, which are lent out and thereby transferred into interest-bearing assets, explains Exim's profitability. Table 7.3 shows the income earned on these funds, computed by multiplying each year's "capital and reserves" times that year's average rate of return on outstanding Exim loans, which are shown in Table 7.2. In four of the six years considered, these earnings exceeded the Bank's net income, that is, Exim's cost of borrowed funds plus operating expenses actually exceeded, in those four years, its earnings on those funds. The difference was passed on to its users as a subsidy.

During congressional hearings in May, 1979, Exim was asked how it contin-

Table 7.3. *Exim's income (loss) on borrowed funds ($ millions)*

	Fiscal year					
Net income	1970	1971	1972	1973	1974	1975
Net income	111	120	148	140	110	81
Income on capital and reserves	125	132	138	140	138	144
Difference	(14)	(12)	10	0	(28)	(63)

Source: Data from Exim annual reports, calculations by author.

ued to remain financially self-sufficient in a period when market interest rates had risen substantially above Exim's lending rate. In its response, Exim admitted, as of March 31, 1979, the average cost of Exim's past borrowings exceeded average earnings on all outstanding loans; however, the "blended cost" of borrowed funds and of funds available from the Bank's capital and retained earnings was still less than the average earnings on outstanding loans.[9]

Exim's costs, therefore, are reduced by holding a large capital stock on which it pays a dividend of only 5 percent or less, a large and growing, interest-free reserve—and by receiving borrowed funds at cost or less from the U.S. Treasury. The Bank's profitability is also enhanced by having fewer costs—most notably, no taxation—than a private lending institution. Chairman Kearns candidly admitted this in congressional testimony:

Eximbank as a government corporation is not subject to payment of either U.S. or foreign taxes. A private corporation, on the other hand, would be subject to an entire array of taxes, including income taxes, border taxes, foreign withholding taxes, and foreign income taxes . . . A private corporation would be subject to the Securities and Exchange Commission's laws and regulations, with all the attendant filings and reportings leading to increased costs of operations.[10]

For any lending institution, one of the costs of doing business is loan losses, which are deducted from income. Yet, since inception, Exim had written off only $4.8 million, net of recoveries, at the end of FY1978.[11] The Bank prefers to carry "delinquencies" on its books: thus, as of September 30, 1978, $468 million in loans were delinquent, including $36 million in claims against Cuba, and $26 million against Mainland China. Another method to avoid write-offs is rescheduling a loan: At the end of FY1978, $618 million, or over 5 percent of total loans receivable, had had their maturity schedules lengthened. Neither the delinquent nor the rescheduled loans were recorded as charges against Exim's income.

Exim has avoided recording loan losses by labeling long-overdue receivables "delinquencies," but the Bank's excellent loss record is also attributable to its ability to extract guarantees from foreign governments and to acquire such assurances as currency convertibility. Exim's position, moreover, as a banking institution within the U.S. Government, has enabled it to divert some more questionable loans to the Agency for International Development (AID). But perhaps the most important reason for Exim's ability to collect is the actual backing of the U.S. Government. In the testimony of Henry Kearns:

Now the [low] loss is not really due completely to astute management, I will assure you of that. A good bit of it is due to the tremendous leverage that you have in the Export–Import Bank. Because of its size and importance in the international field, no private business that intends to stay in business or government that intends to borrow again can really afford to default to us, because if we are no longer willing to loan, guarantee or insure few others will. So it is the strongest possible collection tool that anyone could have, in my humble opinion.[12]

Exim and the U.S. business cycle

Supporters of official export subsidies often argue that the additional orders placed by foreign buyers are a stimulant to U.S. domestic economic activity. Proponents of this view seem to be contending not that the U.S. economy suffers from a chronic, structural weakness in economic activity, but rather, they seem to imply that Exim has acted as a stabilizer of aggregate demand, serving to smooth demand over the ups and downs of the business cycle.

From a theoretical perspective, Exim's ability to act as a macrostabilizer is questionable. First, Exim is relatively small in relation to the U.S. economy as a whole. Second, the volatile nature of investment decisions makes cancellations more likely, and final Exim loan disbursements have been actually for lesser amounts than original authorizations. More important, the size of the projects and products regularly introduces substantial lags between loan authorization and disbursement. This hiatus may not be, however, a fatal flaw, because it is the loan authorization that results in an "order" being placed for the product; it is these loan approvals, rather than final delivery of the goods, "which typically set the first-round economic effects into motion."[13]

Another potential problem with using Exim loans as stabilizers is that the "demand" side retains a voluntarism outside of Exim's direct control. Exim, of course, could seek to induce borrowers by offering more favorable interest rates—but until 1974 Exim's interest rate varied little. Whether insufficient demand has, at times, frustrated Exim attempts to expand business is unclear. Exim administratively could increase demand by easing its creditworthiness criteria, although the Bank must feel constrained by its desire to avoid defaults. To judge by the congressional testimony of business groups urging Exim be expanded, the availability of Exim's supply, rather than loan demand, would appear to be the more serious restraint. When Congress reviews and amends Exim's enabling legislation every few years, it places broad limitations on Exim lending and insurance levels; each year the OMB and Congress fix annual ceil-

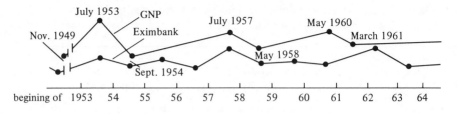

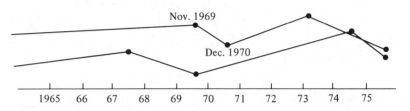

Figure 7.1. Peaks and troughs of U.S. GNP business cycles and of Eximbank loan authorizations (FY). (*Source:* National Bureau of Economic Research; Department of Commerce, *National Income and Product Accounts;* and Eximbank.)

ings on Exim activity. Thus, although Exim can reduce its lending levels at will, it still confronts an upper boundary imposed by external institutions. This upper boundary is not definitive, however, and during the course of the fiscal year Exim can request the OMB and Congress to revise their decisions.[14] The obstacles to using Exim as a macrostabilizer may be considerable. Nevertheless, it is instructive to examine the historical level of Exim loan authorizations as they have varied with respect to the U.S. business cycle.

The peaks and troughs of the U.S. business cycle since World War II, as defined by the National Bureau of Economic Research (NBER), are drawn on Figure 7.1, and compared to the changing levels of Eximbank loan authorizations (drawn from Table A.1). These comparisons reveal fluctuations in Exim activity, notwithstanding a secularly upward trend, have been much greater than GNP fluctuations, and no apparent correlation exists between the variations in GNP growth and Exim authorization levels.

Figure 7.1 gives the following Exim history: In four recessions—roughly equivalent to FY1949, FY1954, FY1957, FY1975—Exim's lending levels fell in phase with the downswing; in two national declines—FY1946, FY1961— Exim actually improved its performance despite the poor prevailing economic conditions; and in two cycles—in the immediate postwar period, and in the late 1960s—Exim's activity levels at first increased, but they dropped off too soon, and Exim earned a rating of "neutral." The conclusion must be that Exim has failed to pivot countercyclically; if anything, Exim has tended to reinforce the ups and downs of the business cycle.[15]

While it was preparing to enter the 1980s, Exim decided that providing U.S. exporters with continual assistance to meet foreign competition was a more important objective than playing a countercyclical role in macroeconomic policy. Eximbank Chairman John Moore, Jr., told Congress:

There are some analysts who argue that Eximbank is a means for expanding employment when overall unemployment levels are high and that, in turn, Eximbank should be trimmed back when the employment rate drops. We reject this view and stress that Eximbank cannot be asked to meet incompatible objectives. If the United States is to meet effectively foreign competition and provide a consistent set of export development programs, then the Bank must give assurance to its customers that it will be available in a predictable fashion. This role of providing consistent, predictable trade finance should be maintained throughout the business cycle.[16]

Although this emphasis on meeting foreign competition—especially subsidized competition—was greater than in other periods, the rejection of a countercyclical role was consistent thoroughly with Exim's historical record.

Costs and benefits

The costs of Exim to the U.S. economy can be defined as the "implicit interest-rate subsidy." The benefits, not evident in macroeconomic stabilization, are often discussed in terms of "additionality," that is, the additional exports that Exim lending makes possible. Unfortunately, no satisfactory methodology has been developed to quantify "additionality." The task is complicated by the numerous variables affecting an export sale, the lack of certain knowledge regarding some of them, and the difficulty of determining whether a sale might have gone forward in the absence of Exim support.

In a study of Exim's FY1978 authorizations, the Treasury Department argued that an export would not have gone forward without Exim's assistance if foreign competition were present, or if the loan maturity exceeded ten years.[17] The Treasury properly admitted that this methodology had shortcomings, and urged caution in interpreting the findings that approximately 70 percent of Exim's FY1978 loans had promoted additional exports. Exim offered financing in excess of ten years but that does not prove that the export might not have proceeded on private terms of somewhat less duration. The Treasury relied on Exim to indicate when official foreign competition was present, and accepted the assumption that this foreign presence meant the U.S. seller would be unsuccessful without Exim subsidies.

Other studies have been less charitable to Exim. Douglas Bohi used regression analysis to conclude, "Eximbank loans are less than 50 percent effective in achieving their objective of promoting additional exports."[18] But Bohi's four-variable equation, which attempted to trace the influence of a few discreet Exim loans on the recipient countries' total level of imports from the United States, clearly was too crude to trace any Exim influence.

A comprehensive examination of Exim's promotional efficiency would need to disaggregate Exim activities by sector or even by product. Firms with a monopoly advantage, or in a collusive relationship with potential competitors, well may be in a position to capture a portion of the subsidy for themselves. Failure to consider such cases can lead to the serious fallacy of assuming the full subsidy is being passed on to the buyer through lower prices. No study yet has attempted such a detailed, microbased approach. Nevertheless, President Reagan seemed to have had such cases in mind when, in his first State of the Union Message, delivered to Congress on February 19, 1981, while calling for reductions in a series of government programs, he stated: "We are asking that another major business subsidy, the Export-Import Bank loan authority, be reduced by one-third in 1982. We are doing this because the primary beneficiaries of taxpayer funds in this case are the exporting companies themselves—most of them profitable corporations."

Studies such as those just discussed may be focused too narrowly and may be too static to capture the full benefits of Exim activity to the United States. Additional gains, for example, could include providing for a more dynamic U.S. capital good sector, helping to assure the U.S. lead in aerospace and nuclear energy, or the attainment of certain foreign policy objectives. Relevant to many U.S. firms is the phenomenon of increasing returns to scale, such that profits earned on the additional sale exceed that on intramarginal sales, as will be shown to occur in the aircraft sector. Exim loans can also result in future benefits, not measurable in the immediate sale, by assisting in initial market penetration, or from the financing of an LDC's industrial infrastructure, which can lay the groundwork for future sales. Nor has proper consideration been given to Exim's role in foreign investment and overseas expansion of U.S. banking.

The complexity of these factors makes it virtually impossible to determine, quantitatively, whether the various benefits of Exim activity are greater or less than the costs of its subsidies. Certain activities, such as expanding subsidies to meet official foreign competition, contain within themselves both benefits and costs that can be intangible and that can alter over time. A subsidy today may help a current sale, but may also increase the likelihood of the competing government offering more generous subsidies tomorrow. Although not of over-riding importance, conflicts over export subsidies add one more tension to the alliances among the Western industrial states.

Chapter 8

In support of overseas investment

Nowhere in the Bank's act is the issue of the transnational corporations (TNCs)[1] addressed directly. The Bank rarely discusses the connection; its task of export promotion is presented as being separate from the business of U.S.-based TNCs. On those few occasions when Exim has confronted its relationship to TNCs, it has sought to minimize the situation. For example, in the supplement to the FY1975 *Annual Report,* the Bank, for the first time, lists credits authorized to support an export sale by a U.S. firm to one of its foreign subsidiaries. The data are manipulated to yield a low figure, suggesting some squeamishness, or at least an awareness of congressional sensitivity to official stimulation of "runaway" shops.[2]

Exim has not always been so shy. *The Semi-Annual Report for the Period January–June, 1953* reads:

A loan by the Bank for a sound project overseas not only provides the private investor with some of the dollars needed to purchase capital equipment and technical services in the United States, but also encourages the investment of private funds in projects abroad which might not have been undertaken in the absence of credit assistance by this Government (pp. 3–4).

The *FY1960 Annual Report* contained a table listing unguaranteed "private loans and investments accompanying Eximbank credits" (p. 9), for the six-month period from January 1 to June 30, 1960. Accompanying bank loans totaled $11.8 million, and "other"—assumedly investments—totaled $32.8 million, for projects in thirteen countries. During congressional testimony in 1967, Chairman Harold Linder stated, "We make direct loans to foreign borrowers, public and private—not infrequently, companies in which U.S. citizens or corporations have substantial equity interests."[3] More recently, in a brief aside in the *FY1973 Annual Report,* Exim commented that a measurement of the benefits from its operations should consider "substantial private equity investment—and other activities that have been called forth" (p. 8).

The closest Exim's legislation comes to broaching the issue of TNCs is in a 1968 amendment exhorting the Bank to consider any "adverse effects" on the U.S. economy of its authorizations. In most cases, Exim's fulfillment of this directive has been to repeat peremptorily in loan documents that the supported exports will provide jobs, foreign exchange, and so forth, and perhaps that the borrower has indicated, at least for the most part, its future sales will not compete with future U.S. exports.

Commentators on Exim, whether private or official, also have failed generally to draw any connection between the Bank and the evolution of the TNCs. An exception has been the American Federation of Labor and Congress of Industrial Organizations (AFL–CIO), whose Andrew Biemiller broached the issue before the Congress in 1973.[4] In its denunciation of the TNCs' export of U.S. technology, jobs, and capital, the AFL–CIO concentrated its attack on Exim loans to the USSR and Eastern Europe, but also listed ten loans authorized in FY1973 to subsidiaries of U.S.-based TNCs. Biemiller's statement emphasized the list was illustrative only, and was by no means an attempt to disclose all such transactions.

Exim's publications do not reveal the ownership of the borrowing firms. Data on stockholders of foreign corporations are difficult to come by. Fortunately, the U.S. Treasury Department did make one attempt to unveil the equity ownership of the recipients of Exim loans.[5] The study found that, of Exim direct, nonmilitary credits authorized in calendar year 1969 (CY 1969), $97 million, or 13 percent of the total, were to firms where U.S. private equity was present. If, however, loans to firms where government agencies hold a participation are excluded, that is, if only 100 percent private firms are considered, then 42 percent of Exim credits were awarded to borrowers with U.S. equity.

Transnationals and U.S. exports

The assessment is still to come on the impact the overseas expansion of U.S. firms will have on U.S. trade. One extensive, statistically oriented study concluded by finding no statistically significant relationship across industries between foreign investing and U.S. exports or imports.[6] What is clear, however, is that a major portion of U.S. exports goes to the affiliates of U.S.-based TNCs, which should dissipate any surprise aroused by Exim's authorizations to TNCs.

According to a comprehensive survey of TNCs and U.S. trade undertaken by the U.S. Tariff Commission, U.S. merchandise exports to majority-owned foreign affiliates (MOFAs) of U.S. companies totaled $12.99 billion in 1970, or 30 percent of all U.S. exports (approximately 75 percent were intracompany transactions, that is, from the parent to the MOFA).[7]

How does this ratio compare to Exim lending patterns? The Treasury study of 1969 Exim authorizations found only 13 percent going to firms with U.S. equity. Given the leverage the large U.S. corporations exert at Exim, this relatively low figure appears paradoxical, until one realizes many of the exports of the large U.S. firms Exim does support are sold not to their own affiliates but to foreign governments. In 1969, according to the Treasury study, 68 percent of loan authorizations were to enterprises with state participation. In CY1974, Exim classified 67 percent of authorizations as going to public buyers.[8]

In the Treasury study, when only purely private borrowers were considered, 42 percent of Exim credits were accounted for by firms with U.S. equity participation. This figure is high, but is not out of line with the 30 percent participation of MOFAs in U.S. exports. Lack of a statistical breakdown of U.S. exports by type of buyer—public versus private—prevents knowing what percentage of U.S. exports to private firms are to MOFAs. It could be postulated that 25 percent of U.S. exports go to public-sector firms, because the government share of GNP is roughly one-quarter in many countries (although obviously more in Eastern Europe). Under this assumption, as a percentage of activity with private buyers/borrowers, Exim's loans to MOFAs approximately equaled their share of U.S. exports. If anything, it is somewhat surprising they did not capture a relatively higher share of Exim's largess.

On the surface, Exim does business with TNC affiliates because they buy U.S.-made equipment and only happen, incidentally, to be U.S. owned. Exim itself has decided, as a matter of internal policy, that *not* to lend to U.S.-based TNC affiliates would be "discriminatory." This chapter argues that Exim's dealings with TNC affiliates, at times, are related only incidentally to export promotion. The involvement of the official U.S. export credit agency serves multiple purposes for overseas affiliates; purposes range from making available a significant percentage of the long-term capital loaned by the U.S. for use by MOFAs, to deterring expropriation—and when that fails, to financing nationalization settlements. For the commercial banks, numerous Exim loan and guarantee programs have sought to hasten the development of their international divisions, and branch banking—a natural follow-up to trade finance—complements and supports TNC affiliates doing business in the "real" sector.

Exim as a source of funds

How significant is Exim as a source of funds for TNCs' overseas operations? Definitional problems, corporate secrecy, and uncertain data make this question impossible to answer with any adequate degree of certainty. The following analysis should be considered a first approximation only.

The *Survey of Current Business* publishes data on the sources of funds used by MOFAs of U.S.-based firms.[9] Because these data cover only majority-owned firms, they are not comparable exactly to the Treasury survey. The 1966 Benchmark study[10] of overseas investments suggested, however, that MOFAs account for the large portion of TNC sales. Sales for MOFAs plus "allied" firms (defined as the parent holding a 25–50 percent equity share) totaled $111 billion, of which the MOFAs accounted for $98 billion.

The *Survey's* data on MOFAs' source of funds encompass only about 50 percent of the universe of MOFAs. Unfortunately, it does not indicate the relative sales volume of those included in the sample. Because, however, the MOFAs in the sample are listed for $8.5 billion in expenditures on property, plant, and equipment for 1972, whereas another series[11] covering the universe of MOFAs estimates such expenditures at $16.3 billion for the same year, the

Table 8.1. *Sources of MOFA finance*

Breakdown	$ (Billions)
U.S. sources[a]	3.0
Foreign external	7.6
Non-MNC[b]	6.8
Financial institutions	0.6
Long term	0.8
Other long term	1.2

Source: Commerce Department, *Survey of Current Business* (see notes 9 and 11 to this chapter).
[a]Of funds from U.S. sources, nearly all appear to come from the parent. This suggests that the data are attributing to the parent loans originally borrowed from banks by the parent.
[b]Non-MNC excludes other affiliates of the same parent firm.

sample would appear to capture approximately half of the MOFAs' investments. Consequently the data from the sample survey for MOFAs' source of funds are doubled.

In 1972, the funds from all sources used by MOFAs totaled $26.6 billion (computed by doubling the figure listed in the *Survey's* sample). Of this, $14.2 billion was generated internally, $11 billion generated externally, and $1.6 billion "other." Those funds generated externally to the MOFA were broken down by source, as shown on Table 8.1.

The relative impact of Exim as a source of funds for TNCs overseas can be determined by computing some ratios. An approximation of Exim authorizations given to firms with U.S. equity participation in FY1972 will be computed by extrapolating from the Treasury study. (The author of the study justified examining only one year on the basis that other years would not yield significantly different results.) For example, 13 percent times $3.3 billion (FY1972 loan authorizations) equals $429 million (assuming 13 percent of discount and Cooperative Financing Facility (CFF) loans are for TNC affiliates, which is probably conservative). Thus, in 1972, the ratio of Exim funds authorized to TNC affiliates to the total of funds generated externally to the firm of MOFAs was 4 percent.

Disaggregating further, Exim funds as a ratio to funds from U.S. sources (which assumedly include Exim) are 14 percent. As a source of funds from the home country, Exim is a noticeable, but not overwhelming contributor. Exim's percentage of U.S.-sourced funds, however, would increase some 40 percent if its guarantees of participating commercial finance are included.

United States funds are not broken down by length of maturity, but the *Survey* does reveal that, of the $7.6 billion generated externally from non-MNC sources outside the U.S., only $2 billion or 26 percent, were long term. Although a highly conjectural operation, extrapolating the same percentage to all funds ($11 billion) generated from sources external to the firm gives 26 percent times $11 billion, equals $2.9 billion. Virtually all of Exim's funds fall in the long-term range. The ratio of estimated Exim funds applied to MOFAs to the long-term funds generated from all external sources is 15 percent. In the area of its special y—long-term lending—Exim would, again, appear to be a noticeable but not an overwhelming source of funds. The weight of Exim loans in the group of long-term funds originating in the U.S. and available to MOFAs, however, is significant: The ratio of Exim loans to long-term funds from the U.S., as extrapolated, is an impressive 55 percent. This finding accords with the earlier conclusion that Exim is a major source of long-term finance, especially for trade, in the U.S. financial markets.

Data problems have made the previous analysis necessarily freewheeling in its use of the statistics available. Nevertheless, certain facts do appear clear. As a percentage of total funds applied by MOFAs, Exim's role is minor. As a portion of external sources used, Exim remains small. These findings largely reflect the fact that MOFAs rely for the large majority of their funds—90 percent in the sample year—on sources outside the United States. As the analysis focused on funds originating in the United States, Exim's influence loomed considerably larger, especially if Exim-guaranteed loans were considered. Finally, Exim became a major force in the area of long-term loans flowing from the U.S. capital market.

If it were possible to disaggregate Exim loans to MOFAs on an industry or, better yet, a firm basis, and compare that data to equally unavailable disaggregated data for all MOFAs, Exim's impact on particular industries and firms would, no doubt, be great. Such a finding would parallel the study of Exim loan allocation by economic sector, which concluded that although Exim finances only a small percentage of total U.S. exports, the greater the degree of disaggregation, the more imposing Exim's contribution becomes, until, arriving finally at the firm level, Exim may cover a major share of foreign sales.

It is clear Exim's contribution to MOFAs in less-developed countries (LDCs) will be even more significant than its contribution for the rest of the world. Only some 25–35 percent of all TNC investment has been located in the LDCs, but Exim has concentrated the majority of its loans in those areas.

The political "subsidy" in Eximbank support

An overseas affiliate of a U.S.-based TNC derives those same benefits from an Exim direct credit or guarantee that accrue to any borrower, including the fixed interest rate, extended terms, and other implicit subsidies. When the transaction is between the parent firm and its own affiliate, the TNC captures the entire financial subsidy (except for any portions captured by the financial intermediary). In addition, Exim support can have special advantages for TNCs in the form of hidden political "subsidies." They include deterring expropriation, assisting in the "working out" of a nationalization exercise, and providing backing to U.S.-based construction and engineering firms who hold equityless contracts with foreign nations.

Exim as a deterrent to expropriation

The arm of the U.S. Government that formally offers insurance to U.S. TNCs against expropriation is the Overseas Private Investment Corporation (OPIC). Those who have sought to oppose the socialization of the risk incurred by TNCs as they move abroad have focused their wrath on OPIC.[12] Because Exim insures loans, and not equity, the Bank has escaped criticism on this score.

Those who think the government should divorce itself from insuring foreign investment should take another look at Exim. In business, investment normally is defined to include equity plus long-term debt. The terms of Exim loans, stretching out for fifteen years and more, make Exim an active party to the foreign affiliate over a good portion of its productive life; certainly during such a period most of the machinery will be depreciated, and equity investors will expect to have earned back their capital with interest. So long as Exim remains a creditor to the project, any expropriatory action will bring the official export credit agency of the U.S. Government into the fray.

The TNCs consciously seek to keep Exim a party to the investment over an extended time frame. For example, in 1954, Exim lent $126 million to Southern Peru Copper Corporation (SPCC) for the construction of the Toquepala copper mine complex. The SPCC's majority stockholder, American Smelting and Refining (ASARCO), wanted the U.S. Government involved for as long as possible, at least for the full length of the Exim loan, which ran for twenty-one years.[13] Therefore, although the acceleration agreement allowed for most of the loan to be rapidly prepaid in the event of sufficiently high copper prices, a portion would remain on the books for the full duration of the loan. The loan was still active at the end of 1975. In the interim, major investments of U.S.-based TNCs—including those of International Petroleum (IPC) and Marcona Mining—had been expropriated by the reformist military regime that took power in Lima in 1968. Marcona received an $11 million loan from Exim in 1968, but it matured in June, 1975. Expropriation occurred shortly afterwards. The Toquepala investment remained disturbed. In 1974, when SPCC decided to open another mine at Cuajone, it again sought and received Exim involvement.

Corporate awareness of the value of Exim participation, as a form of assurance against expropriation, was noticed by Sidney Robbins and Robert Stubaugh in their book, *Money in the Multinational Enterprise*. They concluded that "some managers believe that they get extra benefits from borrowing from the Export-Import Bank," and quoted one executive:

> If you go into a new country with a new venture and have an Exim loan, I think you've got the support of the United States behind you. I know of no case where a foreign government hasn't given foreign exchange to serve an Export-Import Bank loan. So to me this puts you in good shape.[14]

Another example of corporate consciousness of the role of Exim as investment insurance appeared in an article in the American Mining Congress journal. The manager of Bechtel's Financing Services Department wrote:

> Also warranting mention is the special and growing role of worldwide government export credits in project financing, not only as a source of financing but also as risk spreading devices and inhibitors of confiscatory action. Therefore, if the Eximbank is involved in transactions, and to multinationalize it somewhat, Eximbank's counterparts in the United Kingdom and in Japan are also involved as financing agencies, I think there are additional inhibiting factors.[15]

One very practical reason for corporations connecting Exim involvement with investment insurance is the "cross-default" clause routinely contained in Exim loans. In short, cross-default clauses convert a default made against any one party to the particular loan—as well as against any loan made by any U.S. Government instrumentalities—into a default against Exim on the particular loan. Reasons for "default" may be limited to nonpayment of a loan, but also may include expropriatory action: Expropriatory action against a firm with Exim involvement immediately becomes cause for default against all other firms covered by cross-default clauses. This "spread effect" is certainly an inhibitory factor.

Should Exim declare default, it has the right to call in the full amount of the outstanding loan(s), and if payment is not made the Bank can move against any liens or pledged collaterals, as well as against any guarantors.

Even when not involved directly in an expropriation dispute, Exim will not lend to the offending country if so instructed by the U.S. Government.[16] An example is Peru, which, although a country well known and liked at the Bank, had only one loan authorized between 1968 and 1974 (for two cargo Hercules aircraft manufactured by Lockheed, to be used by the Peruvian Air Force). Despite the existence of applications for creditworthy projects, the various investment disputes between U.S. firms and the Peruvian government kept Exim out of Peru until the signing of the Greene Agreement in 1974, which settled on a general compensation formula.[17] The Greene Agreement was signed in February—in March Exim finally acted on the long-standing application of SPCC and approved a $55 million loan.

Exim's withholding of loans is a stick with a carrot. The perception of an Exim withdrawal can have a negative effect on private capital's outlook toward the punished country. On the other hand, a "just" settlement may earn the reconciled nation a fresh authorization—which might even be used to help pay the agreed upon compensation.

Exim as work-out artist

When a U.S.-based TNC is confronted with political hostility overseas, it expects the U.S. Government will be prepared to render assistance to American citizens and their property. The form that assistance may take, however, is far from predetermined. In the extreme case, as in Cuba, the U.S. Government can respond to expropriatory action with an economic blockade, and the use of military force even may be considered. In such politically heightened situations, Exim's role would be minor. But when relations between the foreign government and the United States are less hostile, and when the dispute over equity ownership is susceptible to resolution through financial deals, Exim can take centerstage.

When an affiliate of a U.S.-based TNC is facing nationalization, it naturally eschews risking more of its own capital. Yet it is this very refusal to contribute to fresh investment that worsens relations with the host country. By offering to risk public monies, Exim can help smooth relations between the TNC and the partner government. Exim's $110 million loan for expansion of Kennecott's copper mine in Chile in 1966 illustrates the Bank's willingness to lend to a firm in the process of nationalization.

Eduardo Frei, the reformist Christian Democrat, came to power in Chile in 1964 with campaign promises to "chileanize" and expand copper production. Frei's only important opponent, Salvador Allende, had also advocated nationalization. The tone of the campaign naturally alarmed Kennecott, whose subsidiary, Braden Copper Company, had been operating the largest underground copper mine in the world, El Teniente, since 1915. Together with Exim, Kennecott was able to work out a strategy that would provide financing for expansion without Kennecott putting up one penny. Kennecott would sell a 51 percent share to the Chilean government, but only after gaining several quid pro quos.[18]

To increase production at El Teniente from 180,000 to 280,000 tons, the following financial package was drawn up:

Eximbank	$110,016,000
Chilean government equity	27,482,000
Braden loan and interest	80,000,000 + 12,743,000
Total	$230,241,000

The Braden loan did not come from Kennecott's own purse. Rather, Kennecott was to return to Chile the $80 million the Chilean government was to pay the firm for its acquisition of controlling equity. Only Chile and Exim were putting up fresh capital.

Kennecott lost control of El Teniente, although it maintained a ten-year management contract (a concession Exim conditioned its loan on) as well as the arrangements for selling the increase in output. Kennecott won several other financial advantages. The property was revalued from $67 million to $370 million and a tax reduction decreed. As Moran concluded, "From a cash-flow perspective, Kennecott would be receiving 49 percent of the proceeds from an operation exporting almost 64 percent more output at a tax rate reduced from over 80 percent to 44 percent."[19] The loan document noted the tax reduction would result in the sum of taxes and dividends accruing to Chile being equal approximately to the rate of return the government used to receive from taxes alone.

Exim and Kennecott also insisted an escrow account be established abroad into which sufficient proceeds from copper sales would be placed to service the foreign obligations, including loans, and dividends. Should the price of copper permit, foreign debt would be repaid with accelerated payments; Exim calculated that, with a copper price of thirty-five cents per pound, nearly all of its loan would be repaid in seven years of operations, with a price of thirty-nine cents per pound in four years. Should the price of copper fail to rise, the loan's generous fifteen-year payback schedule—the last Exim maturity stretching until 1986—would prevail. (These price estimates proved to be extremely conservative, although irrelevant, as the election of Allende in 1970 resulted in complete nationalization. In 1974, Exim would reschedule Chilean debt.)

Exim's role was crucial to the successful (as it seemed at the time) work out by Kennecott. According to the loan document, as early as February, 1964, even before Frei was elected, Kennecott had initiated conversations with Exim. Exim served Kennecott in three ways. First, the Bank's provision of over $100 million freed Kennecott from any financial responsibility, and also surely helped Kennecott's relations with the Frei government; Kennecott's access to Exim was one reason for not removing the firm from the mine entirely. Second, although the exact role played by the Bank in the negotiations would be difficult to unravel, the loan document suggested Exim stood firm on gaining concessions benefiting the lenders, including Braden, notably the escrow account and accelerated repayment clauses, as well as the assurance of Chilean government guarantees.

Third, Kennecott's anxieties were eased by the Exim presence. The corporation also insured its $80 million loan (later assumed by OPIC) with a Contract of Guarantee against expropriation from the U.S. Agency for International Development (AID). The TNC also entered into long-term supply contracts with European and Asian customers. "The aim of these arrangements," explained Robert Haldeman, executive vice-president of Kennecott's Chilean operations, "is to insure that nobody expropriates Kennecott without upsetting relations to customers, creditors, and governments on three continents."[20] These words, spoken in May, 1970, were prophetic, for Allende's expropriation of El Teniente did produce the sort of multiple reactions Kennecott had planned.[21]

Harold Linder, President of Exim in the 1960s, stated that the copper expansion project "constitutes one of the more important examples of creative cooperation between U.S. private enterprise and Latin American governments."[22]

Assistance to construction and engineering firms

A common practice in developing countries is for a public agency to retain full ownership of an investment, while farming out the work normally associated with management. Such U.S.-based firms as Bechtel, Pullman–Kellogg, Louis Berger, and Fluor specialize in these contracts. The U.S.-based construction and engineering firms have developed massive overseas business—a business that does not involve the firm in equity. Although the firm's income might be registered as "exports of services" in the U.S. balance of payments, the nomenclature fails to capture properly the scope of the firms' activities. Once the U.S.-based firms are contracted by a government, and although ownership of the project may remain with a state agency, their responsibilities can range from engineering and designing to being prime contractor, procuring imported components, and arranging of the necessary financial package. The U.S.-based construction firm may also be asked to help bring together the parties who will sign long-term marketing contracts, and may even provide any specialized transport vehicles that may be required.

Construction TNCs receive no equity, but they also are not expected to pay in any capital from their own treasuries. Part of their task, however, is often to arrange the necessary foreign finance. Much of their attraction to LDCs arises from their superior access to capital markets in the industrial countries, as well as to their official export credit agencies. Exim has responded favorably to dozens of requests to help finance projects where U.S.-based construction TNCs were involved.

Exim is also willing to finance feasibility studies the construction TNCs wish to undertake, although the amounts involved usually are not great and could be financed on the commercial market. These smallish credits, however, are a good indication Exim itself will be agreeable to providing finance for the project. Therefore when the U.S.-based TNC arrives with Exim financing for the feasibility study, its position is enhanced with the project's local management, who properly assume more Exim finance will follow—if the construction and engineering contract is given to the U.S. firm.

Rescheduling

When a debtor country has been faced with a balance-of-payments crunch, Exim has been willing on numerous occasions to reschedule, that is, to restructure the debt to allow for later repayment. A rescheduling may cover only payments due that year, or may cover future maturities as well. As of September 20, 1978, Exim's "Statement of Financial Condition" showed that of $11 billion in loans receivable, $618 million had been rescheduled at one time or another.[23] In other years, an even higher percentage of loans had been rescheduled; for example, at the end of FY1974, $929 million, or 12 percent of all loans receivable, had maturity schedules that had undergone alteration. Loans may be rescheduled with particular borrowers or as part of a countrywide relief exercise. In the case of the latter, Exim sometimes has rescheduled alone, sometimes in conjunction with other U.S. agencies, and sometimes as part of a multilateral rescheduling under the auspices of the Paris Club, an ad hoc meeting of creditor governments with the debtor country. In recent years, Exim has participated in several Paris Club reschedulings, including those of Chile, Zaire, Peru, and Turkey.

The net effect of rescheduling maturities of a public agency is to release foreign exchange to purchase imports, or to pay debts to foreign commercial lenders (unless they, too, reschedule on equivalent terms). Firms may need the foreign exchange to import inputs, or, in the case of TNCs, to be a medium for profit remittances to the parent. The frequency with which Exim has been willing to reschedule, and the large quantities involved, suggest the Bank has been willing to sacrifice its own cash flow for the welfare of others. By stretching out repayment on public-sector debts, foreign exchange is made available for payments of private and corporate accounts.

In earlier times, Exim was willing to risk fresh funds to provide liquidity to a bankrupt country, permitting it to make hard-currency payments to foreign traders and investors. In frank statements in its annual reports, Exim admitted lending for this purpose to Argentina and Brazil in the early 1950s. "In May 1950, the Bank authorized a credit of $125 million to a consortium of Argentine banks to assist Argentina in the liquidation of past-due dollar obligations to United States commercial creditors both on private and governmental account."[24] And again: "A credit of $300 million to Brazil was authorized in 1953 to assist that country in liquidating its past due dollar accounts in order that Brazil might place its commercial transactions on a current basis."[25] The Bank has since ceased extending large general lines of credit, however, and its individual loans are of insufficient magnitude, given today's levels of accumulated indebtedness, to save most countries in danger of going under.

Other Exim programs and the TNCs

The short- and medium-term insurance programs of Exim and the Foreign Credit Insurance Association (FCIA) can be used, of course, to cover shipments to affiliated firms overseas. The FCIA encourages TNCs making short-term shipments to their subsidiaries to use "political only" coverage. Because the transaction is intracompany, commercial risk is irrelevant.

Promise of access to Exim's discount-loan window makes it easier for U.S.

exporters to "factor," or discount, their medium-term foreign receivables. This opportunity applies equally for shipments to TNC affiliates. Exim's annual report for FY1975, despite its overly narrow definition of intra-TNC trade, listed numerous examples, which totaled $20.9 million to credits. A broader, more appropriate definition would capture a much higher percentage (it was unclear if the list covers all discount loans approved or only those disbursed).

Similarly, the CFF can be used to provide buyer credits for overseas affiliates. The FY1975 annual report lists some examples. This less significant Exim program will be discussed further in the upcoming section on Exim's relation to the transnational banks.

The "product cycle" of commercial banks

Earlier chapters have commented on Exim's concern to stimulate the international activity of the commercial banks. Financial guarantees and FCIA insurance (most FCIA-insured paper probably ends up with a commercial bank) absorb the risk, whereas the profit remains private. Chapter 3 noted some considerable portion of all foreign claims held by banks in the U.S. had Exim/ FCIA coverage. This section will mention several other Exim programs fostering international lending, and will put forward, tentatively, the hypothesis that trade finance, which Exim helps stimulate, is an important step toward eventual direct investment of the banks in their foreign branches. Through trade financing the banks penetrate markets that eventually become sites for branches or subsidiaries, much in the manner that Raymond Vernon and others have described the "product cycle" in manufacturing, where a firm enters a foreign market through exports followed later by a direct investment.[26] This extension of the "product cycle" thesis to international banking and Exim's role in that process will only be sketched here; they offer a promising area for future research.

In addition to its financial guarantees and FCIA coverage, two current programs Exim uses to stimulate international lending are its commercial bank guarantees and its discount window.

Formally instituted in the early 1960s, the commercial bank guarantee program offers Exim's guarantee of repayment on medium-term (180 days to five years) export obligations acquired by U.S. banks from U.S. exporters, with the exporters and banks retaining small portions of the risk. Total authorizations had reached $5 billion by 1978, with annual authorizations in the 1970–78 period ranging from $265 million (FY1970) to a high of $564 million (1976).[27]

Under its medium-term discount program, Exim will make advance commitments to purchase export paper from commercial banks.[28] Application must be made before shipment, and the commercial bank may sell—and repurchase—its export paper at any time before final maturity. In the event of default by the borrower Exim retains unconditional recourse on the commercial bank, but the bank may also insure its credit under another Exim or FCIA program. The facility began in earnest in late 1969, at the time of a sharp credit squeeze, to guarantee the banks immediate liquidity upon demand for covered export credits. As Exim's *Annual Report* for FY1973 explains:

The purpose of establishing (the discount loan facility) was to alleviate the shortages of funds which were constraining commercial bank financing of medium-term (one to five years) exports, and in so doing, encourage even more commercial bank participation in export financing (p. 12).

From FY1970–FY1978, $8.1 billion in discount loan commitments have been authorized. In the FY1970–FY1975 period, only 20–25 percent were actually discounted, although Exim argues the authorization figure indicates the true impact of the program on stimulating export finance.

Both these programs have predecessors in much earlier Exim initiatives. In the immediate postwar period, Exim entered into "agency agreements" with the commercial banks; by December of 1946, Exim had guaranteed $182 million in commercial bank export credit.[29] By 1954, Exim had three separate programs with commercial banks, which the *Annual Report for the Period July–December 1954* lists at the following levels (pp. 67–70):

	Outstanding balances ($ million)
1. Letters of credit guaranteed by Exim	24.3
2. Loans under agency agreements whereby Exim agrees to take out the disbursing bank in the event of default	90.7
3. Loans under agency agreements whereby Exim agrees to take out disbursing bank at any time	28.1
Total	143.1

Items 1 and 2 are guarantee programs, whereas item 3, Exim's agreement to take out the creditor at any time, sounds similar to Exim's commitment under its current discount program.

Unfortunately, Exim's annual reports fail to indicate the maturities of these Exim-covered loans. If, in keeping with Exim's general practice, it is assumed that the loans primarily had maturities of over one year, they would represent 32 percent of the $441 million in long-term claims against foreigners reported by banks in the United States as of December 31, 1954.[30] Exim was, therefore, in this period of recovery and growth playing a role for international banking, whose outstanding foreign claims more than doubled in the 1954–58 period alone.

Exim guarantees improve the quality of the commercial banks' portfolio by absorbing the risk on the covered loans. Exim also allows a bank to extend its total lending to a market: Because a government-guaranteed loan is not part of a bank's risk exposure, it need not count, or will count only fractionally, against exposure ceilings for that market, whether the ceiling be internal to the bank or determined by bank examiners.

By encouraging trade finance, Exim loans and guarantees help to introduce the banks to foreign clients. The import needs of these clients are just one of their many financial demands. To serve best both TNC clients abroad, as well as contacts made in the export–import trade, the commercial banks will, if possible, move to establish a nearby branch office or subsidiary.[31]

Exim no longer publishes the names of the banks whose loans it insures, but its annual reports of the 1940s and 1950s did. The prime users of Exim guarantees were, and presumably still are, the same select number of large banks that dominate international lending. For example, according to an official of one of the leading U.S. banks, Citibank, Exim's encouragement of trade finance most definitely contributed to his own bank's overseas development.[32]

In FY1971, Exim moved directly to help overseas bank operations by instituting the CFF, whereby Exim will finance 50 percent of the credit extended by an overseas banking institution, including branches or representative offices of U.S. banks.

Exim is willing to establish lines of credit to an overseas branch bank—which can be mixed into discrete credits of local customers without Exim approval—if a discretionary authority has been granted; the credits, however, must be for U.S. exports. Until 1978, the "cooperating institution" was limited to a 2.5 percent markup on the Exim portion of the loan, but this ceiling was eliminated to make the CFF more attractive to the banks. By the end of FY1974, Exim had approved $302 million in CFF loans, net of cancellations, for a total export value of nearly $600 million[33] (with Brazil accounting for about one-third of the volume), although use of the facility waned somewhat before the 1978 reform. Exim has not released data to show what percentage of CFF loans has passed through branches of U.S. banks. In any event, the CFF should be seen as the latest in a long history of Exim programs that have stimulated and supported the international thrust of U.S. banking, from trade credits to branch banking overseas.

These various Exim programs, some old, some new, tie in directly to specific transactions. In addition, and perhaps even more important, Exim's direct loans improve the international financial climate *generally,* by supplying a portion of the financial needs of the international trade and payments system. Other official lending institutions, such as the World Bank and bilateral agencies, perform a similar function of cushioning the system, especially through their willingness to undertake the less attractive exposure. In discussing the frailty of the international financial system, several commentators have noted the relation between the stability of the commercial banks and official loan activities. For example, Richard Debs, first vice-president of the Federal Reserve Bank of New York, sought to assure an assembled group of foreign-exchange traders concerned about the burgeoning debts of the LDCs by stating

Table 8.2. *Ownership of Brazilian borrowers*

Borrower by equity type	Authorizations ($ thousands)	(%)	Number of loans
U.S. equity	125,422	(24)	23
Foreign, non-U.S. equity	42,944	(8)	11
Private Brazilian	128,882	(25)	23
Brazilian State	225,650	(43)	19
Total	522,898	(100)	76

Source: Richard E. Feinberg, "The Export-Import Bank in the U.S. Economy." Ph.D. dissertation, Stanford University, 1978, tables 9.3A–9.3E, 242–8.

that "the creditworthiness of many borrowers had been strengthened by enlarged official financing facilities."[34]

Case studies of Exim support for TNCs in four countries

Brazil

Brazil has been a favored Exim client since the early 1940s, when Exim took up a challenge turned down by United States Steel Corporation, to help Brazil finance its infant iron and steel industry.[35] By 1964, over 20 percent of Exim's total loan portfolio was concentrated in Brazil. Harold Linder, President of Exim in the 1960s, purposely reduced this exposure.[36] Nevertheless, by 1975 Brazil was still easily the Bank's leading borrower. In FY1974–1975, Brazil accounted for 10 percent of new Exim loan authorizations.

Table 8.2 breaks down, by ownership of the borrower, Exim direct loans (excluding CFF) authorized to Brazil from July, 1973 through December, 1975, and still active on that date. The four categories of borrower were: discernible U.S. equity; foreign (i.e. non-Brazilian) non-U.S. equity; equity apparently controlled by Brazilian nationals; and borrower a state agency.

Of seventy-six loans authorized in the thirty-month period, twenty-three were to firms where U.S. equity clearly was present; the $125 million so authorized was 24 percent of the total. Forty-three percent of the amount loaned was earmarked for Brazilian state agencies. If just loans to private firms are counted, 42 percent were approved for firms where U.S. equity was present. Of those loans to private Brazilian firms, $112 million, or 87 percent, were for aircraft purchases. Excluding this favored Exim product, of the remaining loans to private firms, 68 percent were captured by firms with U.S. equity.

The U.S.-equity firms are concentrated in four activities: mining and refining, chemicals, and automotive. Exim was willing to lend for plant expansion or initiation, in large and small amounts, and to firms with diverse ownership patterns, including to wholly owned subsidiaries (Dow Chemical, GM, Celanese, Goodyear, and Monsanto) as well as to any mixture of U.S., foreign, private Brazilian, and government shareholders. Five of the borrowing firms with U.S. equity had state participation and two included foreign (non-U.S.) capital. ISAM Eluma, S. A. was owned primarily by a single Brazilian. Mineracoa Rio de Norte combined all four types of equity.

Table 8.2 indicates Exim will lend to foreign, non-U.S. (i.e., European and Japanese) TNCs: The firms supported include the more traditional cement and tire activities as well as the "Light," the Canadian-owned electricity distributor that enjoys a dominant market position in the Rio and Sao Paulo regions;[37] but Exim also aided German-owned steel manufacturing, Japanese-owned petrochemicals, and even a Japanese industrial equipment firm.

As mentioned previously, loans to private Brazilians were largely for aircraft: The Brazilian flag carrier Empresa Viacao Aerea Rio-Gradense (VARIG), like the domestic carrier, Vacai Aerea Sao Paulo (VASP), is held privately. Exim also supported the purchase of smaller jets for the use of Brazilian executives. (Dozens more have been financed through the CFF program). Most of the remaining loans to nationals were for construction and media equipment, with the borrowing firms being among the most prominent in their sector.

Two recipient national firms in the "modern sector"—Romi and Metal Level—had direct business ties to U.S. firms. Romi, which exports machine tools to other Latin American countries, was licensed by Package Machinery Company of East Longmeadow, Massachusetts. Metal Level was to manufacture pistons for incorporation into the products of the local subsidiaries of GM, Ford, and Volkswagen.

Turning to the state agencies, the sectoral distribution of loans was as follows:

Sector	Loan amount ($ thousands)
Railroads	64,769
Iron and steel	55,815
Electricity	44,621
Petrochemical	29,025
Subways	23,360
Automobiles	7,000

These loans illustrate Exim support for infrastructure, which, as in the Brazilian case, commonly is provided by state corporations. Because of the significant TNC presence in Brazil, these infrastructure facilities bore direct relationships to U.S.-owned firms. For example, the $12 million loan to the Sao

Paulo railways was ultimately for the purchase of diesel electric locomotives manufactured by General Electric do Brasil, using components supplied by the GE parent firm. The same railway was the recipient of another Exim loan to purchase signaling equipment to be manufactured in Brazil by a joint venture between a Westinghouse Air Brake subsidiary (Fresinbra) and a local firm, using components supplied by Westinghouse from the United States. Similarly, U.S.-made components for the subway cars were to be assembled into the final product in Brazil by Metrocarro Rio, a consortium consisting of Westinghouse; the Budd Company of Troy, Michigan; Industrias Villares (partially owned by the Dana Corporation, and recipient of a separate Exim loan); and a Brazilian firm, Material Ferroviario. The same consortium supplied the Sao Paulo subway, where Exim support had also been forthcoming.

The state-owned company, Vale do Rio Doce, is the largest iron-ore exporter in the world. Exim began to support the firm in 1942, as an alternative source of supply during World War II; all told, Exim had extended the government firm $177 million in credits and financial guarantees. United States Steel Corporation had a long-standing working relation with Vale, and the two firms recently had entered into a joint venture (49 percent United States Steel, 51 percent Vale)—Amazonia Minerocoa, S.A.—to develop a multibillion dollar export-oriented iron-ore project at Serra dos Carajas. Exim was considering lending to Amazonia.

Various of the Exim-financed U.S.- and foreign-owned firms operating in the chemicals sector were part of a massive petrochemical complex whose core was being constructed by the state-owned Companhia Petroquimica do Nordeste, an Exim borrower. For example, Petroquimica was to supply Oxiteno (partially owned by Halcon International) with ethylene and oxygen. Oxiteno's product, monoethylene glycol, was to be used by Celanese do Brasil in its polyester plant.

In addition to supplying such infrastructure support, the Brazilian state offered TNC affiliates other advantages. Government support for Estireno do Nordeste (owned partially by Foster Grant Company), being part of the Petroquimica complex, was to include import restrictions on competing products, official loans and investment incentives, and the unconditional repayment guarantee of the National Treasury of Brazil. The government guarantee would be a condition of Exim finance.

Exim has been shown to be directly and indirectly supporting U.S.-based (as well as foreign) TNCs in Brazil, directly through copious loans and accompanying financial guarantees, and, indirectly, by developing the requisite infrastructure. In some cases Exim was even seen to be facilitating the sales of the overseas affiliates, by financing the assembly of components made in the United States, in what were partially intracompany transactions. Affiliates were aided also by Exim's willingness to finance firms producing complementary products, such as pistons for automobiles.

Table 8.3. *Ownership of British borrowers*

Borrower–equity ownership	Authorizations ($ thousands)	%	Number of loans
United States	46,370	(15)	4
Foreign (non-U.S.)	56,424	(19)	6
Private British	58,753	(19)	11
British government	142,180	(47)	4
Total	303,727	(100)	25

Source: Richard E. Feinberg, "The Export-Import Bank in the U.S. Economy," Ph.D. dissertation, Stanford University, 1978, tables 9.4A–9.4B, 254–5.

United Kingdom

Exim support for U.S.-based TNCs has been concentrated in, but not limited to, the LDCs. Loans to France, Germany, and Japan have been predominantly to airlines and electric utilities. In the United Kingdom (and Canada), however, Exim loans have been somewhat more diversified. An examination of loans outstanding to the United Kingdom as of December 31, 1975, authorized over the preceding two-and-one-half years, reveals considerable direct and indirect financing of the overseas activities of U.S. affiliates. Four loans went to affiliates of U.S.-based TNCs. Getty and Occidental Petroleum received Exim finance, primarily for their drilling and laying of pipeline in the North Sea. Exim lent to an Alcoa aluminum plant, to a can manufacturing plant wholly owned by National Can Corporation, and to a Channel Islands branch of Citibank for the purchase of two Boeing jets to be leased by the Citibank subsidiary to Britannia Airways.

Table 8.3 indicates that these four loans to U.S. affiliates accounted for 15 percent of the loans surveyed. Another 19 percent were authorized to affiliates of foreign-based (non-British and non-U.S.) firms: Thirty-six million dollars of this $56 million was for the development of the Frigg fields in the North Sea, where the French government was the major actor. Another $11 million was lent to Shell International Petroleum of the Royal Dutch Shell Group, to which the Shell Oil Company of Delaware is affiliated. Of the $59 million in loans classified as being to private British-owned firms, $21 million were to British Petroleum (BP): Although a majority of BP's stock was held by the British government, the government agreed not to interfere with the firm's operations, and the rest of the equity was held publicly. Excluding BP and the Frigg fields (worked by firms controlled by the French government), of loans to private firms in Great Britain (U.S., foreign, and national) 44 percent were to firms where substantial U.S. equity was present. That is, Exim loans primarily went either to firms with considerable or total government support, or to firms owned by U.S. investors.

Several of Exim's loans to private firms owned by European or British citizens indirectly supported U.S.-equity affiliates. The French-owned firms operating in the Frigg gas and oil fields had contracted the British subsidiary of Brown and Root (B&R) to lay and cover the pipeline. Exim chose to finance those services the B&R subsidiary contracted from the United States. Among the loans to firms owned by British nationals was $2.7 million for a subsidiary of Crown Agents (Four Millbank Investments, Ltd.), to purchase a drilling rig from Marathon Shipbuilding Company of Great Britain, a wholly owned subsidiary of Marathon Manufacturing Company of Houston, Texas.

Presumably, the use of Exim by affiliates was motivated more commercially in Great Britain than in Brazil, where politics was influential. The emphasis in the United Kingdom was on capturing the financial subsidies implicit in Exim loans, with a large portion, or even the entire subsidy, falling into the hands of the borrowing affiliate and its parent. Political motives, however, were not absent. Rising nationalist pressures in Scotland and the uncertain policies of the then governing Labour Party had created concern about government interference or even expropriation in the North Sea oil and gas fields. Foreign-exchange problems of the United Kingdom were another country risk.

One distinction between Exim lending to the U.K. and to Brazil is that, because Britain is a (former) global power, Exim's loans sometimes supported the overseas activities of British firms. Aircraft and helicopters were sold to firms with international activities, including British and Commonwealth Shipping Company, Ltd., and Lonrho, Ltd. The drilling rig being built by the Marathon Shipbuilding company was to be contracted out for drilling in Abu Dhabi by a firm two-thirds owned by BP. And, although Sena Sugar was London based, its sugar cane growing and processing interests were in Mozambique and Portugal. Exim lent Sena $1.6 million for sugar harvesting equipment to be shipped to the then Portugese colony.

The Dominican Republic

In some smaller countries, such as the Dominican Republic, Exim's dealings with the private sector have been devoted almost exclusively to foreign-owned firms. In the period from July, 1973 to December, 1975 four loans were extended to private borrowers in the Dominican Republic. One loan of $3.6 million was authorized to Gulf and Western Industries (G&W) for expansion of a furfural chemical plant run by Central Romana By-Products, a wholly owned subsidiary of G&W. Another G&W affiliate, Cementos Nacionales, received $7.1 million for expansion of its cement facilities. Two other loans, totaling $8.8 million, went to the Compania Dominicana de Telefonos, which was wholly owned by Anglo-Canadian Telephone Company of Montreal, which is, in turn, owned by General Telephone and Electronics (GT&E). The major supplier for both loans, which included an earth–satellite station, was to be GT&E. During the two-and-half-year period surveyed, the only borrower that warranted Exim credits, other than firms controlled by G&W or GT&E, was the state-owned electricity company, which received two loans totaling $41.5 million.

The Bahamas

Exim has not shied away from supporting affiliates acting in the Bahamas, where the absence of corporate and income taxes render the islands a major tax haven. For the two-and-half-year period ending on December 31, 1975, Exim authorized four loans for $25,552,000. Of this, $22,320,000 was for a desulfurization facility to be owned equally by Standard Oil of California (through its subsidiary, Chevron) and New England Petroleum Company, which has marketing networks in the northeastern United States, where the processed Arabian and Iranian light crude oil was to have been sold. Two other loans to the Bahamas were to the European firm, Deutag International ($1.5 million) for oil drilling, and for an engineering study of a prospective desalination plant ($450,000) to be conducted by Kaiser. Finally, Exim authorized in early 1974 a loan for $1,260,000, to Manufacturers Hanover Leasing, Nassau Ltd., to purchase one used DC-9 from Ozark Air Lines, to be leased to Linea Aeropostal Venezolano. (Manufacturers Hanover Leasing eventually decided not to use the Exim loan.) The Exim Board was aware that the Bahamian location of the proposed obligor was merely a shell setup to facilitate international transactions. Country conditions in the Bahamas were relevant only to the extent that there were no restrictions on the international flow of capital.

Implications of the case studies

The revelation that massive support is given by a state agency for overseas activities of U.S. firms provides grist for a wide range of comments, but the discussion will remain within the boundaries of this work. A parallel has been discovered between the types of firms whose exports Exim finances, and those firms that are the buyers: Both groups are composed of large firms with strong market positions, although the skewness toward bigness probably is greater among the buyers. Although smaller U.S. firms do have some access to Exim's direct credits, smaller and even medium-sized foreign firms apparently do not. Among suppliers, the parallel to the borrowing state agencies are the nuclear and aircraft firms with close relations to the U.S. state, as will be discussed in Chapter 9.

The extensive nature of Exim lending to affiliates raises questions about the efficiency of the distribution of Exim resources in terms of the stated objective of export promotion. Affiliates of U.S. subsidiaries have preferential access to the euro-currency markets—to judge by the low interest rates they are charged relative to other borrowers, including governments.[38] With their relatively easy access to capital, both local and international, affiliates are in the least need of official export finance. They are the most likely, moreover, to purchase in the United States, from suppliers with which the parent has a standing relationship. True, TNCs increasingly are able to source on a global scale, and the ability of affiliates in Brazil to buy from European or Japanese competitors could justify Exim supporting the U.S. supplier. This argument would be harder to make in the case of the Dominican Republic, where G&W could source from the nearby United States and no potential foreign competition was apparent.

Exim has lent to affiliates for the same reason that the international capital markets offer them preferential interest rates: their high credit rating. The affiliates generally enjoy strong market positions themselves, while having the financial backing of the parent, who also may serve as guarantor. As well, the parent may be in a position to approach the Bank directly and may have political allies in the executive branch or Congress who exert influence at Exim.

A conflict exists, then, between Exim's official purpose—to supply finance where the private market is unwilling—and its preference for making low-risk loans to affiliates of U.S. corporations. In part, this reflects the fundamental tension in an agency mandated to undertake relatively risky ventures, while remaining self-sustaining financially. An additional factor, however, comes into play with Exim: An asymmetry exists between an unconnected firm overseas and one with a parent domiciled in the United States. The two-pronged approach a TNC can take toward Exim gives it a distinct advantage.

Another reason the Exim board may prefer funding a TNC has to do with foreign relations. The State Department, with its considerable influence at the Bank, views favorably the expansion of U.S. firms abroad, because it furthers the vision of an integrated one-world economy, and advances the parochial interest of each embassy that sees its own influence enhanced by the presence of U.S. affiliates. These reasons of State are related no more necessarily to export promotion than are the complex financial, political, and managerial motivations a TNC may have for wanting Exim support in the first place.

The case studies illustrated Exim's penchant for lending to public-sector firms.[39] This practice was not accepted always as natural. In Exim's early days, the State Department frequently opposed Bank loans to governments, fearing government-to-government entanglements.[40] In a 1941 policy release, Exim stated, "In all of its operations, the Export-Import Bank is guided continually by the desire to restore and maintain the widest possible scope for private enterprise in foreign trade. The Export-Import Bank prefers to extend credits to private entities rather than to foreign governments or their agencies."[41] Exim now clearly concentrates on lending to state agencies and TNCs, with the remainder going to the larger private firms. The Bank implicitly is fostering development models emphasizing state and transnational capital, with private local capital playing a subordinate role.

Chapter 9

Aircraft and nuclear power: problem siblings

At first glance, a commercial airplane and a nuclear power plant might not appear to have much in common. When examined from a political economy perspective, however, the similarities between the two products are apparent. Their commercial applications were preceded by military usage, and ties between oligopolistic industries and powerful government agencies have been close. The research and design costs for commercial jets and nuclear reactors have measured in the billions. Production, moreover, exhibits a declining marginal cost curve; heavy initial costs per unit of output argue for large sales volumes, larger, it will turn out, than the respective domestic U.S. markets have been able to absorb. The resulting search for additional markets overseas inevitably has important foreign policy implications: Both products function, at the same time, as symbols of harnessed technology and potential weapons of modern war.

These political, economic, and foreign policy aspects will be examined in greater depth, first for aircraft and then for nuclear power. In the summating, unifying analyses, Exim will fall into its logical plane, as official sales promotor, government agent in what are largely government-to-government transactions, and everyperson's financier, meeting the particular needs of both sellers and buyers. Exim's policies, however, are not without their contradictions.

Aircraft

The aerospace industry is not a product of market forces. For this reason, the widely used academic text on industrial organization, by economist Frederick Scherer,[1] consciously omits it from its general survey, even although the industries' sales of aircraft, missiles, and space products totaled $23 billion in 1975.[2] The products of the aerospace industry were designed not for selling on the open market, but for meeting the specifications of government contracts. From 1947–61, 84 percent of the research and development of eleven major aerospace companies (the same firms that produce aircraft—military and civilian—also produce missiles and space products), was government sponsored and financed; moreover, another 10 percent, although company sponsored, was financed ultimately by the government through indirect charges to government contracts.[3] The federal government has continued to provide the bulk of the

124

financing for the aerospace industries' R&D, which, incidentally, accounts for about one-quarter of all industrial R&D in the United States.[4]

The financing provided by the Department of Defense (DOD), National Aeronautics and Space Administration (NASA), and the Atomic Energy Commission (AEC) was primarily for military or space purposes, but the resulting technology constituted the foundation for commercial spinoffs, notably civilian jet aircraft. As one study of the links between the economic and military aspects of air transportation stated:

The Government normally has provided the necessary funds for the research and development of new models of transport aircraft, principally through expenditures for military needs. Aircraft manufacturers usually have funneled all of this information into the production of civil transports, a typical example being the Boeing 707 as the by-product of military purchases of B-47 and B-52 bombers.[5]

Another example is the next generation of jets, the wide-bodied Boeing 747, much of whose design was derived from Boeing's unsuccessful contender for the C-5A military transport contract.[6]

The government, of course, has been the major buyer of aerospace products. In 1961, of $14.9 billion in sales made by about 55 aerospace companies, $11.8 billion were to the U.S. Government, in 1970 $16.4 billion of $24.8 billion.[7] By 1975, the U.S. Government still accounted for $17.2 billion of $29.2 billion of the industries' sales, but the declining percentage reflected the increased shipments of arms to foreign governments.

In the 1960s, the U.S. Government was also the main purchaser of aircraft; in 1965 it accounted for $4.6 billion of a total of $7.1 billion in sales.[8] In the mid-1970s, however, the U.S. Government's share fell to somewhat under 50 percent, again reflecting overseas sales of military planes (sometimes under DOD credit programs), as well as increased production of commercial aircraft.

Commercial jet production is the purview of three firms, with Boeing and McDonnell Douglas surpassing by a considerable margin third-place Lockheed. These three firms consistently have scored in the top rankings of the annual listings of DOD contractors. For example, in 1975, Lockheed, Boeing, and McDonnell Douglas held first, second, and fourth places, respectively. In 1975, Boeing attributed 38 percent of its sales to the U.S. Government,[9] McDonnell Douglas 44 percent:[10] For both firms, these sales were primarily for military aircraft and for missiles and spacecraft. The U.S. Government has also served as sales agent for the rising volume of military sales to foreign governments.

In the formative period of the development of aerospace technology, the share of sales to the government was even greater. From 1947–61, over 90 percent of Boeing and McDonnell sales were to the U.S. Government, between 60 and 89 percent of Lockheed's and Douglas's.[11] Herman Stekler, in his classic study of the aerospace industry, counted government protection and favoritism among the barriers preventing other firms from entering the industry.

(Other barriers included learned know-how, massive capital outlays, and demand uncertainty.)[12]

As official procurement of aircraft industry products steadied and even declined in real terms after the Korean War boom, the key to the industry's growth became its ability to adapt the technology developed under government contracts for sale to the civilian markets. In 1957, commercial jets began to roll off the assembly lines at Boeing.

The cost structure of commercial aircraft production has two important characteristics. Much of the technology derives from DOD and NASA contracts, but additional expenditures are necessary to complete the commercial applications. Thus, although the industry does not release exact figures, it has been estimated Lockheed spent $800 million to $1 billion on R&D and fixed costs before production could begin on its L-1011 TriStar, in 1972.[13] Clearly, initial costs are heavy. The second characteristic of production costs is the observed declining costs of each additional plane, a decline attributed to "learning by doing."[14] Heavy initial costs combine with a declining marginal cost curve to make the industry push for a large volume of sales.

Unfortunately, the aircraft industry has been noted for its "perennial overoptimism."[15] For example, in the 1974–5 period, while the utilization rates for all U.S. manufacturing industries varied from 75 to 84 percent, the aircraft industries' was slumped at 64 to 72 percent.[16] The respective ratios of operating rates to desired, or "preferred" rates told a similar story. The commercial aircraft industry has suffered from a chronic marketing crisis.

After World War II, the Air Policy Commission, appointed by President Truman and chaired by Thomas Finletter, argued that the government should help to maintain an aircraft industry to meet the mobilization requirements of a future national emergency.[17] Although the mobilization rationale may no longer be dominant, government support for aircraft sales remains solid. The Finletter Commission specifically suggested the Eximbank be used to promote overseas sales. Other government agencies, including the Agency for International Development (AID),[18] the Civil Aeronautics Board (CAB),[19] and the Central Intelligence Agency (CIA),[20] have also helped aircraft manufacturers improve their cost efficiency.

Sales to domestic carriers have been facilitated by various government initiatives, including the building of airports and Treasury Department rulings on depreciation allowances. A study of airline finance concluded the carriers have been able to expand their fleets at rapid rates in large measure because of rapid depreciation and amortization charges. These charges were "by far the most important source of cash generation for the airlines."[21] Moreover, they facilitated borrowings: "The fact that airlines, in the course of their operations, can convert their principal asset—equipment—into cash through depreciation in relatively short time cycles has been a controlling factor for lenders to waive the requirement that the traditional 1-to-1 debt–equity ratio be maintained." Finally, the financial viability of the carriers was for many years guarded by the Federal Aviation Administration (FAA), whose regulatory rulings limited price competition among the airlines, and set rates to allow for profitability. The aircraft purchased by U.S. carriers have been produced almost completely in the United States, at least until the late 1970s when the European Airbus began to penetrate the U.S. market.

In the joint industry-government international marketing effort, creating demand was more of a problem than foreign competition. A survey of world civil airlines found that, in 1960, 82 percent of aircraft in operation were manufactured in the United States; in 1974, 3,311 of the 4,133 aircraft in operation (80 percent) were U.S. made.[22] In certain categories of aircraft, such as "standard, long-range," U.S. dominance has been almost absolute, and no competition exists at all in the "wide-bodied, long-range" class.

Even in those sales made by foreign manufacturers, U.S. industry is often present. The A-300B Airbus,[23] which is the most serious competition U.S. firms have faced, is powered by two GE CF6-50C engines representing approximately 30 percent of the cost of a commercial jet. (The interagency National Advisory Council (NAC) has forbidden Exim from financing the export of engines for use in the European Airbus.) In the future, increased cooperation between U.S. and European firms is planned in both the design and manufacture of aircraft.[24]

While the U.S. Government was involved heavily in the development and sales of commercial jet aircraft, the buyers were also often related to governments. In many countries, the major international carriers are state owned. Even when the airlines nominally are private, governments may make their influence felt, as the scandal involving the sale of Lockheed TriStars to All Nippon Airways Co. showed. Lockheed evidently felt that it was worth influencing Prime Minister Tanaka, who was jailed on charges of accepting bribes from the U.S. firm in connection with the Nippon sale. (Exim, incidentally, has authorized large sums to Nippon, including $56 million for Lockheed TriStars.)

By selling jet aircraft to foreign countries, the United States earns at once gratitude for helping to create or upgrade the recipient's national airline, and succeeds in tying the purchaser's self-pride to the U.S.-made product. Being the suppliers of foreign airlines also provides U.S. firms (and certain government agencies, including Exim) with detailed information on equipment, financial status, and sometimes on local airports, air routes, and so forth on these airlines. Such information has potential military use, as Thayer, a career air force officer, points out throughout his book.

This discussion of the U.S. aircraft industry has outlined the industry's close relationship with the government, the industry's concentrated structure, its downward-sloping costs of production, its chronic marketing problems, its limited extent of foreign competition, and, briefly, some of its foreign policy and strategic implications. Before explicitly relating these factors to Exim involvement, a similar survey of the nuclear-power generation industry is in order.

Nuclear power

Studies of the nuclear power industry inevitably underline the important role the government has played in the development and promotion of nuclear technology.[25] The initial interest was military: The $2 billion Manhattan Project in the War Department culminated at Hiroshima. Following World War II, both military and civilian development of nuclear technology was housed in the Atomic Energy Commission (AEC). Some of the military-oriented research furthered a nuclear technology that could be adopted for civilian purposes; for example, the nuclear-powered propulsion system that Westinghouse helped develop for the Navy's Nautilus submarine (launched in 1954) laid the groundwork for Westinghouse's reactor technology.[26] The AEC also purposely financed R&D for civilian reactors and directly supported ancillary activities such as fuel exploration[27] and reactor safety research.

In the 1950s the AEC pioneered the development of civilian reactors: Most of the early experimental reactors were government owned, although private firms gained experience as contractors.[28] Many of the first reactors built by public utilities received AEC financial assistance.[29] Nurtured and assisted by the government, the private nuclear industry has grown large—but it is not ready to terminate the "hallowed tradition"[30] of official subsidy. Quite the contrary, the two major producers of nuclear reactor systems, GE and Westinghouse, have continued to seek public aid, to provide infrastructure (uranium supplies and fuel recycling), to absorb externalities (nuclear waste), and to create public support (regulation, safety). The Westinghouse 1975 *Annual Report* makes the following statement:

The future growth of nuclear power in the U.S. will depend greatly on government policy decisions. Decisions are needed on expansion of uranium fuel enrichment capacity, nuclear fuel recycling and waste disposal. In addition, the public needs to be fully informed on issues such as nuclear power safety, cost-savings and the need to conserve dwindling fossil fuels through the expanded use of nuclear power (p 11).

The GE 1975 *Annual Report* makes a similar plea, and also exhorts the government to increase its R&D authorizations:

Greater industry–government cooperation is needed most in those high-technology sectors where the scale and uncertainty of development costs, and the long time-cycles required before these costs can be recovered, make it difficult for individual companies alone to finance the essential R&D (p. 17).

General Electric and Westinghouse dominate the highly concentrated nuclear power industry. Babcock and Wilcox and Combustion Engineering can also deliver reactor systems, but only the two dominant firms are present in overseas sales. Reasons for this exclusivity are probably similar to those that Stekler offered to explain concentration in aircraft manufacturing: government favoritism, demand uncertainty, learned know-how, and massive capital outlays. In spite of massive indirect and direct government support, "reactor manufacturers themselves have had to invest heavily in R&D and manpower training. . . General Electric and Westinghouse together have probably spent more than a billion dollars on light water reactor research, development and training."[31]

Both GE and Westinghouse are more diversified, in terms of product lines and customers, than are the major aircraft manufacturers, but both firms are major government contractors. Their annual reports fail to indicate what percentage of their sales are accounted for by government purchases. Both firms have been among the major Department of Defense (DOD) contractors. In 1975, GE listed "aerospace" sales at $2.0 billion (15 percent of corporate revenues), whereas Westinghouse's "public systems" division, which accounted for $1.3 billion or 22 percent of total sales, was "led by the outstanding performance of the Defense Group."[32] For both firms, the government-nurtured nuclear divisions are major components in the corporate structure.

This study will not attempt to determine the impact of market concentration and other historical characteristics on the development of nuclear reactor technology. The fact is that nuclear power plants have rapidly become very large—often exceeding 1,000 megawatts—as well as very expensive. By 1976, the price of even a modest-sized reactor had surpassed $500 million.[33] Such expensive and large-scale technology surely facilitates concentration. According to the manufacturers, "There is no economic case for 'small and medium' sized reactors because primary fixed costs associated with reactor production are independent basically of size and do not fall in proportion to reductions in the rate of capacity of the unit."[34] The commercial viability of large-scale technology was made possible by the high capacity of the electricity grids in the manufacturers' domestic market, the United States.

The high initial fixed costs incurred in R&D and in acquiring producer goods make the marginal cost of producing each reactor less than the average cost (including fixed and variable costs) of those produced, at least until some counterveiling factor enters to push the marginal cost curve upward. In addition, learning-by-doing is probably present in the nuclear industry, both at the manufacturing and operating stages.

The technology of reactor manufacturing appears to exhibit increasing returns to scale. P. L. Joskow and M. L. Baughman wrote in the 1976 volume of the *Bell Journal of Economics:*

We have not done an independent analysis of the minimum efficient scale for producing nuclear steam supply systems (NSSS). However, our discussions with existing reactor vendors indicated that five reactor sales per year were required to get close to the 'flat' portion of the average cost function.[35]

To benefit from these scale effects, to be able to spread out the heavy initial R&D investments over many reactors, and to improve from learning-by-doing, the manufacturers must realize sales in volume. The AEC has promoted nuclear reactor sales to electrical utilities through various subsidies and inducements: The AEC, for example, lobbied for the Price–Anderson Amendment, which limits the liability of a utility in the event of a nuclear mishap.[36] Also, incidentally, nuclear power, which is very capital intensive (but involving low operating costs), is made relatively attractive to utilities by the regulatory practice of allowing profits as a percentage of capital.[37] But these inducements to domestic buyers have not been sufficient to absorb productive capacity, and GE and Westinghouse have looked to overseas markets.

As of 1974, of eighty-four GE reactor systems in operation or on order, 25 percent were for export, while of eighty-eight Westinghouse systems, 26 percent were for foreign customers.[38] The dependence of the two oligopolists on foreign markets is understated by looking only at U.S. exports. Several of their major foreign "competitors" are partially owned or licensed by the two U.S. giants.[39] This strategy of subsidiaries and royalties was an accommodation to the determination of certain governments to develop their own nuclear reactor technology.

Until the mid-1970s U.S. firms held a dominant role in the global as well as the export market for civilian reactors. As of 1974, U.S. firms had built two-thirds of the reactors (100 megawatts and larger) in operation, and had won 63 percent of the new orders. (One calculation including subsidiary sales under GE and Westinghouse totals found that the four U.S. firms accounted for a full 84 percent of reactors operating and on order.)[40] Excluding the U.S. market, foreign firms had accounted for 127 of the 171 systems operating or on order.[41] Of of the 127 sales to foreign firms, however, 101 were within country: Of sales made to export markets, U.S. firms had won 44 of 60. This strong position of U.S. firms in the export field was made more impressive by the number of lost sales dominated by overwhelming political or geographic factors, such as Swedish sales to Finland, or West German sales to Austria.

Before Canadians and Western European manufacturers began in the late 1970s to challenge GE and Westinghouse's dominance, the principal problem had been to create a market for the U.S. products. To accomplish this, the U.S. Government had provided foreign buyers with extensive technical assistance, guaranteed long-term supplies of enriched fuel at stable prices—and offered Exim credits and financial guarantees.[42] The firms themselves were willing to sell some reactors as "loss leaders" to promote the new technology (although the losses on some fixed-price contracts were made greater than expected by inflating costs).[43]

In foreign sales of nuclear plants, governments have been active in both sides of the transaction. The buyers have been either government agencies or government-regulated utilities. Foreign governments were also brought into the decision process by Section 123 of the U.S. Atomic Energy Act of 1954, which requires that an Agreement for Cooperation be signed between the importing foreign government and the United States (as represented by the AEC—now the Nuclear Regulatory Commission (NRC), and the State Department.[44] For each transaction, export licenses must be obtained from the NRC. The United

States has not required that purchasing governments be signatories of the Non-Proliferation Treaty, but it does seek international safeguards and pledges of "nonmilitary" usage. Nevertheless, operating a reactor helps to develop nuclear know-how, with its inevitable military applications; acquiring this knowledge is one important reason why governments are necessarily interested in being involved in the buying and running of nuclear reactor plants.

Among the foreign policy considerations that lie behind the U.S. Government's interest in civilian nuclear power is its ability to substitute as a source of energy for OPEC oil. The 1973 oil embargo and subsequent oil-price hikes thrust this possibility into the news, but the idea was not new. Mullenbach observed in 1963: "The increasing costs of coal production and the overhanging threat to imported energy supplies—despite the North African discoveries of oil and the transport of liquefied natural gas—have been sufficiently imposing to indicate a need for special assistance to Japan and Western Europe."[45] An Exim vice-president testified before a congressional committee in 1975:

An important indirect benefit of nuclear exports for the U.S. and the world economy is the effect it has in reducing worldwide reliance on fossil fuels, particularly oil and most especially OPEC oil. Each one million kw nuclear power plant results in a savings of the equivalent of 9.4 million barrels of oil per year (or 2.5 million tons of coal or 56 billion cubic feet of natural gas). The $100 billion in worldwide nuclear investment projected for the 1976–78 period represents 140 million kw of new capacity. This translates into a yearly savings of 1.3 billion barrels of oil (or about 364 million tons of coal or 7.84 trillion cubic feet or natural gas) which is roughly twice the annual crude oil production of a major oil producer such as Kuwait.[46]

Some nuclear-importing countries worry that they may only be replacing dependency on OPEC oil with dependence on U.S. nuclear technology and fuel—the U.S. is, by far, the major supplier of "yellow cake." Nuclear power exports also have propaganda value. A foreign policy study commissioned by the U.S. Government concluded:

In certain cases there may be legitimate economic advantages to nuclear power. . . But it is surely at least equally as important that reactors, for better or worse, have become the visible symbol of technical progress and national attainment. Even more than a national airlines, ownership of reactors is almost universally seen as the most direct route to stature in the world community.[47]

The role of Exim

From the inception of overseas sales of commercial jets in 1957 through 1975, Exim authorized $5.4 billion in direct credits to support $13.6 billion in export sales. (During the 1970–5 years, these authorizations for jet aircraft, averaging $637 million annually, accounted for between 24 percent and 39 percent of all Exim direct credits.) In addition, Exim guarantees frequently covered a portion of the private finance, and Exim always guaranteed Private Export Funding Corporation (PEFCO) loans, which often financed aircraft. In response to the increased tempo of competition in the aircraft industry anticipated for the 1980s, Exim announced in 1979, it expected to allocate approximately half of its total authorizations in FY1980 and FY1981, (about $4.2 billion) for air-craft financing.[48]

In the 1970–5 period, Exim participated in the financing of about 75 percent of commercial jet exports.[49] During those five years, about 60 percent of all commercial jets manufactured in the United States were exported; therefore Exim helped finance about 45 percent of all commercial jet aircraft produced in the United States.

Until Lockheed's TriStar entered production, Boeing and McDonnell Doug-las accounted for nearly all Exim credits for commercial jets. According to Exim's last "Aircraft Report" (released March 3, 1972), from July 1, 1956 to December 31, 1971, Exim authorized $1.6 billion in direct credits to finance $4.4 billion in Boeing jets, and authorized $1.2 billion in support of $3.1 billion worth of McDonnell Douglas commercial jet aircraft.

Exim direct credit and guarantee authorizations for nuclear power plants and training centers have been extended to more than sixteen countries. From 1959 through FY1976, Exim supported $4.7 billion in equipment exports and $1.6 billion in fuel by authorizing $3.1 billion in direct loans and $1.5 billion in financial guarantees. The large portion of the equipment exports were accounted for by GE and Westinghouse. Exim has helped finance virtually every nuclear power plant exported from the United States; the only major plants not covered by Exim, namely, two plants to India, were financed by AID.[50]

The previous discussion of the aerospace and nuclear power industries pro-vides the background making Exim's concentrated financing activity a per-fectly logical affair. The substantial government commitment to the ongoing development of aerospace and nuclear power sets the stage for Exim's entrance. Exim is part of the same state structure that has nurtured these industries, and although the Bank has a certain degree of independence, it is ultimately accountable to the President: Exim's loans and policies are reviewed by the interagency National Advisory Council (NAC), whose principals are cabinet members; Exim's board is appointed by and serves at the pleasure of the Pres-ident. Given the level of official commitment to aerospace and nuclear tech-nology, the inclusion of Exim is to add but one more state agency to the general endeavor. In the early postwar period, the Finletter Commission publicly called for Exim to finance aircraft exports, and by the early 1950s the AEC had Exim financing uranium mining in South Africa. In 1956, Exim and the AEC issued a special public announcement of the Bank's willingness to finance atomic reactor plants, including reactors for research and training.[51] Exim support has been continuous and generous, since those early days of each industry.

The five major firms of the two industries—GE, Westinghouse, Boeing, McDonnell Douglas, and Lockheed—are among the nation's largest, all falling well within the ranks of the top 100 U.S. corporations in terms of sales. With so much productive power concentrated within unified corporate structures, the firms' impact on the state apparatus is potentially great. The firms can claim to represent the livelihood of tens and even hundreds of thousands of workers, and have the financial resources to try to influence the political process.

If their size and government connections[52] place the aircraft and nuclear power plant manufacturers in a position to gain Exim support, their cost structure and marketing problems give them the incentive. Stephen Hymer explained the motivation of large, high-technology firms for whom R&D expenditures represent an original fixed cost, to look to export markets:

> The actual cost of production [i.e., marginal cost] is thus typically well below selling price and the limit on output is not rising costs but falling demand due to saturated markets. The marginal profit on new foreign markets is thus high, and corporations have a strong interest in maintaining a system which spreads their products widely. Thus, the interest of multinational corporations in underdeveloped countries is larger than the size of the market would suggest.[53]

The insufficient absorptive capacity of the U.S. market relates to the non-market origins of aerospace and nuclear products. Unable to find a sufficient market domestically, the firms have naturally turned to their parent, the state—who had shielded them from the marketplace in the first instance. The domestic market could not absorb sufficient quantities of the commercial spin-offs (sufficient in terms of the financial and technological requirements of production), so the government—through its official export credit agency—was asked to help boost sales abroad. Exim was especially suited to compensate for a major marketing problem facing planes and nuclear plants—the need for plentiful and long-term finance.

In both industries, the U.S. oligopolists initially dominated the noncommunist markets, so that official export promotion could not generally be justified logically on the basis of meeting the foreign competition, although the Bank occasionally invoked the doctrine of preemptive competition. In fact, official support has often aimed at expanding or creating markets that might have foregone the purchase (or, as loan documents often state, "deferred" or "cancelled") of aircraft or nuclear plants in the absence of official prodding. By providing long-term, fixed interest-rate finance (at times with a substantial subsidy component), Exim contributes to this prodding. As an official agency, the Bank places the power and prestige of the U.S. Government behind the sale. Because the buyers are generally official or quasi-official institutions, Exim's presence elevates the sale to a government-to-government status.

This official prodding has been especially important in selling to developing countries, not only because they are more in need of trade finance, but also because the products are often ill-suited to their markets. Exim has supported aircraft sales to many lesser developed countries (LDCs), but the World Bank has refrained from doing so because "there are questions as to the priority of such investment. International airlines in many developing countries are operated as a matter of national prestige; with some notable exceptions, they tend to lose substantial sums of money and often involve net foreign exchange losses as well."[54] The World Bank also notes that airlines "serve foreigners to a large extent," and the "aircraft types [have been] determined by the needs of other countries." Thayer wrote in 1965 that the airlines of the developing countries "may become the real gypsies of international aviation; they seldom will land in their home countries,"[55] since such a high percentage of their travel time is spent on routes outside domestic borders. In the area of nuclear power generation, the indivisible, high per-unit capacity of the plants makes them efficient only in the presence of large electric grids, which only a handful of developing countries possess.[56] In its defense, to date Exim has financed nuclear plants only to industrial countries and the more developed nations in the Third World.

Although Exim aids the overseas marketing efforts of the two industries, their technology creates another financial need Exim is willing and able to meet. The long construction periods required for commercial jet aircraft and nuclear reactor systems create a demand for substantial working-capital financing before delivery to the buyer. Once a loan agreement has been signed, Exim, like DOD, is willing to begin disbursements during the construction period. Such progress payments are important sources of finance for the five firms. For example, in 1975 McDonnell Douglas's balance sheet *(1975 Annual Report)* showed "contracts in process and inventories" to be $2.7 billion, $1.1 billion of which was being financed by progress payments (p. 11). Such progress payments were the firm's primary source of current capital: The firm's "open lines of credit" with its sixteen U.S. banks totaled only $300 million (*1975 Annual Report,* Note D). Although McDonnell Douglas' annual report failed to reveal the sources of the progress payments, it did state that $555 million worth of commercial aircraft were in process (p. 16), and Exim must have accounted for a substantial share of the advanced payments financing those aircraft. For its part, GE's *1975 Annual Report* value "progress collections and price adjustment accrued" at $1.1 billion, as compared to "short-term borrowings" of $650 million (p. 29). Exim's early disbursements on GE's nuclear and conventional power plants accounted for a good portion of the $1.1 billion,[57] some of which may have been received through subcontracts with aircraft firms using GE engines. Exim, by helping to pay weighty preshipment financial requirements, meets the special needs of these firms.

Although promoting the export of planes and reactors fosters the interests of the producing firms, makes visible U.S. technological prowess, and cements diplomatic and military alliances, such exports are not without their dangers. Thayer argues heatedly that placing a high percentage of commercial jets in foreign hands is prejudicial to the U.S. capacity to mobilize military aircraft, and is financially detrimental to U.S.-owned carriers,[58] an argument Pan American Airways has been quick to make. Similarly, exporting nuclear technology threatens to quicken the pace of nuclear proliferation, as other nations learn to develop their own nuclear military capability. Nevertheless, the government–industry dynamics in aerospace and nuclear power, of which Exim is but a part, will make it extremely difficult to reverse the politics of promoting overseas sales. The stiffening pace of foreign competition facing both industries in the 1980s will add a further justification to their long-standing relations with Exim.

Chapter 10

Conclusion: trends and alternatives

The scope of Exim activity

Over the years, Exim has designed a wide and sometimes bewildering diversity of credit and guarantee programs to meet different needs. Existing programs were altered or new ones created in response to changes in the structure of the U.S. economy, the domestic and international capital markets, and the relative competitive position of the United States in world markets.

As private capital markets expanded, programs designed to stimulate private export credit proliferated, under such names as "discount loans," "bank guarantees," "financial guarantees," and the "cooperative financing facility" (CFF), while the Foreign Credit Insurance Association (FCIA) offered another set of insurance programs. The heart of Exim activity, however, remains its direct loan program.

If the official intent of these programs has always been the promotion of U.S. exports, they have also generated a series of secondary effects that were not always foreseen. Given the close relationship between U.S. capital goods exports and the overseas thrust of U.S.-based transnational corporations (TNCs), it is not surprising that Exim has been party to these investments. Frequently, government programs designed originally for other purposes were used creatively to support the overseas march of U.S. firms, and Exim proved to be a willing partner. Similarly, while Exim did not look on its stimulation of trade finance as an instrument to foster the globalization of U.S. banking, U.S. banks were able to use Exim programs to assist them in their overseas expansion.

In some instances, the ultimate effect of Exim activities has been contrary to original intentions, at times because of alterations in the environment. In the 1930s and 1940s, the extention by the United States of export credit added to world liquidity and promoted the stability and growth of international trade. But after World War II, the function of assisting countries with balance-of-payments problems was officially assigned to the International Monetary Fund (IMF), and, by the 1970s, the specter of a "subsidy war" among export credit agencies was an additional irritating factor in an already uncertain environment.

Exim has not primarily pursued economy-wide objectives. The Bank has not published any coherent analyses of its macroeconomic impact on the economy,

136

and statistics listing the employment attributed to Exim-supported exports suffer fatally from a partial equilibrium framework. The bank does not work to stabilize overall U.S. economic activity, nor to balance the trade account, and in a world of flexible exchange rates, the effect of increased exports on the dollar would have to be considered to determine the complete impact of Exim activity on the trade balance. In fact, Exim has been working at the level of the firm. As was described in Chapter 9 on aircraft and industry, Exim programs can have important unanticipated benefits for firms, such as providing working capital and assisting them to move out on a declining marginal cost curve. At the same time, the support that Exim has extended to some large and important firms has had implications for the national economy.

Multiplicity of interests

If Exim is primarily oriented toward assisting U.S. firms and banks, it has additional interests to consider, including its own institutional concerns. As a financially self-sustaining agency, Exim seeks to protect its solvency by avoiding undue risk, while behaving like most bureaucracies in trying to grow in size. As a government agency with financial resources, Exim is subject to pressure from individual politicians or politically connected firms, and must also pay attention to broader political issues. For example, in recent years, Congress has actively pressed Exim to consider human rights before lending to certain authoritarian governments, and to avoid job loss from potential imports coming from projects abroad. Exim turned down a loan for a steel mill in Trinidad and Tobago under pressure from the U.S. steel industry and labor unions, who feared Trinidadian steel imports would gain shares of the U.S. market.

Over the years Exim has assisted the State Department in pursuing a wide variety of diplomatic objectives. As in the case of Chile, Exim can serve as one instrument in a broader effort to effect internal political conjunctures. In South Africa, the refusal of Exim services is part of a more long-term policy demonstrating disapproval of a society's basic legal structures. Exim can help improve relations with nationalist governments (Algeria) or show support for conservative authoritarian regimes (South Korea, the Philippines under Marcos). Exim loans to communist countries serve the dual purpose of opening new markets and building economic ties that can later be used for political leverage. Exim largess can be used as a quid pro quo for a single issue like the opening of a military base, or may contribute to an effort to fundamentally alter the political economy of a country. The Inga–Shaba transmission line project in Zaire was intended to give President Mobutu and Kinshasa control over the vital energy sources of the rebellious province of Shaba (formerly Katanga).

Finally, personalities can matter in determining Exim policies. The sharp drop in lending in FY1975–1976 reflected Chairman Dubrul's priority concern to avoid competing with private capital. DuBrul was supported by a Republican Administration that believed that market mechanisms, in the form of flexible exchange rates, were preferable to export subsidies as instruments to correct balance-of-payments disequilibria. DuBrul was especially instrumental in restricting Exim support to guarantees, for aircraft not facing foreign competition.

These various economic interests or points of view are articulated within the U.S. Government by agencies that participate in the interagency NAC, which oversees Exim.[1] The Commerce Department, with its close association to U.S. industry, is the strongest proponent for an expansive Exim, and rarely opposes individual Exim loans. The Treasury Department, responsive to the concerns of the financial community, scrutinizes Exim activity to be certain it is complementing and not competing with private capital. The Treasury's fiscal responsibilities, and interest in avoiding "credit wars" that are disruptive to the international financial system, place it on the side of moderation—although at times Treasury's concern about a deteriorating trade position can place it behind an expansionist Exim policy. The State Department, of course, makes its diplomatic concerns known through the NAC and directly to the Exim Board, as can the National Security Council (NSC) and the White House. The labor unions, however, do not have a strong advocate within the administration well positioned to influence Exim. The Labor Department, although sometimes present at the NAC, has had little effect. On issues such as the potential adverse effects of Exim projects on U.S. employment, congressional oversight has been a more effective instrument for labor than Exim.

Exim's statute created an advisory committee of nine members, consisting primarily of representatives of business and finance, but it served more as a lobbying tool for Exim than as an instrument of business to affect Exim policies.[2] The Carter Administration abolished it in 1978. Business interests have taken their concerns individually and directly to members of Exim's Board of Directors, worked through their trade associations, or sought to mobilize pressure via their contacts in Congress or other executive branch agencies.

Contradictions

With so many diverse pressures on it, Eximbank not surprisingly confronts a number of sometimes contradictory objectives. Throughout this study, the tension between Exim's institutional need to be self-financing and therefore limit risk has come into conflict with its fundamental purpose, as a public-sector institution, to undertake activities the private sector considered too risky or insufficiently profitable. The creation of the soft-loan windows in the World Bank and the regional development banks, and of the Agency for International Development (AID), has relieved some of the pressures for Exim to venture into the poorest developing countries, or to undertake projects with a less certain internal cash-flow projection. The dilemma nevertheless remains, and may become even more acute should the international financial environment become more uncertain in the 1980s.

The most immediate threat to Exim's solvency comes from pressures from industry for the Bank to offer terms competitive with those provided to foreign exporters by their own countries' export credit and insurance agencies. Sharply fluctuating interest rates on international capital markets and vascillating exchange rates leave considerable uncertainty as to the competitiveness of Exim's terms. Although Exim's maturities are as favorable as those of other official export credit agencies, its interest rates have sometimes been higher. Some governments, including Great Britain, France, and Italy provide their export credit agencies with budgetary appropriations permitting routine subsidization. Sizable capital and reserves, on which it pays only a nominal dividend to the U.S. Treasury, permit Exim to offer below-market rates, but massive subsidies would force it to eat into this capital base.

A meaningful international agreement to restrain the subsidization of export credit would clearly relieve pressure on Exim's financial structure, but Exim claims foreign credit agencies have blocked progress on such an understanding.[3] Export credit subsidization disrupts U.S. efforts to harmonize national and international financial stability and economic growth. An Eximbank correcting market failures, for example, by providing the long-term credit the banking system fails to supply, can be seen as acting on behalf of global welfare. An Exim subsidizing trade for national advantage is disruptive of international cooperation.

Offering cut-rate loans to meet foreign competition also conflicts with a central Exim tenet: not to compete with private capital. In the case where a shared financial package is made competitive by Exim's subsidy, Exim's below-market rates can actually increase business for U.S. banks. As U.S. banks increasingly act on a global basis, however, and are as capable of financing exports from Western Europe as from the United States, their interest in winning such competition diminishes.

Export subsidies also distort the prices facing potential importers. Exim's decision to abandon its earlier concern for development to concentrate exclusively on U.S. commercial advantage may be shortsighted if it results in decisions by governments in developing countries that prove detrimental to longer-term economic growth.[4] United States diplomatic objectives regarding the political stability of the recipient country may also be compromised.

The withholding of Exim loans, as a diplomatic sanction, will normally come into conflict with export promotion objectives, at least in the short run. For example, U.S. exports to Chile fell off, partly because of Exim's closure, during and in the immediate aftermath of the Allende government. If such sanctions succeed in reversing the policies of the government in question, or altering the government itself, the export loss may be temporary and short lived. But as relative U.S. economic strength in an increasingly multi-polar world declines, the ability of the U.S. to use economic leverage to obtain diplomatic objectives will suffer. As this reality becomes more apparent, the sacrifice of export promotion objectives on the behalf of unattainable diplomatic objectives will arouse increasing opposition. Criticisms of the use of Exim in the pursuit of human rights policies were based partly on the readiness of other exporting nations to replace quickly U.S. exporters in the abandoned markets. This is not to deny, however, that Exim may still serve foreign policy objectives in numerous circumstances.

Making Exim more efficient

In the process of analyzing Exim's various functions, this study has at several points suggested reforms in Exim policies that could render the Bank a more effective export promotion agency. The following reforms could be implemented without unduly jeopardizing Exim's financial solvency.

Exim has continued to devote roughly one-quarter of its loans to developed countries. The borrowers are generally public-sector agencies and firms, or else major private firms with excellent credit ratings. The superior access of such borrowers to the private capital market suggests Exim should take steps to guarantee official credit as necessary. Exim can encourage such borrowers to seek Exim lending only as a last resort if its interest rate to such markets is fixed slightly above current market rates. The borrower might still prefer Exim finance for its fixed rates or political overtones, but in many cases borrowers would be stimulated to attempt to tap first the private markets. Exim could thereby assure a more effective allocation of its limited financial resources among global markets.

The large U.S.-based TNCs are another class of borrowers with excellent credit ratings and ready access to private financing. An additional reason for carefully scrutinizing loans to TNCs is the greater likelihood that they will source in the United States in any event. Exim must also be wary of TNCs, with their ability to source globally, coaxing official export credit agencies into bidding against one another. A clever TNC may have already decided where it will produce the capital goods for its subsidiary, but will try to get that country's eximbank to offer more favorable terms by appearing to consider sourcing from another country whose eximbank has already offered advantageous terms. In lending both to TNCs and to industrial states, Exim may be needed to provide lengthy maturities, to finance an unusually risky or large-scale project, or to serve political purposes, but the potential deal should be approached with a healthy skepticism.

By staying safely in the stream of private capital and trade flows, Exim has concentrated on the industrial nations and the more advanced of the developing countries. A public-sector agency should seek to move ahead of the private market and assist in the penetration of new, lesser-known regions. Consistent with this reasoning, Congress in 1968 authorized Exim to open a special Export Expansion Facility (EEF) to grant loans and insurance to markets that promised not the usual "reasonable assurance of repayment" but only a "sufficient likelihood of repayment." Exim lent, under the $500-million-facility, from its own ordinary monies in a very different pattern from its normal operations. The market distribution of the EEF, by export value of transactions supported by loans, as of September 30, 1974, compared to that of regular Exim loans, as of January 1, 1975, is shown in the following table:

	A(%)	B(%)	C(%)	D(%)
EEF loans (as of Sept. 30, 1974)	2	12	52	34
Regular loans (as of Jan. 1, 1975)	39	38	14	8

"A" markets are lowest risk, "D" highest risk.
Source: Unpublished Eximbank memoranda.

This distribution is somewhat misleading, as the concentration of EEF loans in the C and D categories reflected the presence of Turkey, South Korea, and the Philippines. Loans were also extended, however, to the less traditional markets of Afghanistan, Bolivia, Burma, the Central African Republic, Guinea, Jordan, Ecuador, Guyana, Liberia, Nigeria, and Uruguay.

Exim has not shown enthusiasm for the EEF, which has stagnated. This is unfortunate, for the distribution of loans resulting from "sufficient" assurance of repayment is what a forward-looking, public-sector Bank should produce.[5] Nor does the risk taken appear to have been excessive: The FCIA reported that insurance policies issued under the EEF through CY1975 had a loss of only 0.4 percent.

The tendency of the FCIA to seek profits for its shareholders is detrimental to its original conception to service exporters and their creditors. National export credit agencies are generally expected to break even on their operations, generating a surplus only for purposes of building up a reserve against potential losses.[6] The FCIA is reinsured by Exim and, by implication, the U.S. Government; the absence of private risk taking removes the justification for private profitability.

Exim should follow the lead of FCIA and cease to charge regressive premium rates. Although the logic (if not, as the FCIA found, the actuarial evidence) of private capital markets might argue for charging the poorer, less-developed markets more, the public sector ought not to reproduce this behavior, which also restrains exporters from penetrating new markets.

Both Exim and FCIA ought to explore whether insured lenders are shaving interest spreads to compensate for the reduced risk. Lenders that continue to levy high interest charges when the risk has been socialized are displaying their superior market power: Their behavior has no academic or social justification. France, in fact, places restrictions on interest rate practices of lenders covered by its official insurance agency, Compagnie Française d'Assurance de Commerce Extérieur (COFACE).

Finally, Exim should recognize that the dichotomy between export and development finance is often artificial. Exim's large loans can have a significant impact on the investment patterns of the borrowing country, and the Bank ought to consider this impact in its loan analysis. To carry out such "impact" studies in a meaningful way, Exim would have to enlarge its staff of economists and other analysts.

The common thread of these reforms is the attempt to overcome some of Exim's institutional interests, and the narrower purposes of particular clients, to the benefit of the U.S. export sector as a whole. The proposals seek to distinguish Exim as a public-sector agency serving broad interests.

Future trends

The direction and even the continued existence of Exim shall depend heavily, as it always has, on the evolution of the private capital markets. In the 1970s, the international financial markets expanded tremendously, and commercial banks showed increasing willingness to extend maturities of five, seven, and even ten years. For the first time since the Depression, a widening number of developing countries gained access to the international bond market. In the late 1970s and early 1980s, soaring market interest rates widened the subsidy element in Exim's loans, whose interest charges remained substantially below commercial bank rates. Exim for the first time faced the danger of its cost of funds exceeding its total earnings, despite the absence of interest costs on its large reserve and capital base. While Exim is capable of absorbing even substantial losses, it cannot indefinitely eat into its capital reserves. Exim will have to close the gap between its cost of funds and its lending rates even if its competitors continue to offer highly subsidized rates. The alternative would be for Congress to provide Exim with direct authorizations, but this would run counter to the dominant trend toward federal budgetary stringency. OMB has been restraining Exim's loan disbursements, which count as outlays in the fiscal budget.

These developments confront Exim with perhaps the greatest challenges to its mission since its founding in the 1930s. Nevertheless, Exim stalwarts can point to countertrends to justify the Bank's continued existence.

While private capital markets have expanded, they are not capable of meeting the full financial needs of the developing world. Especially when countries face balance of payments disequilibria, commercial banks still hesitate to extend the seven- to fifteen-year loans needed for some big ticket items or large projects. The international bond market is still cautious about lending to most developing countries, and bonds are not well suited to the phased disbursement more appropriate to export financing.

Other official institutions have come into being and matured in the postwar period, but none exactly replaced Exim. The World Bank and the regional development banks grew rapidly in the 1970s, but their resources still do not match the demand for investment funds in the developing world. The World Bank's emphasis on meeting the basic needs of the poor, especially in rural areas, diverts resources away from the large, capital-intensive equipment in which Exim specializes.

The World Bank, and to a substantial degree the commercial banks, are multinational actors, but Exim is a bilateral agency whose loans are tied to U.S. products. AID and its Economic Support Fund (ESF) also are tied to U.S. products, but the real funding levels for development loans have been stagnant and substantially oriented toward basic needs projects, and ESF, which provides ten-year money for military and economic purposes, has been concentrated heavily in a few politically sensitive regions. These programs do not have the flexibility needed to respond to export opportunities as they arise.

No national or international agency has the capability to provide the export credit insurance offered by Exim and the FCIA. Both the World Bank and Overseas Private Investment Corporation (OPIC) have the legal authority to guarantee private finance, but the World Bank has not yet done so and OPIC financial insurance has been offered in very limited amounts and targeted exclusively to affiliates of U.S.-based TNCs.

The increasing tensions in the international environment are likely to rebound in Exim's favor. In a world of expanding and increasingly competitive international trade, the demand for export finance will surely increase. Unless a meaningful international arrangement to restrain the subsidization of official export credits can be negotiated, the pressure from U.S. exporters for Exim to "meet the competition" will continue to mount. In an age of heightened anxiety over national security, Exim will be well suited to assist industries vital to defense and the broader national industrial base.

As it has been in the past, Exim will be caught up in many of the major issues that will confront the United States in the 1980s. Exim will be touched by the debates over the role the U.S. Government should play in subsidizing high-technology industries that contribute to employment and the trade balance. Critics will scrutinize Exim's impact on technology transfer and the overseas spread of nuclear know-how. The collapse of the Shah's regime in Iran raises the specter of political instability in the upper-tier developing countries where Exim's exposure is concentrated heavily. An increase in uncertainties in the international financial markets would yield a demand for more active official-sector finance. The Bank may also want to become more active in the next layer of developing countries, as they become more integrated into the international trade and capital systems. Exim has already been called on to help open new markets in China. The search for raw materials will, once again, produce a need for Eximbank support. In confronting these issues, Exim will undoubtedly need to revise particular programs, while preserving its essential purposes.

With its breadth of activities, the multitude of vested interests with a stake in its existence, and the continuing inability of the private capital and insurance markets and other official institutions to fully reproduce Exim's functions, it seems certain that Exim will remain a significant if unsung institution serving particular needs of the U.S. economy.

Appendixes

Appendix A

Statistical tables

Table A.1. *Eximbank annual authorizations*

Fiscal year	Gross authorizations	Loans	Guarantees and insurance
1934–45	1,269	—[a]	—[a]
1946	2,197	—	—
1947	279	—	—
1948	466	—	—
1949	174	—	—
1950	406	—	—
1951	395	—	—
1952	551	—	—
1953	571	—	—
1954	250	—	—
1955	632	—	—
1056	235	—	—
1957	1,067	—	—
1958	857	—	—
1959	890	—	—
1960	551	500	51
1961	1,414	1,242	172
1962	1,862	1,093	769
1963	1,474	680	794
1964	1,743	778	964
1965	1,859	852	1,008
1966	2,142	1,149	993
1967	3,607	2,724	884
1968	3,534	2,526	1,008
1969	2,517	1,295	1,222
1970	3,968	2,209	1,759
1971	5,397	2,362	3,034
1972	7,230	3,285	3,946
1973	8,514	4,054	4,461
1974	9,100	4,905	4,195
1975	8,315	3,813	4,502
1976	8,620	3,489	5,131

Table A.1. *(cont.)*

Fiscal year	Gross authorizations	Loans	Guarantees and insurance
Transition quarter	1,451	448	1,003
1977	5,600	1,221	4,379
1978	7,376	3,425	3,952
1979	9,491	4,475	5,016
1980	12,609	4,578	8,031
1981[b]	12,884	5,428	7,456

[a]Before 1960, the Eximbank did not publish a clear breakdown between loans and guarantees/insurance.
[b]Preliminary.
Source: Eximbank, Annual Reports, Washington, D.C.: 1945–80.

Table A.2. *Distribution of outstanding Eximbank loans by economic sector*

Economic sector	As of Dec. 31, 1975		As of July 31, 1979	
	$ (millions)	%	$ (millions)	%
Agriculture	263	2	159	1
Communication	278	2	305	2
Construction	234	2	335	2
Electric power	3,687	25	4,987	28
Nuclear power	2,532	17	3,397	19
Manufacturing	1,399	10	1,451	8
Mining and refining	2,971	20	3,457	20
Transportation	4,546	31	5,334	30
Commercial jet aircraft	3,431	23	4,071	23
Miscellaneous	1,306	9	1,631	9
Total	14,686[a]	100	17,661	100

[a]Totals may not add due to rounding.
Source: Eximbank, *Annual Report 1979,* Washington, D.C., 13.

Table A.3. *Exim lending patterns by product group*

Product groups	Exim disbursements FY1974 ($1,000s)	Total value of exports financed	Exports financed as percentage of total U.S. exports
Agriculture	85,449	102,688	0
Intermediate manufactures	7,938	18,704	0
Consumer manufactures	18,709	37,432	1
Armaments	157,163	310,050	—
Machinery and transport equipment	1,927,106	4,402,629	12
Power	388,603	687,970	16
Hydroelectric	49,691	108,819	558
Nuclear	270,123	425,131	290
Thermal	37,580	81,063	10
Special industry	282,823	633,016	25
Construction and mining	148,002	325,955	19
Foundry	19,986	43,665	7
Telecommunications	15,629	33,647	2
Railroad vehicles	65,603	143,528	51
Aircraft	726,695	1,821,388	32
Commercial jet	710,451	1,782,654	40
Other electrical	47,400	103,478	2
Other transport	8,198	18,922	0
Other nonelectrical	417,169	917,015	9
Chemical processing	17,411	38,446	—
Petroleum refining and processing	89,484	196,495	—
Total	2,241,365	4,871,503	5

Source: Eximbank unpublished data.

Table A.4. *Product groups*

═══

Agriculture: food, live animals, beverages, tobacco, crude materials, minerals, fuels,
    oils, and fats (SITC 0–4)
Intermediate manufactures: chemical and manufactured goods classified chiefly by
    materials (SITC 5–6)
Consumer manufacturers: miscellaneous manufactured articles (SITC 8)
Military equipment: armaments (SITC 95)
Machinery and transport equipment: machinery and transport equipment (SITC 7)
  Power: power-generating machinery, electric power machinery, and switch gear
      (SITC 711, 722)
    Hydroelectric: hydroelectric power plant and equipment (SITC 7118)
    Nuclear: nuclear power plant and equipment (SITC 7117)
    Thermal: thermal power plant and equipment (SITC 7221)
  Special industry: machines for special industries (SITC 718)
    Construction and mining: construction, excavation, and mining equipment
        (SITC 7184)
  Foundry: metalworking machinery (SITC 715)
  Telecommunications: telecommunications apparatus (SITC 724)
  Railroad vehicles: railway vehicles (SITC 731)
  Aircraft: aircraft (SITC 734)
    Commercial jet: commercial jet aircraft (SITC 7341)
  Other electrical: other electrical machinery (SITC 72 except 722, 724)
  Other transport: other transport equipment (SITC 73 except 731, 734)
  Other nonelectrical: other nonelectrical machinery (SITC 71 except 711, 715,
      718)
    Petroleum: petroleum refining and processing equipment (no SITC number
    equivalent)

═══

Source: Eximbank, unpublished data.

Table A.5. *Maturity distribution of disbursements, 1974*

Category	Less than 1 year	1–5 years	5–7 years	7–8.5 years	8.5–10 years	10–12 years	More than 12 years	Total
I. Agriculture, etc.	4	96	0	0	0	0	0	100
II. Chemicals, paper, rubber	0	0	10	58	20	13	0	100
III. Misc. manufactures	0	8	7	9	6	14	56	100
IV. Armaments	0	0	0	1	98	0	1	100
V. Machinery & transport. equip.	0	2	5	8	8	36	42	100
A. Power generation mach. electrical	0	0	1	2	9	5	83	100
1. Hydroelec. power plant & equip.	0	0	2	1	0	0	98	100
2. Nuclear power plant & Equip.	0	0	0	0	12	0	88	100
3. Thermal power plant & equip.	0	0	0	6	2	1	91	100
B. Mach. for special industries	0	6	19	13	15	12	36	100
1. Constr., excav., mining equip.	0	11	30	23	17	7	13	100
C. Foundry equip.	0	4	17	7	0	33	39	100
D. Telecom. equip.	0	0	9	9	36	23	22	100
E. Railroad vehicles	1	0	2	8	6	67	16	100

Table A.5. *(cont.)*

Category	Less than 1 year	1–5 years	5–7 years	7–8.5 years	8.5–10 years	10–12 years	More than 12 years	Total
F. Aircraft								
1. Commercial jet aircraft	1	0	1	7	8	66	17	100
G. Other elec. mach.	0	0	1	12	0	0	87	100
H. Other trans. mach.	0	5	47	17	13	19	0	100
I. Other Nonelec. equip.	0	4	4	11	4	26	52	100
1. Chem. processing plant & equip.	0	0	0	29	18	54	0	100
2. Petrol. refining & processing equip.	0	13	0	22	1	11	54	100
Total	0	5	5	8	14	32	37	100

Source: Eximbank, memoranda, unpublished.

Table A.6. *Geographical distribution of Eximbank loans as of Dec. 31, 1975, and July 31, 1979*

	As of Dec. 31, 1975		As of July 31, 1979	
Location	$ (thousands)	% of total	$ (thousands)	% of total
Lesser developed countries				
Africa/Mideast	2,378,407	16	2,945,621	17
Asia (except Japan)	2,679,316	18	4,342,106	25
Latin America	3,444,813	24	3,815,733	22
Total	8,502,536	58	11,103,460	63
Developed countries				
Canada	318,833	02	270,169	02
Japan	753,510	05	733,428	04
Europe	4,622,896	32	4,434.543	25
Australia/New Zealand	438,415	03	255,280	01
Total	6,133,654	42	5,693,420	32
Miscellaneous	—	—	863,761	05
Total all areas	14,636,190	100	17,660,641	100

Source: Eximbank, *Annual Report 1979,* Washington, D.C., 13.

Table A.7. *Foreign assets of U.S. commercial banks reporting under the VFCR guidelines (millions of dollars)—data as of end of month*

Category	Dec.[a] 1969	Dec.[a] 1970	Nov. 1971	Dec. 1971	Dec. 1972	Oct. 1973	Nov. 1973
1. Foreign assets held for own account	10,143	10,424	11,698	12,902	14,529	16,007	16,201
A. Loans, acceptances, deposits, and other claims	9,273	9,437	10,515	11,700	13,130	14,322	14,438
B. Long-term securities	161	141	116	119	108	91	95
C. Invest. in foreign subs.	628	781	1,005	1,021	1,222	1,473	1,542
D. Other long-term holdings	81	65	62	62	69	121	126
2. Less: VFCR exempt assets	794	1,120	3,111	3,947	5,339	6,967	6,988
A. Canadian assets (change since 2/68)	164	266	218	536	927	1,005	867
B. Del. subs. liab. offset	—	—	104	112	199	261	261
C. Export credits other than to residents of Canada	522	791	2,789	3,299	4,213	5,700	5,860
(1) Participated in, or guaranteed, by Eximbank or insured by FCIA			e1,388	e1,429	1,612	1,759	1,837
(2) Guaranteed by Department of Defense			e31	e32	148	242	218
(3) Other			e1,370	e1,838	2,453	3,699	3,805
D. Deferred payment letters of credit[b]	180	63					
3. Assets subject to VFCR (1-2)	9,349	9,304	8,587	8,955	9,189	9,040	9,214
4. Aggregate ceilings	10,092	9,968	9,876	10,032	10,276	10,365	10,338
5. Aggregate net leeway (4-3)	743	664	1,289	1.078	1,087	1,324	1,124
6. Number of reporting banks	169	173	184	194	222	231	226
Memorandum items: Claims held for account of customers	1,541	1,563	1,737	1.918	2,166	2,456	2,462
Total own and customers' claims	10,814	11,000	12,252	13,619	15,296	16,778	16,900

Source: Federal Reserve, "Survey of Export Credit as a Portion of U.S. Bank Credit to Foreigners,"
[a]Data do not include Export Term-Loan Ceiling (ETLC) and assets subject to that ceiling. On December 31, 1969, the aggregate ETLC was $1,264 million, with total outstanding loans of $16 million. On December 31, 1970, the aggregate ETLC was $1,423 million with total outstanding loans of $190 million.
[b]Deferred payment letters of credit held on April 30, 1968 and currently outstanding. e = estimated.

Table A.8. *Foreign assets of U.S. agencies and branches of foreign banks reporting under the VFCR guidelines (millions of dollars)—data as of end of month*

Category	Nov. 1971	Dec. 1971	Dec. 1972	June 1973	Oct. 1973	Nov. 1973
1. Foreign assets held for own account	2,838	3,009	4,812	6,770	7,630	7,860
A. Loans, acceptances, deposits, and other claims	2,817	2,987	4,794	6,745	7,604	7,835
B. Other holdings	21	22	18	25	26	25
2. Less: VFCR exempt assets	964	1,066	1,819	2,699	2,639	2,719
A. Canadian assets	250	273	409	548	464	436
B. Export credits other than to residents of Canada	714	793	1,410	2,151	2,175	2,283
(1) Participated in, or guaranteed by, Eximbank or insured by FCIA	—	—	38	38	44	43
(2) Guaranteed by DOD	—	—	11	11	10	10
(3) Other	—	—	1,361	2,102	2,121	2,230
C. Other VFCR exempt assets	—	—	—	0	0	0
3. Assets subject to VFCR (1–2)	1,875	1,943	2,994	4,071	4,991	5,142
4. Foreign liabilities	—	—	—	—	10,193	10,421
5. Net foreign position(3–4)	—	—	—	—	− 5,202	− 5,280
6. Net foreign position as of 6/30/73	—	—	—	—	− 4,551	− 4,605
7. Leeway (6–5)	—	—	—	—	650	675
8. Number of reporting institutions	49	51	62	68	69	71
Memorandum items: Claims held for account of U.S. customers	232	233	447	352	377	392
Total own and customers' claims	3,049	3,220	5,241	7,097	7,981	8,227

Source: Federal Reserve "Survey of Export Credit as a Portion of U.S. Bank Credit to Foreigners," press release, 1974.

Table A.9. *Eximbank financial guarantees ($ millions)*

Fiscal year	Financial guarantee
1969[a]	112.3
1970–1	335.8
1971	1,076.7
1972	1,219.8
1973	1,529.7
1974	1,191.0
1975	1,144.2
1976	1,082.5
Transition quarter	156.9
1977	489.0
1978	242.6

[a]Prior to FY1979 Exim did not clearly distinguish between "bank guarantees" on purely private credits and "financial gaurantees" on credits participating with Exim direct credits.
Source: Eximbank, Annual Reports, Washington, D.C., 1969–79.

Table A.10. *FCIA authorizations by year and policy*

Policy	1971	1972	1973	1974	1975	1976	1977	1978
Short-term policies	886.6	960.1	1,404.8	1,611.9	1,831.6	2,103.2	2,291	2,026
Medium-term policies	412.8	571.8	544.7	460.3	472.6	432.8	454	910
Master policies	314.3	668.4	523.3	529.1	672.4	888.9	826	957
Total authorizations	1,613.7	2,200.3	2,472.8	2,601.3	2,931.6	3,425	3,571	3,893

Source: Eximbank, Annual Reports, Washington, D.C., 1971–9; Foreign Credit Insurance Association, *Annual Reports,* New York, 1971–9.

Appendix B

The country distribution of Eximbank loans: statistical analysis

The following statistical analysis uses the data from Table 5.1.

Equation 1 regresses each country's relative portion of Exim loans on its portion of foreign debt and U.S. capital goods exports:

$$\frac{\text{Exim}^i}{\text{Exim}_{30}} = \frac{.01}{(1.5)} + \frac{.33}{(1.7)} \frac{\text{Debt}^i}{\text{Debt}_{30}} + \frac{.33}{(1.8)} \frac{\text{Exports}^i}{\text{Exports}_{30}} \qquad R^2 = .41 \qquad (1)$$

where Exim = outstanding Exim loans, Debt = outstanding foreign debt, Exports = 1973 U.S. capital goods exports, superscript i = the ith country, and subscript 30 = the sum for all 30 LDCs. Figures in parentheses are t-statistics.

As might be anticipated, a country's absorption of U.S. exports (or of foreign goods in general) upon testing turns out to be correlated significantly with its level of foreign debt (for the twenty-nine LDCs, the correlation coefficient is .52). See Table B.1 for the matrix of correlation coefficients for the five variables shown in Table 5.1. Note that both a country's foreign debt and its absorption of U.S. capital goods are correlated significantly with its GNP. If Exim loans are regressed on all four variables, for the thirty LDCs, the multicollinary pulls down the t-statistics, but all coefficients are positive and (except for Aid's) are of approximately equal statistical significance:

$$\text{Exim}^i = 3.6 + \underset{(.6)}{.07} \quad \underset{(1.4)}{\text{Debt}^i} + \underset{(1.3)}{.27\text{Exports}^i} + \underset{(1.5)}{5.4\text{GNP}^i} + \underset{(.67)}{.01\text{Aid}^i} \qquad (2)$$
$$R^2 = .5$$

As the low correlation coefficient between Exim loans and aid per country suggested, the regression coefficient on the aid variable is quite insignificant, although positive.

To avoid multicollinary between the right-hand variables, Exim loans were regressed on exports alone:

$$\text{Exim}^i = \underset{(.7)}{40.2} + \underset{(5.2)}{1.14} \text{Exports}^i \qquad R^2 = .50 \qquad (3)$$

The regression coefficient is highly significant and is greater than one. That is, it appears that, as a country's importation of capital goods from the United

Table B.1. *Matrix of correlation coefficients for the five variables in Table 5.1*

	Loans (1)	Debt (2)	Exports (3)	GNP (4)	Aid (5)
1. Exim loans	1.00000				
2. Debt	0.56957	1.00000			
3. U.S. exports	0.70687	0.51675	1.00000		
4. GNP	0.56816	0.40210	0.46022	1.00000	
5. U.S. aid	0.22634	0.04809	0.14411	0.39795	1.00000

States increases, Exim's attention to that country increases disproportionately. Although the slope of the fitted equation is greater than one, the equation fails to capture all of the favoritism Exim has shown toward the bigger buyers: The residuals for the seven biggest-buying countries were notably positive.

Notes

Introduction

1. Data on the various program levels can be found in Agency for International Development, *U.S. Overseas Loans, Grants, Obligations, and Authorizations,* an annual AID release.
2. This estimate is derived from the National Advisory Council on International Monetary and Financial Policies, *Annual Report FY1974* (Washington, D.C.: Government Printing Office, 1975), 229, 233.
3. U.S. Congress, House, Committee on Ways and Means, *Second Annual Report of the Department of the Treasury on the Operation and Effect of the Domestic International Sales Corporation* (for FY1973), 94th Cong., 1st sess., April 15, 1975, Table 4-1, 21.
4. Overseas Private Investment Corporation, *Annual Report,* Washington, D.C., 1973–8.

1. The birth and historical evolution of the Bank

1. Export-Bank File, 1933–54, Records of the Department of the Treasury, RG 56, National Archives, Washington, D.C.
2. Commerce Department, Bureau of the Census, *Historical Statistics of the United States: Colonial Times to 1970,* vol. 2 (Washington, D.C.: Government Printing Office, 1970) ser. U 249–63.
3. Whether the large U.S. trade surplus and resulting dollar gap was caused by underlying structures in the U.S. and world economy or by government policies is debated in M. E. Falkus, "United States Economic Policy and the 'Dollar Gap' of the 1920s," *Economic History Review, 29,* no. 4 (November, 1971), 599–623; and Sean Glynn and Alan Lougheed, "A Comment on U.S. Economic Policy and the 'Dollar Gap' of the 1920s," *Economic History Review, 26,* no. 4, (November, 1973), 692–4.
4. For a vision of the Edge Act as part of the halting but irrepressible overseas thrust of U.S. financial capital, see Carl Parrini, *Heir to Empire: United States Economic Diplomacy, 1916–1923* (University of Pittsburgh Press, 1969), chap. 4, 72–100.
5. This account of the trading corporation follows Richard N. Owens, "The Hundred Million Dollar Foreign Trade Financing Corporation," *Journal of Political Economy, 30,* no. 3 (June, 1922), 346–62.
6. See Glynn and Lougheed, "U.S. Economic Policy and the 'Dollar Gap'," 692–4.
7. Parrini argues that important U.S. banking and investment interests, notably the House of Morgan, were tied closely to British capital and were less concerned

with financing U.S. exports. This led to calls for the U.S. Government to require U.S. banks to tie their loans to U.S. exports. *Heir to Empire,* chap. 7, 172–211.

8. Commerce Department, *Historical Statistics of the United States,* ser. U 1–25.
9. Remarks before the 47th annual conference of the National Association of Supervisors of State Banks, September 23, 1948, Eximbank File, 1933–54.
10. Mentioned in James McHale, "National Planning and Reciprocal Trade: The New Deal Origins of Government Guarantees for Private Exporters," *Prologue, 6,* no. 3 (Fall, 1974), 194.
11. U.S. Congress, Senate, Banking and Currency Committee, *Inquiry into the Operations of the Reconstruction Finance Corporation and its Subsidiaries* under S. Res. 132, 80th Cong., 1st sess. (December 3–12, 1947). As of June 30, 1947, only 14.5 percent (or $1.2 billion) of total RFC disbursements had gone to public agencies (p. 162), with $202 million earmarked for Exim (p. 165).
12. General Correspondence File of the Export-Import Bank, Reconstruction Finance Corporation, RG 234, National Archives (Washington, D.C.). [hereafter GCF].
13. Ibid.
14. The first Eximbank was established with the intent to extend credit to the newly recognized Soviet Union, but failure to reach an agreement on outstanding debt claims left the Bank inactive. The second Eximbank was formed, also in early 1934, to handle a loan to Cuba, and then to deal with all countries except the USSR. The personnel of the two banks overlapped, and they were consolidated formally in 1935–6. Hawthorne Arey, "History of Operations and Policies of the Export-Import Bank of Washington," mimeo. (Washington, D.C., 1953), 175.
15. Peek to Senator Morris Sheppard, July 16, 1935, GCF.
16. St. Louis Chamber of Commerce, Foreign Trade Bulletin, (January, 1935), speeches by George N. Peek, Office of the Special Advisor on Foreign Trade, Eximbank File, Records of the Department of the Treasury, RG 20, National Archives, Washington, D.C.
17. Address by Charles Stuart before the Export Managers' Club of New York, August 21, 1934; Eugene Thomas to Earl Schwulst of the RFC, GCF.
18. McHale, "National Planning and Trade," 192.
19. Address before the National Foreign Trade Convention in Houston, Texas, November 19, 1935, Eximbank File, 1933–54.
20. Frederick C. Adams, *Economic Diplomacy: The Export-Import Bank and American Foreign Policy, 1934–39* (Columbia, University of Missouri Press, 1976) 90–3.
21. Thomas to Schwulst, GCF.
22. U.S. Congress, Senate, Committee on Banking and Currency, *To Continue the Functions of the Commodity Credit Corporation, the Export-Import Bank of Washington, and the Reconstruction Finance Corporation,* 76th Cong., 1st sess. (February 14 and 21, 1939) 60–1.
23. J. Maynard Keynes and some New Dealers believed that the "imperialist wars" resulting from foreign trade competition could be avoided by substituting expanding domestic markets for foreign customers, thereby reducing the pressures for overseas sales. Leon Trotsky, however, argued such strategies were "both reactionary and utterly utopian." He correctly foresaw productive forces were pressing inevitably toward an internationalized economy. "Imperialism has withdrawn into its own national lair to gather itself for a new leap," he predicted. Leon Trotsky, "Nationalism and Economic Life," *Foreign Affairs, 12,* no. 3 (April, 1934) 400.

24. Eximbank File, 1933–54, Charles Stuart to Marvin McIntyre, Assistant Secretary to the President (September 6, 1935).
25. Adams, *Economic Diplomacy,* chaps. 5 and 7, 129–59, 188–225.
26. Address before the Export Managers' Club of New York, August 21, 1934, GCF.
27. This section relies heavily on Hawthorne Arey, "History of Operations and Policies of the Export-Import Bank of Washington," in U.S. Congress, Senate, Committee on Banking and Currency, *Hearings, Study of Export-Import Bank and World Bank,* 83rd Cong., 2nd sess. (January 25–February 2, 1954), 83–170; Eleanor Lansing Dulles, *The Export-Import Bank of Washington: The First Ten Years* (Washington, D.C.: Government Printing Office, 1944), 27.
28. F. Adams, *Economic Diplomacy,* chap. 4, 98–128.
29. The closure of Exim to the USSR after a flurry of credits in 1973–4 by the "Jackson" amendment to the Trade Act of 1974 is described in Paula Stern, *Water's Edge: Domestic Politics and the Making of American Foreign Policy* (Westport, Conn.: Greenwood Press, 1979), 242.
30. Arey, *History of Operations and Policies,* 110.
31. One government study noted that, in addition to financing raw materials projects directly, Exim frequently assisted in developing the complementary infrastructure, such as transportation, communication, and power installations. The President's Policy Commission, *Resources for Freedom, 5* (Washington, D.C.: Government Printing Office, 1952), 122.
32. Eximbank, *FY1959 Annual Report,* 104–9.
33. Eximbank, *FY1959 Annual Report,* 8.
34. Testimony of Eximbank chairman, Harold Linder, in U.S. Congress, Senate, Subcommittee on International Finance, Committee on Banking and Currency, *Hearings, Export-Import Bank Act Amendments of 1967,* 90th Cong., 1st sess. (May 16, 1967), 40; Eximbank annual reports (FY60–73) of the period.
35. See Eximbank, "Report to the U.S. Congress on Export Credit Competition and the Export-Import Bank of the United States," semiannual reports, various. For detailed descriptions of export credit programs, see OECD, *The Export Credit Financing Systems in OECD Member Countries* (Paris: OECD, 1976).
36. For a discussion of the panoply of U.S. Government actions against the Allende government, see U.S. Congress, Senate, Select Committee to Study Governmental Operations with Respect to Intelligence Activities, *Covert Action, 7,* 94th Cong., 1st sess. (December 4–5, 1975).

2. Eximbank's mainstay: the direct loan program

1. Exim formally requires the applicant for a loan to be the prospective borrower, but not the applicant for a preliminary commitment, which precedes many formal loan applications. A preliminary commitment, once approved, generally is considered a moral obligation by Exim to finalize eventually the credit *(ceteris paribus).*
2. The Private Export Funding Corporation (PEFCO) was incorporated in 1970, and its shareholders consist of some fifty commercial banks and seven manufacturing firms including four aircraft companies. It borrows on private capital markets, and its loans are guaranteed unconditionally by Exim, which approves all PEFCO transactions. Originally, PEFCO was conceived to handle medium-term maturities, and to complete financial packages where banks were taking shorter maturities and Exim was waiting for the last repayments, although PEFCO has

also moved into the long-term range. As of December 31, 1978, export loan commitments totaled $1.5 billion. See PEFCO, *Annual Report,* various years.
3. Exim estimated its programs were touching about 16 percent of the U.S. non-agricultural exports. Eximbank, *Annual Report* (FY1976), 2. In the late 1970s, despite the relative decline in Exim lending levels, the Bank claimed involvement in over 20 percent of U.S. capital goods exports. Statement by Eximbank President John Moore, Jr., U.S. Congress, House, International Finance, Subcommittee on Banking, Housing, and Urban Affairs, *Hearings,* 95 Cong., 2nd sess. (March 20, 1978).
4. The leading twenty-five suppliers in order of magnitude of authorizations were: Boeing, GE, McDonnell Douglas, Westinghouse, Chemical Construction Corp., Morrison-Knudsen, Fluor-Ocean, GM, Bethlehem Steel, Ford Motor Co., Foster Wheeler Corp., Chemtex Fibers, Inc., Epstein, A. Companies, Eastern Airlines, Koppers Co., Lang Engineering Corp., Lockheed Aircraft Corp., Dravo Corp., Allis Chalmers, Bucyrus-Erie, Fuller Co., Mitsubishi, Arthur G. McKee and Co., General Tire, and Continental Airlines.

3. Eximbank and the U.S. capital market

1. For some examples, see Edward Mason and Robert Asher, *The World Bank since Bretton Woods* (Washington, D.C.: Brookings Institution, 1973), 496–504.
   Exim noted the similarity, in its FY1968 Annual Report: "In its role as relatively long-term lender, Eximbank's operations parallel those of the multinational banks; but whereas these institutions serve the interests of all their shareholder governments, Eximbank's activities serve the export interests of the United States" (p. 3). A statement released by Exim around the time of the founding of the World Bank sounded a similar theme: "The facilities of the Export-Import Bank, an agency of the United States, and those of the International Bank for Reconstruction and Development, an institution of which the United States is a member, are intended to be complementary. To this end, the activities of the Export-Import Bank and the policies of the United States representatives on the International Bank are coordinated by the National Advisory Council, as provided in the Bretton Woods Agreement Act." "General Policy Statement, revised August 1, 1947" (Washington, D.C.: Government Printing Office, 1947). A former vice-president of Exim, B. J. Middleton, and a former World Bank official, N. McKitterick, teamed together to write a monograph arguing that the similarities between development aid and export finance were great and should be recognized officially. See *The Bankers of the Rich and the Bankers of the Poor: The Role of Export Credit in Development Finance* (Washington, D.C.: Overseas Development Council, 1972), 58, esp. chap. 4.
2. For the commercial banks, Table 3.2 lists outstanding, that is, disbursed loans, whereas for Eximbank, total committed loans (undisbursed and disbursed) are listed. For Exim, total committed loans is a useful indication of economic impact, because in most cases at least a portion of a committed loan has been disbursed, and the undisbursed portion will be drawn as the ongoing project is completed. The quantitative difference between total committed and disbursed loans would be greater presumably for Exim than for the commercial banks, which publish only outstanding loan figures, because of the slow drawdown on Exim's long-term maturities.
3. Citicorp, *1978 Annual Report,* New York, 38.

4. Ibid., 46.
5. "Foreigners" include all institutions and individuals domiciled abroad; the foreign branches, subsidiaries, and offices of U.S. bank and business concerns; and international and regional organizations, wherever located.
6. U.S. Treasury Department, *Treasury Bulletin,* December 1978 (Washington, D.C.: Government Printing Office), Table CM-II-4, 99.
7. Ibid., Tables CM-V-3, CM-V-7, various. "Nonbanking concerns" include exporters, importers, and industrial and commercial firms in the United States other than banks and brokers. Intercompany accounts of multinational corporations are excluded, as are capital transactions of the U.S. Government.
8. The VFCR guidelines define "export credit" as any claim on a foreigner for the demonstrable financing of the export of U.S. goods and services. To be demonstrable, the financing must relate to a specific, individual, identifiable export for which shipping documents or other documents evidencing the export are obtainable.

   Export credit may be direct or indirect. Direct credit is a credit resulting in the direct acquisition of a debt obligation of a foreigner obligor. An indirect credit is one extended to a foreign financial institution that, in consequence, acquires debt obligations of obligors resident outside the United States. Also, an export credit may be extended through purchase of documented loan paper. The VFCR methodology for measuring bank attention to export credit has two flaws, which the Federal Reserve press releases (3n.) saw as serious but not fatal. Funds from open lines of credit that actually were used for trade finance, but without the extending bank having demonstrable knowledge, would not be captured by the VFCR reporting system. Also, U.S. banks support export trade indirectly, by lending to the U.S. supplier who, in turn, extends credit to the foreign importer. The extent of such activity is unknown, but certainly is less common for long-term transactions, where direct bank loans to importers would be the normal method of finance. This holds in part because longer-term obligations are not readily marketable instruments, unlike short-term letters of credit, or drafts, which promise the exporter liquidity if needed.
9. "Claims on foreigners" include claims on foreigners held for an institution's own account as well as for accounts of customers. The VFCR forms also captured "long-term securities," reported normally on a separate form.
10. "Survey of Export Credit as a Portion of U.S. Bank Credit to Foreigners," Federal Reserve, press release (March 3, 1971), 8.
11. Board of Governors of the Federal Reserve System, *Annual Report, 1973* (Washington, D.C.: Board of Governors, 1974), 229.
12. U.S. Treasury Department, "Financial Operations of Government Agencies and Funds," *Treasury Bulletin,* October 1974 (Washington, D.C.: Government Printing Office), Table GA-II-2, Fn. *55,* 138.
13. Eximbank, "Eximbank Programs," *3,* pamphlet, 6–7.
14. Federal Reserve, *Federal Reserve Bulletin, 57,* no. 2, (Washington, D.C., February, 1971), A19.
15. See the Board of Governors of the Federal Reserve System, *Annual Report,* from 1965–74, which contain chapters on the VFCR, esp. *Annual Report* 1974, 230–1.
16. So admitted by a Citibank officer in an interview in New York, 1975; and by the late Exim veteran and director Walter Sauer at a roundtable discussion on Exim and East–West Trade, at Eximbank, 1975.

17. John Maynard Keynes, *The General Theory of Employment, Interest and Money* (New York: Harcourt, 1964), 155.
18. For a discussion of the "customer relationship" in bank behavior, see Donald Hodgman, *Commercial Bank Loan and Investment Policy* (Champaign, Ill.: Bureau of Economic and Business Research and University of Illinois, 1963), 181.

4. The Foreign Credit Insurance Association

1. FCIA, *Report of Operations 1972* (Washington, D.C.), 1.
2. FCIA, "Export Credit Insurance Manual," 1 (Washington, D.C.: 1972). According to Edward Hoyt, who helped write the FCIA charter, it was modeled after the government-backed British Export Credits Guarantee Department (ECGD), which was established in 1919. Exponents of government trade insurance can also refer to Ricardo, who argued that the uncertainties resulting from ignorance of foreign markets reduced international commerce to suboptimal levels.
3. The sources for the sections on Exim's insurance agency include the FCIA's "Export Credit Insurance Manual," FCIA annual reports, the brochure "FCIA: Export Credit Insurance—the Competitive Edge," and interviews with FCIA officials and users of FCIA programs.
4. A commercial bank obtains FCIA-covered export paper either directly from credits extended to buyers by the bank, or indirectly by purchasing already insured export paper from the original insuree. Most of FCIA's policies probably end up being "assigned" to commercial banks.
5. For a discussion of the sometimes artificial distinction between commercial and political risk, see Chapter 6.
6. To the extent the increase in premium costs was related to the losses sustained in Chile, the cost of overthrowing Allende was being spread over the entire U.S. export community and their foreign customers. The losses in Chile occurred, in part, because the U.S. public and private sectors had conspired to deprive Allende of credit, so that Chile was forced into default.
7. Stated in an interview of an FCIA officer in New York, July 21, 1976, by an experienced Eximbank official, and by a ranking officer in an international marketing and credit firm that insures almost all its business with FCIA. In its 1979 *Annual Report,* the FCIA flatly stated that "many exporters will pass the cost of the insurance along to the foreign buyer" (p. 5).
8. To the extent banks, despite insurance coverage, continue to charge rates of interest in excess of their costs of funds (and an allowance for operating expenses), it would be difficult to justify their profit margin on the basis of risk.
9. See Federal Reserve, *Federal Reserve Bulletin,* A-27.

5. Determinants of loan authorizations to developing countries

1. "LDCs" for this chapter will be the World Bank list of eighty-six developing countries, which includes all of Africa (except South Africa), Latin America, and Asia (except for mainland China, Japan, Australia, and New Zealand), as well as parts of southern Europe. The inclusion of southern Europe would give the LDCs a percentage of total Exim loans in excess of the 57 percent as calculated in Chapter 2.
2. As of July 31, 1979, the top ten Exim borrowers were identical to the 1974 leaders shown on Table 5.1, except that Chile and Argentina had been replaced by Indo-

nesia and the Philippines, two countries that had missed narrowly an earlier ranking in the leading ten. The relative decline of Chile and Argentina reflected their poor credit ratings, because of political and economic instabilities during portions of the intervening years, and because of the denial or delay of Exim credits because of human rights violations or, in the Chilean case, official harboring of international terrorists.

3. Taiwan had been able to avoid heavy foreign borrowing in part because of massive U.S. grant aid and a phenomenal export growth based partially on the affiliates of TNCs; Exim held a major portion of the liabilities Taiwan had acquired. The EEC had kept Franco's Spain from being integrated into the European economic system, although Spain was among the tenth largest holders, among all countries, of long-term liabilities to U.S. banks. U.S. Treasury Department, *Treasury Bulletin,* October, 1976 (Washington, D.C.: Government Printing Office), Table CM-II-6, p. 101. Private nonguaranteed debt held by affiliates of foreign corporations, not captured in the World Bank data, might be significant.

4. World Bank, World Bank Debt Tables (EC-167/75), *1* (Washington, D.C.: World Bank, 1975), v–viii.

5. Robert D. Hormats, speech delivered before the brokerage firm of G. Tsai and Co., September 2, 1976, New York, "The Growing Economic Influence of the Third World and its Likely Impact on the United States in the Coming Decade."

6. William Appelman Williams, *American–Russian Relations, 1781–1947* (New York: Rinehart, 1952), 239; Frederick C. Adams, *Economic Diplomacy: The Export-Import Bank and American Foreign Policy, 1934–39* (Columbia, Mo.: University of Missouri Press, 1976), chap. 4, 98–128.

7. Hawthorne Arey, "History of Operations and Policies of the Export-Import Bank of Washington," mimeo. (Washington, D.C., 1953), 6.

8. Adams, *Economic Diplomacy,* 137.

9. U.S. Congress, House, Subcommittee on International Trade, Investment, and Monetary Policy, Committee on Banking, Finance, and Urban Affairs, Oversight Hearing on the Export-Import Bank, 96th Cong., 1st sess. (May 21, 1979), 66.

6. Creditworthiness

1. Cited in Howard Blum, "Rating Games: The Trial of New York," *Village Voice* (April 21, 1975), 8.

2. Kalman Cohen, Tom Gilmore, and Frank Singer, "Bank Procedures for Analyzing Business Loan Applications," in Kalman Cohen and Frederick Hammer (eds.), *Analytical Methods in Banking* (Homewood, Ill.: Richard D. Irwin, Inc., 1966), 219–51.

3. John Maynard Keynes, *The General Theory of Employment, Interest, and Money* (New York: Harcourt, 1964), 161–2.

4. One writer has suggested that the geographic site of bond-raters' homes help determine their judgments as to districts' creditworthiness. See Blum, "Rating Games," 8.

5. For example, in 1975, of the five board members, three had extensive experience in private banking: R. Alex McCullough had been vice-president and senior vice-president of the South Carolina National Bank (1957–69); John C. Clark had been senior vice-president of Wachovia Bank in Winston–Salem before being appointed by Nixon, and had worked previously for Chase Manhattan (1947–51); and Mitchell P. Kobelinski came from Parkway Bank and First State Bank of

Chicago, both of which he helped found. The fourth board member, Walter Sauer, a lawyer, had been with Exim since 1941. The fifth member, President Casey, was a partner in the New York law firm of Hall, Casey, Dickler, and Howley, specializing in corporate and financial law. His 1976 replacement, Stephen DuBrul, Jr., came from the investment house of Lazard Freres, and attended Harvard Business School. Coincidentally, both Casey and DuBrul had intelligence experience; Casey with the predecessor of the CIA, the OSS, and DuBrul with the agency itself, in the early 1950s.

By 1979, the Board had turned completely over. The Carter-appointed chairman, John L. Moore, Jr., came from an Atlanta, Georgia, law firm, where he specialized in corporate finance and tax and securities law. Of the three other Carter appointees, two were alumni of the world of private finance: H. K. Allen had headed several Texas banks and had been director of a large Dallas financial holding company; Thibaut de Saint Phalle had worked with several New York investment banking firms and been a senior partner of Coudert Brothers, an international law firm. The other Carter selection, Donald Stingel, was formerly president of Pullman Swindell. The fifth board member, Margaret W. Kahliff, named by President Ford in October, 1976, had been in small business, and was the sister of Senator Dale Bumpers from Arkansas.

6. For a critical discussion of the State Department's economic expertise, see John F. Campbell, *The Foreign Affairs Fudge Factory* (New York: Basic Books, 1971), esp. chap. 8, 204–27.

7. An analysis of the DuPont project can be found in Jack Baranson, "International Transfers of Industrial Technology by U.S. Firms: An Evaluation of the U.S. Export-Import Bank Review of Potential Economic Impact," contract no. J9K60033 (Washington, D.C.: U.S. Department of Labor, 1977), 6–16.

8. In response to a congressional inquiry, Kearns listed only eight denials for $11 million worth of direct and CFF loans, from January 1, 1969 to April 31, 1971. U.S. Congress, House, Subcommittee on International Trade, Committee on Banking and Currency, *Hearings, The Export Expansion Act of 1971*, H.R. 5846, 92nd Cong., 1st sess. (May 18–26, 1971), 108.

9. Edward Gramlich, "The New York City Fiscal Crisis: What Happened and What is to be Done," *American Economic Review, Papers and Proceedings, 66*, no. 2 (May, 1976), 415–20.

10. In a paper published in 1978, two Exim economists offered a quick sketch of the variables considered by the Bank in judging a country's health, including: current-account performance, export commodity dependence, GNP per capita and growth rate, the capital-output ratio, investment level, inflation rate, and the fiscal balance. In addition, country analysts attempted to assess "management competence and policy", "work ethic", repayment record and physical resources. The Bank also reported working to develop an "early warning" econometric model, as one input in helping the Bank foresee repayment problems. Alice Mayo and Anthony Garrett, "An Early-Warning Model for Assessing Development-Country Risk," in *Financing and Risk in Developing Countries,* ed., Stephen Goodman (New York: Praeger, 1978), 81–7.

11. Citibank, in its *1975 Annual Report,* offers an explanation for this private-market behavior similar to Exim's explanation: "Risk is also significantly reduced, regardless of maturity, where the financing is directly related to a self-liquidating transaction" (p. 19).

12. McDonnell Douglas has admitted paying "commissions" to facilitate the sales of DC-10s to PIA, and has been indicted by a federal grand jury on charges of fraud

and conspiracy, which include having made false statements to Eximbank. Exim has, so far, appeared as an innocent and naive party in the aircraft bribery scandals. "Four Aircraft Executives Indicted," *The Washington Post* (November 10, 1979).

13. See, for example, DuBrul's speech before the 39th Annual Chicago World Track Conference on April 21, 1976, as reported in the *Eximbank Record, 1*, no. 1 (May, 1976).

14. John Maynard Keynes, *General Theory of Employment*, esp. bk. 4. A National Board of Economic Research (NBER) study found a similar problem in macroeconomic behavior, noting that "changes in credit risk and credit difficulties tend to accentuate business cycle expansions and contractions" (p. 6), Edgar Fielder, *Measures of Credit Risk and Experience*, NBER General Series 95, 1971.

15. An International Monetary Fund study on commercial bank lending patterns to LDCs offered the following assessment of their creditworthiness determination: "As the repayment term of the loan is stretched longer . . . banks rely heavily on personal contacts and on *ad hoc* criteria peculiar to each bank. The existence of natural resources is considered generally as sufficient evidence of creditworthiness." Azizali Mohammed and Fabrizio Saccomanni, "Short-term Banking and Euro-Currency Credits to Developing Countries," *IMF Staff Papers, 20*, no. 3 (November, 1973), 612–38.

16. Exim's *FY1960 Annual Report* lists eight credits made under the "Defense Production Act of 1950," (pp. 182–3), primarily for copper, cobalt, and manganese production.

7. Export subsidies, business cycles, and nationalist rivalries

1. U.S. Congress, Subcommittee on Priorities and Economy in Government, Joint Economic Committee, *Federal Subsidy Programs* (Washington, D.C.: Government Printing Office, 1974), 1.

2. Carl Shoup, "The Economic Theory of Subsidy Payments," U.S. Congress, Joint Economic Committee, *The Economics of Federal Subsidy Programs* (Washington, D.C.: Government Printing Office, 1972), 55.

3. The formula to calculate the present discounted value reads:

$$PDV = \sum_{i=1}^{n} \frac{R_t}{(1 + d)^i}$$

where R_t = the expected payment of interest and principal in period t; d = the discount rate; t = the repayment period.

4. Congressional Budget Office, "The Export-Import Bank: Implications for the Federal Budget and the Credit Market," staff working paper (Washington, D.C.: Government Printing Office, 1976), 16.

5. Janos Horvath, "Are Eximbank Credits Subsidized: Toward an Empirical Analysis," in Paul Marer, ed., *U.S. Financing of East–West Trade* (Bloomington, Ind.: International Development Research Center, Indiana University, 1975), 105–37.

6. Congressional Budget Office, "The Export-Import Bank," 16.

7. This subsidy cost to the U.S. economy would be matched by an off-setting benefit of incremental exports only if the potential importers of U.S. goods had foreseen this addition to their subsidy stream.

8. U.S. Congress, House, Subcommittee on International Trade, Committee on Banking and Currency, *Hearings, The Export Expansion Finance Act of 1971*, H.R. 5846, 92 Cong., 1st sess. (May 18, 1971), 14.

9. U.S. Congress, House, Subcommittee on International Trade, Investment and Monetary Policy, Committee on Banking, Finance, and Urban Affairs, *Oversight Hearing on the Export-Import Bank,* 96th Cong., 1st sess. (May 21, 1979), 54.

10. U. S. Congress, *Hearings, The Export Expansion Act,* 92nd Cong., 1st sess. (May 18, 1971), 14.

11. Calculation based on the financial notes of Exim's annual report, and a summary statement in the FY1974 report (p. 36).

12. U.S. Congress, Senate, Subcommittee on International Finance, Committee on Banking, Housing, and Urban Affairs Committee, *Hearings on S.1890,* 93rd Cong., 1st sess. (October 29 and 30, 1973), 14.

13. George F. Break, *Federal Lending and Economic Stability* (Washington, D.C.: Brookings Institution, 1965), 117. In a confused discussion of Exim loans, Break goes on to argue that the loans "are subject to long and highly variable lags and hence cannot be classified as flexible stabilizers" (p. 118).

14. A recent study by the CBO argues that Congress cannot control closely Exim's "outlays," because the congressional ceilings limit Exim authorizations rather than disbursements, which involve the actual flows (outlays). The CBO paper fails to address the relevant issue, namely, whether the lag between Exim's authorizations and disbursements is really disqualifying. Also, Congress *could* address itself to Exim's disbursements, which flow as a result of authorizations in a predictable pattern. *The Export-Import Bank: Implications for the Federal Budget and the Credit Market,* staff working paper (Washington, D.C.: Government Printing Office, October 27, 1976).

15. Regression analysis confirmed this finding. Introducing time leads and lags—which would allow Exim to be responding to rather than predicting levels of economic activity—and scrutinizing rates of change of Exim and GNP levels, rather than just absolute fluctuations, failed to produce evidence that Exim had been acting countercyclically. The strongest statistical relationship was found to be between the growth of GNP over time and Exim lending, i.e., both have increased secularly.

16. U.S. Congress, *Oversight Hearing on the Export Import Bank,* 96 Cong., 1st sess. (May 21, 1979), 14.

17. U.S. Treasury, "'Additionality' in the Activities of the Export-Import Bank of the United States", unpublished memorandum submitted to Congress in 1978.

18. U.S. Congress, Senate, Subcommittee on International Finance, Committee on Banking, Housing, and Urban Affairs, *Hearing on the Export-Import Bank of the United States,* 93rd Cong., 1st sess. (October 29–30, 1973), 108.

8. In support of overseas investment

1. The term "transnational corporation," which will be employed here with its abbreviation TNC, uses "transnational" rather than "multinational" to avoid the false impression that many nations have equity participation; the use of "corporation" is preferred to "enterprise," because it is more exact legally and less normative.

   A "TNC-related firm" will be defined as a foreign firm with which a U.S.-based TNC has either an equity, licensee, or management relationship. To limit the definition to an equity relationship is to give a false impression of the scope of TNC business as practiced today.

2. The Eximbank table (unnumbered) lists $68.2 million in such credits authorized

in FY1975. The report fails to define "subsidiary", but apparently uses the strictest definition of 100 percent ownership. Only direct parent-sub sales are considered, thereby omitting sales by a nonaffiliated U.S. firm to an overseas subsidiary of another U.S. TNC. In the event, moreover, that the Bank authorized a loan for a parent-sub transaction, only those sales made directly by the parent are considered. Because the Bank will sometimes omit such sales from coverage in a loan, an entire loan for a parent-sub transaction can be omitted easily.

3. U.S. Congress, Senate, Subcommittee on International Finance, Committee on Banking and Currency, *Hearings,* 90th Cong., 1st sess. (May 16, 1967), 8.
4. See U.S. Congress, Senate, Subcommittee on International Finance, Committee on Banking, Housing, and Urban Affairs, *To Extend the Export-Import Bank Act, S1890,* 93rd Cong., 1st sess. (November 16, 1973), 240–72.
5. Treasury Department Memorandum, "Ownership of Firms Benefitting from EIB Direct Non-Military Credit Authorizations to Overseas Borrowers—CY1969," 1970.
6. Fred Bergsten, Thomas Horst, and Theodore Moran, *American Multinationals and American Interests* (Washington, D.C.: Brookings Institution, 1978), summarized in T. Horst, "American Multinationals and the U.S. Economy," *American Economic Review, Papers and Proceedings, 66,* no. 2 (May, 1976), 149–54.
7. U.S. Tariff Commission, report to the U.S. Congress, Senate, Committee on Finance, *Implications of Multinational Firms for World Trade and Investment and for U.S. Trade and Labor* (Washington, D.C.: Government Printing Office, 1973), 177; the report is summarized in Commerce Department, "U.S. Foreign Trade Associated with U.S. Multinational Companies," *Survey of Current Business, 52,* no. 12 (December, 1972), 20–8.
8. Calculated from Eximbank, "Statement of Active Loans," December 31, 1975. The publication classified loans as either to public or private buyers; in the case of a joint venture, Exim judges which shareholder is dominant; generally, but not necessarily, this would be the majority partner. In CY1974, that two-thirds of Exim loans went to the public sector held equally for industrial nations and for LDCs. These percentages should give a good indication of general trends, but errors were detected in specific loan classifications.
9. See, for example, Commerce Department, "Sources and Uses of Funds of Majority-Owned Foreign Affiliates of U.S. Companies, 1965–1972," *Survey of Current Business, 55,* no. 7 (July 1975), 29–52.
10. U.S. Tariff Commission, *Implications of Multinational Firms.*
11. Department of Commerce, "Property, Plant, and Equipment Expenditures by Majority-Owned Foreign Affiliates of U.S. Companies," *Survey of Current Business* (September, 1975), 29. The universe is defined as approximately 350 U.S. direct investors and their 3,500 MOFAs.
12. For critical analyses of OPIC, see Comptroller General of the U.S., *Management of Investment Insurance, Loan Guarantees, and Claim Payments by the Overseas Private Investment Corporation,* B-173240, 1973; Congressional Research Service, Library of Congress, *The Overseas Private Investment Corporation: A Critical Analysis* (Washington, D.C.: Government Printing Office, 1973), 165; U.S. Congress, Senate, Committee on Foreign Relations, *Report: The Overseas Private Investment Corporation Amendments Act, S.2957,* 93rd Cong., 2nd sess. (February 5, 1974), 66.
13. Stated in an interview in Washington, D.C., on March 20, 1975, by Thomas Doughty, a veteran Exim loan officer specializing in Latin America. Doughty said that "SPCC was an old friend. In 1954, the purpose of Exim participation was

just to get the U.S. Government involved." The press release of November 5, 1954, however, suggested an additional reason: "The U.S. Government would have the right to purchase a portion of the copper upon reasonable notice."

14. Sidney Robbins and Robert Stubaugh, *Money in the Multinational Enterprise* (New York: Basic Books, 1973), 70.
15. Ralph M. Dorman, "The Influence of Expropriation on Mining Company Investments," *Mining Congress Journal, 59,* no. 10 (October, 1973), 40. Dorman also suggested maximizing debt as opposed to equity, because "when a host country is concerned about its credit rating, it is much more likely to honor international debts to foreign investors than externally imposed obligations for compensation for equity investments" (p. 39).
16. Stated, as a matter of firm policy, to the author by a veteran Exim official.
17. Convenio Peru-Estados Unidos de America (Lima: Oficina del Primer Ministro, February 19, 1974).
18. The sources for this account are the Loan Memorandum no. 02382, November, 1966; and Theodore H. Moran, *Multinational Corporations and the Politics of Dependence: Copper in Chile* (Princeton University Press, 1974), chap. 4, 119–52.
19. Ibid., 134.
20. Quoted in Moran, ibid., 136.
21. See North American Congress on Latin America, "Chile: Facing the Blockade," *7,* no. 1, *Latin America and Empire Report* (January, 1973), 22–3.
22. Eximbank, "Eximbank Authorizes $110 Million Loan to Chilean Copper Producer," press release (April 10, 1967).
23. Eximbank, *FY1978 Annual Report,* 36.
24. Eximbank, *Semi-Annual Report for the Period January–June, 1950,* 3.
25. Eximbank, *Semi-Annual Report for the Period January–June, 1953,* 1.
26. Raymond Vernon, *Sovereignty at Bay: The Multinational Spread of U.S. Enterprises* (New York: Basic Books, 1971), 65–77.
27. Eximbank, *Annual Report,* FY1970–1978.
28. Eximbank, *Eximbank Programs, 3,* 21–4.
29. Eximbank, *Semi-Annual Report for the Period July–December, 1946,* 51.
30. Federal Reserve, *Federal Reserve Bulletin, 51,* no. 2 (January, 1966), 100–1.
31. I am indebted to John Swett of Citibank for pointing out to me that the normal cycle of international banking "moves from trade finance to MNC financing to, finally, local real estate and stock markets."
32. Interview with John Swett, New York, August 2, 1975.
33. Eximbank, *The CFF Courier* (summer, 1974), 4.
34. "Petro-dollars, LDCs, and International Banks," Federal Reserve Bank of New York, *Monthly Review, 58,* no. 2 (January, 1976), 16.
35. Hawthorne Arey, "History of Operations and Policies of the Export-Import Bank of Washington," mimeo. (Washington, D.C., 1953), 42–50.
36. Donald E. Syvrud, *Foundations of Brazilian Economic Growth* (Stanford: Hoover Institution Press for American Enterprise Institute-Hoover Research Publications, 1974), 205.
37. A discussion of the symbiotic relationship between the "Light" distribution network and the state-owned power-generation agencies can be found in Judith Tendler, *Electric Power in Brazil: Entrepreneurship in the Public Sector* (Cambridge: Harvard University Press, 1968), 264.
38. See World Bank, *International Capital Markets* (Washington, D.C.: World Bank), quarterly report.

39. In 1969, for example, of all direct credits authorized globally, 41 percent were allocated to borrowers owned 100 percent by governments; another 28 percent were to firms with public-sector participation. In CY1974, approximately 67 percent of authorizations were to public buyers, in 1972–3, 60 percent. Calculated from Eximbank, "Statement of Active Loans" (December 31, 1975).
40. Frederick C. Adams, *Economic Diplomacy: The Export-Import Bank and American Foreign Policy, 1934–39* (Columbia, Mo.: University of Missouri Press, 1976), passim.
41. Eximbank, *General Policy Statement, Revised August 1, 1947* (Washington, D.C.: Government Printing Office, 1947), 15.

9. Aircraft and nuclear power: problem siblings

1. *Industrial Market Structure and Economic Performance* (Chicago: Rand McNally, 1970). However, Frederick Scherer has written an essay entitled "The Aerospace Industry," which he describes as lying in "the gray area between private and public enterprise," in Walter Adams (ed.), *The Structure of American Industry*, 4th ed. (New York: Macmillan, 1971), chap. 12, 443–84.
2. Aerospace Industries Association of America, *Aerospace Facts and Figures 1967–77* (New York: McGraw-Hill, 1976), 2.
3. Stanford Research Institute, *The Industry-Government Aerospace Relationship*, report no. AD 617 885/6, 1 (Menlo Park, Calif.: Stanford Research Institute, 1963), 45.
4. Aerospace Industries, *Facts and Figures*, 94.
5. Frederick C. Thayer, Jr., *Air Transport Policy and National Security: A Political, Economic and Military Analysis* (Chapel Hill, N.C.: University of North Carolina Press, 1965), 310.
6. K. Munson, *Airliners Since 1946* (New York: Macmillan, 1972), 172. Boeing still hoped in 1976 to sell the 747 to the air force for use as a tanker-cargo plane, specifically for airborne refueling of heavy bombers. The 747 has also been modified for use as a carrier for space shuttle orbiters and as a flying command-and-control station for the air force, as was the 707. See Boeing, *Annual Report* (1975), 13–15.
7. Aerospace Industries, *Facts and Figures*, 14.
8. Ibid., 33.
9. Boeing Company, *Annual Report* (1975), 18.
10. McDonnell Douglas Corporation, *Annual Report*, 2.
11. Stanford Research Institute, *Aerospace Relationship*, 2, 90–1.
12. Herman O. Stekler, *The Structure and Performance of the Aerospace Industry* (Berkeley: University of California Press, 1965).
13. U. E. Reinhardt, "Break-even Analysis for Lockheed's TriStar: An Application of Financial Theory," *Journal of Finance, 28*, no. 4 (September, 1973), 821–38. Later modifications in the airplane's design drove development costs to $1.5 billion, which Lockheed doubts it will ever recover fully; *Fortune* (December 17, 1979), 64.
14. K. Hartley, "The Learning Curve and its Application to the Aircraft Industry," *Journal of Industrial Economics, 13*, no. 2 (March, 1965), 122–8.
15. Stekler, *Structure and Performance of the Aerospace Industry*, 197.
16. Department of Commerce, *Survey of Current Business, 56*, no. 3 (March, 1976), Table 6.

17. Cited in Thayer, *Air Transport Policy,* 57.
18. See, for example, U.S. State Department, AID, "The U.S. Program Aviation Assistance to LDCs," mimeo. (Washington, D.C.: Agency for International Development, July, 1964).
19. See Thayer, *Air Transport Policy,* passim.
20. John Marks, a specialist on the intelligence community, argues that the CIA financed Libya's national airline. "The CIA's Corporate Shell Game," Washington Post (July 11, 1976) Cl. Exim historically has not been open for business in Libya.
21. Selig Altschul, "Airline Financial Capability to Purchase SST Aircraft Beginning 1 January 1973," a report prepared for the Federal Aviation Agency, contract no. FA-SS-65-9 (December 1, 1964), 1–2.
22. Aerospace Industries, *Facts and Figures,* 20. The survey excluded the USSR, the People's Republic of China, and nonmembers of the International Air Transport Association.
23. For a discussion of European multicountry efforts to compete with U.S. aircraft, see Chapter 2 on aerospace in Raymond Vernon (ed.), *Big Business and the State* (Cambridge: Harvard University Press, 1974), 310.
24. See *The Economist, 260,* no. 6941, (September 11, 1975) 77–82.
25. For example, see Philip Mullenback, *Civilian Nuclear Power: Economic Issues and Policy Formation* (New York: The Twentieth Century Fund, 1963), 406; Richard J. Barber Associates, Inc., *LDC Nuclear Power Prospects, 1975–1990,* a report prepared for the Energy Research and Development Administration, (ERDA-52), esp. chap. 4; Irvin Bupp and Jean-Claude Derian, "The Nuclear Power Industry," in *Commission on the Organization of the Government for the Conduct of Foreign Policy* ("Murphy Commission"), Vol. 1 (Washington, D.C.: Government Printing Office, 1975), 85–100; Abraham Ribicoff, "A Market-Sharing Approach to the Nuclear Sales Problem" *Foreign Affairs, 54,* no. 4 (July 1976), 763–87; Norman Gall, "Atoms for Brazil, Dangers for All," *Foreign Policy,* no. 23 (summer, 1976), 155–201.
26. I. Bupp and J. Derian, "Nuclear Power Industry," 85.
27. At the request of the AEC, Eximbank in the early 1950s, authorized $126 million in credits to mining firms in South Africa to produce uranium for AEC consumption. Eximbank, *Semiannual Report for July–December, 1954,* 16.
28. P. Mullenbach, *Civilian Nuclear Power,* 134.
29. During the industries' formative period, the roles to be played by the public and private sectors were debated hotly, ibid., esp. 9–14. A similar debate occurred in the early days of aviation. Gordon Adams argues that although some favored a strong state role in both production and air transport, private industry succeeded in gaining for itself the more profitable branches of the business; the public sector was instructed to fund R&D, provide infrastructure, stabilize the industry through steady military procurement, and to create confidence among investors and the flying public through regulation. "State-Industry Relations in Advanced Capitalism: The American Aviation Industry, 1916–1926," unpublished ms.
30. A phrase used by N. Gall, "Atoms for Brazil," 191.
31. I. Bupp and J. Derian, "Nuclear Power Industry," 86.
32. Westinghouse, *1975 Annual Report,* 2.
33. I. Bupp and J. Derian, "Nuclear Power Industry," 94.
34. Barber Associates, "Nuclear Power Prospects," xi.

35. "The Future of the U.S. Nuclear Energy Industry," *Bell Journal of Economics, 7*, no. 1 (spring, 1976), 3–32.
36. Investor Responsibility Research Center, "The Nuclear Power Alternative," special report 1975-A (Washington, D.C., 1975), 28–9.
37. The high-capital intensity of nuclear plants also means that Eximbank, whose coverage is limited generally to the imported capital component, is able to finance a higher percentage of nuclear plants as opposed to other sources of energy.
38. In its *1975 Annual Report,* GE attributed 24 percent of its overall business to overseas sales (exports plus subsidiary products) (p. 16); Westinghouse attributed 30 percent, *1975 Annual Report,* 16.
39. See Bupp and Derian, "Nuclear Power Industry," 87–8, and Ribicoff, "Market-Sharing Approach," 782.
40. Bupp and Derian, ibid., 88. This degree of concentration allowed for possible collusion, including market sharing. The Justice Department brought a series of suits against GE and Westinghouse for fixing prices on large turbine generators. See the *Washington Star* (December 11, 1976).
41. Barber Associates, "Nuclear Power Prospects," C-7, C-8.
42. On the role of the U.S. Government in the export promotion of nuclear reactors see Gall, "Atoms for Brazil," 155–201 and Barber Associates "Nuclear Power Prospects," chap. 4, 35–46.
43. Barber Associates, "Nuclear Power Prospects," chapter 4, 36–7.
44. Ibid., 52–4.
45. Mullenbach, *Civilian Nuclear Power,* 18.
46. Stephen Minikes, statement before the U.S. Congress, House, Subcommittee on International Security and Scientific Affairs, Committee on International Relations (October 28, 1975), 6–7.
47. Bupp and Derian, "Nuclear Power Industry," 94.
48. Statement by Eximbank president, John Moore, Jr., U.S. Congress, House, Subcommittee in International Trade, Investment, and Monetary Policy, Committee on Banking, Finance, and Urban Affairs, Oversight Hearing on the Export-Import Bank, 96th Cong., 1st sess. (May 21, 1979), 20.
49. Exim financed about 70 percent of U.S. commercial jets delivered to foreign airlines from 1969 to 1971. See National Advisory Council, "Export-Import Bank Financing of Commercial Aircraft Exports to G-10 Countries," mimeo. 1972, released by Congressperson Henry Reuss, July 23, 1974.
50. Stephen Minikes, Statement before the U.S. Congress, 6–7.
51. Eximbank, *Semi-Annual Report for the Period July–December,* 1956, 6.
52. One useful connection was the Department of Defense (DOD), which had established a working relation with Exim. Between FY1962–74, Exim had authorized $3.9 billion in military credits, some of which were guaranteed by DOD. Exim, however, has since extracted itself from the arms sales business. The primary recipients of Exim military credits were Great Britain, Australia, Iran, Italy, and Spain.
53. Stephen Hymer, "The Multinational Corporation and Uneven Development," in Jagdish Bhagwati (ed.), *Economics and World Order* (New York: Macmillan, 1972), 113–40.
54. World Bank Group, *World Bank Operations: Sectoral Programs and Policies* (Baltimore: The Johns Hopkins University Press for the IBRD, 1972), 174–6.
55. F. Thayer, *Air Transport Policy,* 284.

56. The lengthy Barber Associates study, "Nuclear Power Prospects," argues strongly that "any case for subsidizing nuclear exports to LDCs appears very weak," because of the uncertainties and inappropriateness of the new technology. See esp. the study's conclusions, V-81–6.
57. According to the April, 1971, edition of *GE International,* during 1970 over 30 percent of GE International Sales Division's exports were supported by Exim, including almost all "big-ticket" items. Cited in N. McKitterick and B. J. Middleton, *The Bankers of the Rich and the Bankers of the Poor: The Role of Export Credit in Development Finance* (Washington, D.C.: Overseas Development Council, 1972), 33.
58. F. Thayer, *Air Transport Policy,* esp. 272–84.

10. Conclusion: trends and alternatives

1. See Richard E. Feinberg, "Divisions within the State: A Case Study of the Views of Four Federal Agencies on the U.S. Export-Import Bank," unpublished.
2. The U.S. Chamber of Commerce complained of the Advisory Committee's lack of influence in Congressional testimony in 1977. See The Task Force on Export Policy of the U.S. Chamber of Commerce, House, Subcommittee on International Trade, Investment, and Monetary Policy, Committee on Banking, Finance, and Urban Affairs, Hearings, *To Extend and Amend the Export-Import Bank Act of 1945,* 95th Cong., 1st sess. (March 25 and 28, 1977), 147–9.
3. Eximbank, "Report to the U.S. Congress on Export Credit Competition, and the Export-Import Bank of the United States for the period April 1, 1978 through September 30, 1978" (March, 1979), 39.
4. Exim's support for Zaire's Inga-Shaba power transmission line appears to be one example of a major project that may severely jeopardize a country's future development and balance-of-payments projects. See U.S. Congress, Senate, Subcommittee on International Finance, Committee on Banking, Housing, and Urban Affairs, Hearings, *U.S. Loans to Zaire,* 96 Cong., 1st sess. (May 24, 1979), 68; and Guy Gran (ed.), *Zaire: The Political Economy of Underdevelopment* (New York: Praeger, 1979), 331.
5. In a survey of U.S. exporters and commercial lenders, Exim found that users wanted the Bank to be more willing to take risks in the lesser developed countries. Eximbank, "Report to the U.S. Congress on Export Credit Competition" (March, 1979), 39. Congress found that the Overseas Private Investment Corporation (OPIC) had a similar behavioral tendency to favor more stable markets, and therefore amended its legislation in 1973 restricting OPIC's activities in countries with per capita incomes of $1,000 or more in 1975 dollars, ordering the public insurer of U.S. private equity to "give preferential consideration" to investment projects in LDCs with per capita incomes of under $520.
6. Ibid., 25.

Bibliography

Archival materials

Record Group 20, "Records of the Export-Import Bank," National Archives, Washington, D.C.
Record Group 56, Export-Import Bank Files, "Records of the Department of the Treasury," National Archives, Washington, D.C.
Record Group 234, "Records of the Reconstruction Finance Corporation," National Archives, Washington, D.C.

Government and other official periodicals

Agency for International Development. *U.S. Overseas Loans, Grants and Obligations, and Authorizations*. Washington, D.C.
Bank of England. *Bank of England Quarterly Bulletin*. London.
Board of Governors of the Federal Reserve System. *Annual Report*. Washington, D.C.
Federal Reserve. *Federal Reserve Bulletin*. Washington, D.C.
Office of Management and Budget. *Special Analyses*. Washington, D.C.
Overseas Private Investment Corporation. *Annual Report*. Washington, D.C.
Private Export Funding Corporation. *Annual Report*. New York, N.Y.
U.S. Commerce Department. *Survey of Current Business*, Washington, D.C.
U.S. Treasury Department. *Treasury Bulletin*. Washington, D.C.
World Bank. *Borrowing in International Capital Markets*, Washington, D.C.
World Bank. World Debt Tables, Washington, D.C.

U.S. Government publications and documents

Arey, Hawthorne. "History of Operations and Policies of the Export-Import Bank of Washington." Mimeographed, Washington, D.C., 1953.
U.S. Congress, Senate. Committee on Banking and Currency. *Hearings, Study of Export-Import Bank and World Bank*. 83rd Cong., 2nd sess., 1954.
Commerce Department, Bureau of the Census. *Historical Statistics of the United States: Colonial Times to 1970*. vol. 2. Washington, D.C.: Government Printing Office.
Congressional Budget Office. *The Export-Import Bank: Implications for the Federal Budget and the Credit Market*. Washington, D.C.: Government Printing Office, 1976.
Council on International Economic Policy. *International Economic Report, Report of the President, FY1974*. Washington, D.C.: Government Printing Office, 1975.

Dulles, Eleanor Lansing. *The Export-Import Bank of Washington: The First Ten Years*. Washington, D.C.: Government Printing Office, 1944.

Federal Energy Administration. *Project Independence Report*. Washington, D.C.: Government Printing Office, 1974.

National Advisory Council on International Monetary and Financial Policies. *Annual Report FY1974*. Washington, D.C.: Government Printing Office, 1975.

National Advisory Council. "Export-Import Bank Financing of Commercial Aircraft Exports to G-10 Countries." Mimeographed. 1972.

Office of Management and Budget. "Interagency Report on U.S. Government Export Promotion Policies." Washington, D.C. 1975.

U.S. Congress, House. Committee on Ways and Means. Second *Annual Report of the Department of the Treasury on the Operation and Effect of the Domestic International Sales Corporation*. 94th Cong., 1st sess. 1975.

U.S. Congress, House. Subcommittee on International Trade, Investment, and Monetary Policy, Committee on Banking, Finance, and Urban Affairs. *To Extend and Amend the Export-Import Bank Act of 1945*. 95th Cong., 1st sess., 1977.

U.S. Congress, House. Subcommittee on International Trade, Committee on Banking and Currency. *Hearings, The Export Expansion Finance Act of 1971, H.R. 5846*. 92nd Cong., 1st sess., 1971.

U.S. Congress, House. Subcommittee on International Trade, Investment, and Monetary Policy, Committee on Banking, Finance, and Urban Affairs. *Oversight Hearing on the Export-Import Bank*. 96th Cong., 1st sess., 1979.

U.S. Congress, Senate. Committee on Banking and Currency. *Inquiry into the Operations of the Reconstruction Finance Corporation and its Subsidiaries*. 80th Cong., 1st sess., 1947.

U.S. Congress, Senate. Committee on Banking and Currency. *To Continue the Functions of the Commodity Credit Corporation, the Export-Import Bank of Washington, and the Reconstruction Finance Corporation*. 76th Cong., 1st sess., 1939.

U.S. Congress, Senate. Select Committee to Study Governmental Operations with Respect to Intelligence Activities. *Covert Action, 7*. 94th Cong., 1st sess., 1975.

U.S. Congress, Senate. Subcommittee on International Finance, Committee on Banking and Currency. *Hearings, Export-Import Bank Act Amendments of 1967*. 90th Cong., 1st sess., 1967.

U.S. Congress, Senate. Subcommittee on International Finance, Committee on Banking, Housing, and Urban Affairs. *Hearings on the Export-Import Bank of the United States, S. 1890*. 93rd Cong., 1st sess., 1973.

U.S. Congress, Senate. Subcommittee on International Finance, Committee on Banking, Housing, and Urban Affairs. *To Extend the Export-Import Bank Act, S. 1890*. 93rd Cong., 1st sess., 1973.

U.S. Congress, Senate. Subcommittee on International Finance, Committee on Banking, Housing and Urban Affairs. *Hearings, U.S. Loans to Zaire*. 96th Cong., 1st sess., 1979.

U.S. Congress, Subcommittee on Priorities and Economy in Government, Joint Economic Committee. *Federal Subsidy Programs*. Washington, D.C.: Government Printing Office, 1974.

U.S. State Department. AID. "The U.S. Program of Aviation Assistance to LDCs." Mimeographed. July, 1964.

U.S. Tariff Commission, report to the U.S. Congress, Senate, Committee on Finance. *Implications of Multinational Firms for World Trade and Investment and for U.S. Trade and Labor*. Washington, D.C.: Government Printing Office, 1973.

Eximbank sources

Annual Report. Annual publication, Washington, D.C., 1934–79.
The CFF Courier. Irregular periodical, Washington, D.C.
Cumulative Records. Washington, D.C., 1974.
Eximbank Record. Irregular periodical, Washington, D.C.
"Guide for Drawing Funds under Eximbank Credits." Instruction sheet.
"Report to the U.S. Congress on Export Credit Competition and the Export-Import Bank of the United States." Semiannual report.
"Statement of Active Loans." Quarterly report, Washington, D.C.

Books and pamphlets

Adams, Frederick C. *Economic Diplomacy: The Export-Import Bank and American Foreign Policy, 1934–39.* Columbia, Mo.: University of Missouri Press, 1976.
Aerospace Industries Association of America. *Aerospace Facts and Figures 1976–77.* New York: McGraw-Hill, 1976.
Altschul, Selig. "Airline Financial Capability to Purchase SST Aircraft Beginning 1 January 1973." A report prepared for the Federal Aviation Agency, contract no. FA-SS-65-9. December 1, 1964.
Barber Associates, Inc., Richard J. *LDC Nuclear Power Prospects, 1975–1990.* A report prepared for the Energy Research and Development Administration, Washington, D.C. ERDA-52.
Bergsten, C. Fred, Horst, Thomas, and Moran, Theodore. *American Multinationals and American Interests.* Washington, D.C.: Brookings Institution, 1978.
Break, George F. *Federal Lending and Economic Stability.* Washington, D.C.: Brookings Institution, 1965.
Campbell, John F. *The Foreign Affairs Fudge Factory.* New York: Basic Books, 1971.
Cheng, Hang-Sheng. *International Bond Issues of the Less-Developed Countries.* Ames, Iowa: Iowa State University Press, 1969.
Eximbank. *General Policy Statement. Revised August 1, 1947.* Washington, D.C.: Government Printing Office, 1947.
Foreign Credit Insurance Association. "Export Credit Insurance Manual." New York, New York, 1972.
Foreign Credit Insurance Association. *Report of Operations.* Annual report, New York, 1963–79.
Gran, Guy, ed. *Zaire: The Political Economy of Underdevelopment.* New York: Praeger, 1979.
Hodgman, Donald. *Commercial Bank Loan and Investment Policy.* Champaign, Ill.: Bureau of Economic and Business Research, University of Illinois, 1963.
Investor Responsibility Research Center. "The Nuclear Power Alternatives." Special Report 1975-A. Washington, D.C., 1975.
Keynes, John Maynard. *The General Theory of Employment, Interest, and Money.* New York: Harcourt, 1964.
Mason, Edward and Asher, Robert. *The World Bank since Bretton Woods.* Washington, D.C.: Brookings Institution, 1973.
Middleton, B. Jenkins and McKitterick, Nathaniel M. *The Bankers of the Rich and the Bankers of the Poor: The Role of Export Credit in Development Finance.* Washington, D.C.: Overseas Development Council, 1972.

Mikesell, Raymond. *Foreign Investment in Copper Mining*. Baltimore: The Johns Hopkins University Press, 1975.

Mintz, Ilse. *Cyclical Fluctuations in the Exports of the U.S. since 1879*. New York: Columbia University Press, NBER, 1967.

Moran, Theodore H. *Multinational Corporations and the Politics of Dependence: Copper in Chile*. Princeton University Press, 1974.

Morgan Guaranty Trust. *The Financing of Exports and Imports: A Guide to Procedures*. New York, 1973.

Mullenbach, Philip. *Civilian Nuclear Power: Economic Issues and Policy Formation*. New York: Twentieth Century Fund, 1963.

Munson, K. *Airliners since 1916*. New York: Macmillan, 1972.

Organization for Economic Cooperation and Development. "Tables for Use in Grant Element Calculations." Mimeographed. Paris: OECD, 1972.

Organization for Economic Cooperation and Development. *The Export Credit Financing Systems in OECD Member Countries*. Paris: OECD, 1976.

Parrini, Carl. *Heir to Empire: United States Economic Diplomacy, 1916–1923*. University of Pittsburgh Press, 1969.

Robbins, Sidney, and Stubaugh, Robert. *Money in the Multinational Enterprise*. New York: Basic Books, 1973.

Scherer, Frederick. *Industrial Market Structure and Economic Performance*. Chicago: Rand McNally, 1970.

Stanford Research Institute. *The Industry-Government Aerospace Relationship*. Report no. AD 617 885/6, vol. 1. Menlo Park, Calif.: Stanford Research Institute, 1963.

Stekler, Herman O. *The Structure and Performance of the Aerospace Industry*. Berkeley: University of California Press, 1965.

Stern, Paula. *Water's Edge: Domestic Politics and the Making of American Foreign Policy*. Westport, Conn.: Greenwood Press, 1979.

Syvrud, Donald E. *Foundations of Brazilian Economic Growth*. Stanford, Calif.: Hoover Institution Press for American Enterprise Institute-Hoover Research Publications, 1974.

Tendler, Judith. *Electric Power in Brazil: Entrepreneurship in the Public Sector*. Cambridge: Harvard University Press, 1968.

Thayer, Frederick C., Jr. *Air Transport Policy and National Security: A Political, Economic, and Military Analysis*. Chapel Hill, N.C.: University of North Carolina Press, 1965.

Vernon, Raymond, ed. *Big Business and the State*. Cambridge: Harvard University Press, 1974.

Vernon, Raymond, ed. *Sovereignty at Bay: The Multinational Spread of U.S. Enterprises*. New York: Basic Books, 1971.

Williams, William Appelman. *American–Russian Relations, 1781–1974*. New York: Rinehart, 1952.

Articles

Bupp, Irvin, and Derian, Jean-Claude. "The Nuclear Power Industry." In *Commission on the Organization of the Government for the Conduct of Foreign Policy* ("Murphy Commission"), vol. 1. Washington, D.C.: Government Printing Office, 1975.

Carli, Guido. "Italy's Malaise," *Foreign Affairs, 54,* no. 4 (July, 1976). 708–18.

Cohen, Kalman, Gilmore, Tom, and Singer, Frank. "Bank Procedures for Analyzing Business Loan Applications." In *Analytical Methods in Banking.* Edited by Kalman Cohen and Frederick Hammer, Homewood, Ill.: Richard D. Irvin, Inc., 1966, pp. 219–51.

Debs, Richard. "Petro-dollars, LDCs, and International Banks," Federal Reserve Bank of New York, *Monthly Review, 58,* no. 1 (January, 1976), 16.

Dorman, Ralph M. "The Influence of Expropriation on Mining Company Investments," *Mining Congress Journal, 59,* no. 10 (October 1973), 38–40.

Falkus, M. E. "United States Economic Policy and the 'Dollar Gap' of the 1920s," *Economic History Review, 24,* no. 4 (November, 1971), 599–623.

Feinberg, Richard E. "Divisions within the State: A Case Study of the Views of Four Federal Agencies on the U.S. Export-Import Bank." Unpublished.

Frank, Charles, and Cline, William. "The Debt Service Burden." In Charles Frank, et al. *Assisting Developing Countries: Problems of Debts, Burden-Sharing, Jobs and Trade.* New York: Praeger, 1972. 36–53.

Gall, Norman. "Atoms for Brazil, Dangers for All," *Foreign Policy,* no. 23 (summer 1976), 155–201.

Glynn, Sean, and Lougheed, Alan. "A Comment on U.S. Economic Policy and the 'Dollar Gap' of the 1920s," *Economic History Review, 26,* no. 4 (November, 1973), 692–4.

Hartley, K. "The Learning Curve and its Application to the Aircraft Industry," *Journal of Industrial Economics, 13,* no. 2 (March, 1965), 122–8.

Horst, Thomas. "American Multinationals and the U.S. Economy," *American Economic Review, Papers and Proceedings, 66,* no. 2 (May, 1976), 149–61.

Horvath, Janos. "Are Eximbank Credits Subsidized: Toward an Empirical Analysis." In *U.S. Financing of East–West Trade.* Edited by Paul Marer. Bloomington, Ind.: International Development Research Center, Indiana University, 1975, pp. 105–37.

Hymer, Stephen. "The Multinational Corporation and Uneven Development." In *Economics and World Order.* Edited by Jagdish Bhagwati. New York: Macmillan, 1972, pp. 113–40.

McHale, James. "National Planning and Reciprocal Trade: The New Deal Origins of Government Guarantees for Private Exporters," *Prologue, 6,* no. 3 (fall, 1974), 189–99.

Mayo, Alice, and Garrett, Anthony. "An Early-Warning Model for Assessing Developing-Country Risk." In *Financing and Risk in Developing Countries.* Edited by Stephen Goodman. New York: Praeger, 1978, 81–7.

Mohammed, Azizali, and Saccomanni, Fabrizio. "Short-term Banking and Euro-Currency Credits to Developing Countries." *IMF Staff Papers, 20,* no. 3 (November, 1973), 612–38.

Owens, Richard N. "The Hundred Million Dollar Foreign Trade Financing Corporation," *Journal of Political Economy, 30,* no. 3 (1922), 346–62.

Reinhardt, U. E. "Breakeven Analysis for Lockheed's TriStar: An Application of Fiscal Theory," *Journal of Finance, 28,* no. 4 (September, 1973), 821–38.

Ribicoff, Abraham. "A Market-Sharing Approach to the Nuclear Sales Problem," *Foreign Affairs, 54,* no. 4 (July, 1976), 763–87.

Sargen, Nicholas. "Commercial Bank Lending to Developing Countries." Federal Reserve Bank of San Francisco. *Economic Review* (spring, 1976) 20–31.

Scherer, Frederick. "The Aerospace Industry." In *The Structure of American Industry.* Edited by Walter Adams. New York: Macmillan, 1971.

Shoup, Carl. "The Economic Theory of Subsidy Payments." In U.S. Congress, Joint Economic Committee. *The Economics of Federal Subsidy Programs.* Washington, D.C.: Government Printing Office, 1972.

Spiro, Michael H. "The Impact of Government Procurement on Employment in the Aircraft Industry." In *Studies in Economic Stabilization.* Edited by A. Ando et al. Washington, D.C.: Brookings Institution, 1968.

Trotsky, Leon. "Nationalism and Economic Life." *Foreign Affairs, 12,* no. 3 (1934), 395–402.

Index

additionality, 101
administrative charges, 47
aerospace industry, 102
  U.S. government policy toward and analysis of, 124–7, 132
  see also aircraft industry
African Development Fund (ADF), 39
Agency for International Development (AID), 1, 81, 99, 126, 142
agricultural commodities
  risk to, FCIA and, 50
  wheat, 74
agricultural sector, 77, 81
  creditworthiness and, 85
  direct loans and, 27, 31, 32, 33
Agriculture Department, 1
aid, *see* foreign aid
aircraft, 59, 71, 121, 122
  direct loans and, 34, 35, 36
  exports of, 132, 133
  jet, 30, 32, 66, 85, 120, 125–7, 131–2
  product loans and, 23
aircraft industry, 5
  analysis of, 126–7
  Exim and, 131–5
  loan denials and, 73, 78, 80, 81
  percent of Exim loans and, 85
  see also aerospace industry
Albania, 66
Alcoa, 120
Algeria, 64, 65, 66, 67
  loan denials and, 74–5, 80, 85
Allende, Salvador, 21, 67, 68, 110, 111, 139
Amazonia Minerocoa, S.A., 119
American Bankers' Association, 10, 12–13, 14
American Federation of Labor and Congress of Industrial Organizations (AFL-CIO), 82, 104

American Smelting and Refining (ASARCO), 108
Arey, Hawthorne, 67
Argentina, 18, 63, 65, 113
  loan denial and, 75, 81
armaments, 32
Asian Development Bank (ADB), 39
Atomic Energy Act, 130
Atomic Energy Commission (AEC), 20, 125, 128, 129–30
authorizations (insurance), 51
authorizations (loan), 71, 104
  to Brazil, 117
  disbursements and, 99
  historical level of, 100
  hostile regimes and, 67–8
  LDCs and, 63–5
  sectoral analysis of direct loans and, 27–31
  subsidy estimation and, 93
  U.S. aid and, 65–6

Babcock and Wilcox, 128
Bahamas, 122
balance of payments, 73, 74, 75, 76, 77, 80, 112, 137, 142
  Exim's phasing out of financing for, 21
Bank of America, 39, 76
bank claims, 41
bankers
  economic behavior of, 70
  herd instinct and, 83
  psychological traits of, 47
Bankers Trust, 77
banks
  commercial, 83, 142
    behavior of, 47–8
    cofinancing with Exim and, 43–6
    Exim's direct loans and, 23, 24, 25
    Exim's founding and, 12–13, 16

quotas, 14

railroads, 73, 80, 119
  see also locomotives
raw materials, 2, 18, 20, 79, 80, 84
Reagan Administration, 68
Reagan, President, 102
Reciprocal Trade Act, 9, 14–16
Reconstruction Finance Corporation
  (RFC), 12
refining, *see* mining and refining
reimbursement, 24
repayments, 64, 73, 74, 77, 81
  on cut-rate loans, 97
  direct loans and, 33–4
  loan rescheduling and, 112
  progress, 24, 32, 134
  reasonable assurance of, 20, 141
  subsidy estimation and, 94, 95
  terms of, 48
  see also payments
research and development (R&D), 5,
  125, 128–9, 133
risk, 96
  business, Exim founding and, 13
  commercial banks and, 47
  creditworthiness and
    commercial, 71–2, 78
    political, 84
  FCIA and commercial and political,
    49–50, 53
  financial guarantees and, 46
  sovereign, 70–1
road development, 31, 77, 79, 81, 85
Robbins, Sidney, 108
Romi (Brazilian machine tool
  company), 118
Roosevelt, President Franklin D., 12, 13,
  16, 18
Rumania, 66
rural sector, 85, 86, 87, 142
  power generation and, 31

San Martin, President, 67
Sao Paulo, 119
Scherer, Frederick, 124
Science Management Corporation,
  74
sectors, *see* economic sectors
Sena Sugar, 121
  see also sugar

Shell Oil Company of Delaware, 120
Shoup, Carl, 91
Singer, Frank, 69, 87
Somisa (Argentine steel company), 75
South Africa, 20, 67
Southern Peru Copper Corporation
  (SPCC), 108
South Korea, 65
Soviets, *see* Union of Soviet Socialist
  Republics
Spain, 64
Spicer Philippine Manufacturing
  Company, 76
Standard International Trade
  Classification (SITC), 31, 32
Standard Oil of California, 122
the state, 2
  commercial banks and, 47–8
  see also governments
State Department, 15, 70, 81, 123, 126,
  137, 138
statistical tables, 147–56
steel industry, 80
  Argentine, 75, 81
  Brazilian, 18, 25, 45
  loan denials and U.S., 137
Stekler, Herman, 125, 128
Stuart, Charles, 14, 15, 16
Stubaugh, Robert, 108
subsidy, 4
  defined, 91
  Exim's loans and financial, 121
  Exim's source of funds and, 96–9
  overseas investment and tax, 1
  transport, 85
  see also export subsidy
Sudan, loan denial and, 73–4
sugar, 31
  see also Sena Sugar
suppliers, 81
  risk to, insurance and, 49
  U.S., direct loans and, 23, 34–5

Taiwan, 64
Tanaka, Prime Minister, 127
Tanzania, loan denial and, 77–8, 85, 87
tariffs, 10
taxes, 96
  Bahamas and, 122
  Exim and, 98
  overseas investment and, 1